RICK STEVES'
SPANISH
& PORTUGUESE
PHRASE BOOK & DICTIONARY

3rd Edition

John Muir Publications
Santa Fe, New Mexico

Thanks to the team of people at *Europe Through the Back Door* who helped make this book possible: Dave Hoerlein, Colleen Murphy, Mary Romano, and . . .

Spanish translation: Gloria Villaraviz Weeden with Julio Villaraviz and John Weeden
Spanish proofreading: Angelina Saldaña de Gibbons
Portuguese translation: Luis F. Gonçalves Conde and Maria Antonia Campota
Phonetics: Risa Laib
Layout: Rich Sorensen
Maps: Dave Hoerlein

Edited by Risa Laib and Rich Sorensen

John Muir Publications, P.O. Box 613, Santa Fe, NM 87504

Third edition. First printing October 1996
Printed in the U.S.A. by Quebecor Printing

ISBN 1-56261-315-4

Cover photo by Leo de Wys, Inc./Bob Krist

Distributed to the book trade by
Publishers Group West
Emeryville, California

While every effort has been made to keep the content of this book accurate, the author and publisher accept no responsibility whatsoever for anyone ordering bad beer or getting messed up in any other way because of the linguistic confidence this phrase book has given them.

JMP travel guidebooks by Rick Steves:

Rick Steves' Europe
Rick Steves' France, Belgium & the Netherlands
  (with Steve Smith)
Rick Steves' Italy
Rick Steves' Germany, Austria & Switzerland
Rick Steves' Great Britain & Ireland
Rick Steves' Scandinavia
Rick Steves' Spain & Portugal
Rick Steves' Baltics & Russia (with Ian Watson)
Rick Steves' Europe Through the Back Door
Europe 101: History and Art for the Traveler
  (with Gene Openshaw)
Mona Winks: Self-Guided Tours of Europe's Top Museums
  (with Gene Openshaw)
Rick Steves' Phrase Books: French, Italian, German,
  French/Italian/German, and Spanish/Portuguese
Asia Through the Back Door (with Bob Effertz)

Rick Steves' company, *Europe Through the Back Door,* provides many services for budget European travelers, including a free quarterly newsletter/catalog, budget travel books and accessories, Eurailpasses (with free video and travel advice included), free-spirited European bus tours, on-line travel tips, and a user-friendly Travel Resource Center in Edmonds, WA. For more information and a free copy of Rick's newsletter, call or write:

Europe Through the Back Door
120 Fourth Avenue N, Box 2009
Edmonds, WA 98020 USA
Tel: 206/771-8303, Fax: 206/771-0833
Web: http://www.ricksteves.com

Contents

Appendix

Hi, I'm Rick Steves.

I'm the only mono-lingual speaker I know who's had the nerve to design a series of European phrase books. But that's one of the things that makes them better.

You see, after twenty summers of travel through Europe, I've learned first-hand: (1) what's essential for communication in another country, and (2) what's not. I've assembled the most important words and phrases in a logical, no-frills format, and I've worked with native Europeans and seasoned travelers to give you the simplest, clearest translations possible.

But this book is more than just a pocket translator. The words and phrases have been carefully selected to help you have a smarter, smoother trip in Spain and Portugal without going broke. Spain used to be cheap and chaotic. These days it's neither. It's better organized than ever—and often as expensive as France or Germany. The key to getting more out of every travel dollar is to get closer to the local people, and to rely less on entertainment, restaurants, and hotels that cater only to foreign tourists. This book will not only help you order a meal at a locals-only Sevilla restaurant—it will help you talk with the family who runs the place . . . about their kids, social issues, travel dreams, and favorite *música*. Long after your memories of museums have faded, you'll still treasure the personal encounters you had with your new Iberian friends.

A good phrase book should help you enjoy your Iberian experience—not just survive it—so I've added a healthy dose of humor. But please use these phrases carefully, in a self-effacing spirit. Remember that one ugly American can undo the goodwill built by dozens of culturally-sensitive ones.

To get the most out of this book, take the time to internalize and put into practice my Spanish and Portuguese pronunciation tips. Don't worry too much about memorizing grammatical rules, like the gender of a noun—the important thing is to forget about sex and communicate!

You'll notice this book has a handy dictionary and a nifty menu decoder (to help you figure out what's cooking). You'll also find tongue twisters, gestures, international words, telephone tips, and handy tear-out "cheat sheets." Tear them out and keep them in your pocket, so you can easily memorize key phrases during otherwise idle moments. As you prepare for your trip, you may want to read this year's edition of my *Rick Steves' Spain & Portugal* guidebook.

The Spanish and Portuguese speak less English than their European neighbors. But while the language barrier may seem a little higher, the locals are happy to give an extra boost to any traveler who makes an effort to communicate. If this phrase book helps make that happen, or if you have suggestions for making it better, I'd love to hear from you.

Happy travels,

Getting Started

Spanish

...opens the door to the land of siestas and fiestas, fun and flamenco. Imported from the Old World throughout the New, Spanish is the most widely spoken romance language in the world. With its straightforward pronunciation, Spanish is also one of the simplest languages to learn.

Here are some tips for pronouncing Spanish words:

C usually sounds like C in cat.
    But *C* followed by *E* or *I* sounds like TH in think.
D sounds like the soft D in soda.
G usually sounds like G in go.
    But *G* followed by *E* or *I* sounds like the guttural J in Baja.
H is silent.
J sounds like the guttural J in Baja.
LL sounds like Y in yes.
Ñ sounds like NI in onion.
R is trrrilled.
V sounds like B in bit.
Z sounds like TH in think.

Spanish vowels:

A sounds like A in father.
E can sound like E in get or AY in play.
I sounds like EE in seed.
O sounds like O in note.
U sounds like OO in moon.

Spanish has a few unusual signs and sounds. The Spanish add extra punctuation to questions and exclamations, like this: ¿*Cómo está?* (How are you?) ¡*Fantástico!* (Fantastic!) You've probably seen and heard the Spanish ñ: think of *señor* and *mañana*. Spanish has a guttural sound similar to the J in Baja California. In the phonetics, the symbol for this clearing-your-throat sound is the italicized *h*.

Spanish words that end in a consonant are stressed on the last syllable, as in *Madrid*. Words ending in a vowel are generally stressed on the second-to-last syllable, as in *amigo*. To override these rules, the Spanish sometimes add an accent mark (´) to the syllable that should be stressed, like this: *rápido* (fast) is pronounced **rah**-pee-doh.

When you're speaking a romance language, sex is unavoidable. Even the words are masculine or feminine, and word endings can change depending on gender. A man is *simpático* (friendly), a woman is *simpática*. In this book, we show gender-bender words like this: *simpático[a]*. If you're speaking of a woman (which includes women speaking about themselves), use the *a* ending. It's always pronounced "ah." Words ending in *r*, such as *doctor*, will appear like this: *doctor[a]*. A *doctora* is a female doctor. Words ending in *e*, such as *amable* (kind), apply to either sex.

The endings of Spanish nouns and adjectives agree. Cold weather is *tiempo frío*, and a cold shower is a *ducha fría*.

Plurals are a snap. Add *s* to a word that ends in a vowel, like *pueblo* (village) and *es* to a word that ends in a consonant, like *ciudad* (city). Visit a mix of *pueblos* and *ciudades* to get the full flavor of Spain.

In northern and central Spain, Spanish sounds as if it's spoken with a lisp. *Gracias* (thank you) sounds like grah-thee-ahs. As you head farther south, you'll notice a difference in pronunciation. In southern Spain, along the coast, people thpeak without the lisp: *Gracias* sounds like grah-see-ahs. Listen to and imitate the Spanish people around you.

You'll often hear the Spanish say, *"Por favor"* (Please). The Spanish are friendly, polite people. *Por favor* use *por favor* whenever you can.

¡Buen viaje! Have a good trip!

Here's a quick guide to the phonetics we've used in this book:

ah	like A in father.
ay	like AY in play.
ee	like EE in seed.
eh	like E in get.
ehr	sounds like "air."
g	like G in go.
h	like the guttural J in Baja.
ī	like I in light.
oh	like O in note.
or	like OR in core.
oo	like OO in moon.
ow	like OW in now.
oy	like OY in toy.
s	like S in sun.

Spanish Basics

Greeting and meeting the Spanish:

Hello.	**Hola.**	**oh**-lah
Good morning.	**Buenos días.**	**bway**-nohs **dee**-ahs
Good afternoon.	**Buenas tardes.**	**bway**-nahs **tar**-days
Good evening.	**Buenas tardes.**	**bway**-nahs **tar**-days
Good night.	**Buenas noches.**	**bway**-nahs **noh**-chays
Mr.	**Señor**	sayn-**yor**
Mrs.	**Señora**	sayn-**yoh**-rah
Miss	**Señorita**	sayn-yoh-**ree**-tah
How are you?	**¿Cómo está?**	**koh**-moh ay-**stah**
Very well, thanks.	**Muy bien, gracias.**	**moo**-ee bee-**yehn** **grah**-thee-ahs
And you?	**¿Y usted?**	ee oo-**stehd**
My name is...	**Me llamo...**	may **yah**-moh
What's your name?	**¿Cómo se llama?**	**koh**-moh say **yah**-mah
Pleased to meet you.	**Mucho gusta.**	**moo**-choh **goo**-stah
Where are you from?	**¿De dónde es usted?**	day **dohn**-day ays oo-**stehd**
See you later.	**Hasta luego.**	**ah**-stah loo-**ay**-goh
Goodbye.	**Adiós.**	ah-dee-**ohs**
Good luck!	**¡Buena suerte!**	**bway**-nah **swehr**-tay
Have a good trip!	**¡Buen viaje!**	bwayn bee-**ah**-hay

Survival phrases

Ernest Hemingway fought in the Spanish Civil War using only these phrases. They're repeated on your tear-out cheat sheet near the end of this book.

The essentials:

Hello.	**Hola.**	**oh**-lah
Do you speak English?	**¿Habla usted inglés?**	ah-blah oo-**stehd** een-**glays**
Yes. / No.	**Sí. / No.**	see / noh
I don't speak Spanish.	**No hablo español.**	noh ah-bloh ay-spahn-**yohl**
I'm sorry.	**Lo siento.**	loh see-**ehn**-toh
Please.	**Por favor.**	por fah-**bor**
Thank you.	**Gracias.**	**grah**-thee-ahs
It's (not) a problem.	**(No) hay problema.**	(noh) ī proh-**blay**-mah
Very good.	**Muy bien.**	moo-ee bee-**yehn**
You are very kind.	**Usted es muy amable.**	oo-**stehd** ays moo-ee ah-**mah**-blay
Goodbye.	**Adiós.**	ah-dee-**ohs**

Where?

Where is a...?	**¿Donde hay un...?**	dohn-day ī oon
...hotel	**...hotel**	oh-**tehl**
...youth hostel	**...albergue de juventud**	ahl-**behr**-gay day hoo-behn-**tood**
...restaurant	**...restaurante**	ray-stoh-**rahn**-tay
...supermarket	**...supermercado**	soo-pehr-mehr-**kah**-doh

...bank	...banco	**bahn**-koh
Where is the...?	¿Dónde está la...?	**dohn**-day ay-**stah** lah
...pharmacy	...farmacia	far-mah-**thee**-ah
...train station	...estación de trenes	ay-stah-thee-**ohn** day **tray**-nays
...tourist information office	...Oficina de Turismo	oh-fee-**thee**-nah day too-**rees**-moh
Where are the toilets?	¿Dónde están los servicios?	**dohn**-day ay-**stahn** lohs sehr-**bee**-thee-ohs
men / women	hombres / mujeres	**ohm**-brays / moo-*heh*-rays

How much?

How much is it?	¿Cuánto cuesta?	**kwahn**-toh **kway**-stah
Write it?	¿Me lo escribe?	may loh ay-**skree**-bay
Cheap(er).	(Más) barato.	(mahs) bah-**rah**-toh
Cheapest.	El más barato.	ehl mahs bah-**rah**-toh
Is it free?	¿Es gratis?	ays grah-**tees**
Is it included?	¿Está incluido?	ay-**stah** een-kloo-**ee**-doh
Do you have...?	¿Tiene...?	tee-**ehn**-ay
I would like...	Quería...	keh-**ree**-ah
We would like...	Queríamos...	keh-**ree**-ah-mohs
...this.	...esto.	**ay**-stoh
...just a little.	...un poquito.	oon poh-**kee**-toh
...more.	...más.	mahs
...a ticket.	...un billete.	oon bee-**yeh**-tay
...a room.	...una habitación.	**oo**-nah ah-bee-tah-thee-**ohn**
...the bill.	...la cuenta.	lah **kwayn**-tah

How many?

one	**uno**	**oo**-noh
two	**dos**	dohs
three	**tres**	trays
four	**cuatro**	**kwah**-troh
five	**cinco**	**theen**-koh
six	**seis**	says
seven	**siete**	see-**eh**-tay
eight	**ocho**	**oh**-choh
nine	**nueve**	**nway**-bay
ten	**diez**	dee-**ayth**

You'll find more to count on in the Numbers chapter.

When?

At what time?	**¿A qué hora?**	ah kay **oh**-rah
Just a moment.	**Un momento.**	oon moh-**mehn**-toh
Now.	**Ahora.**	ah-**oh**-rah
Soon.	**Pronto.**	**prohn**-toh
Later.	**Más tarde.**	mahs **tar**-day
Today. / Tomorrow.	**Hoy. / Mañana.**	oy / mahn-**yah**-nah

Be creative. You can combine these survival phrases to say: "Two, please," or "No, thank you," or "I'd like a cheap hotel," or "Cheaper, please?" Please is a magic word in any language. If you want something and you don't know the word for it, just point and say, *"Por favor"* (Please).

Struggling with Spanish:

Do you speak English?	¿Habla usted inglés?	ah-blah oo-**stehd** een-**glays**
A teeny weeny bit?	¿Ni un poquito?	nee oon poh-**kee**-toh
Please speak English.	**Hable en inglés, por favor.**	ah-blay ayn een-**glays** por fah-**bor**
You speak English well.	**Usted habla bien el inglés.**	oo-**stehd** ah-blah bee-**yehn** ehl een-**glays**
I don't speak Spanish.	**No hablo español.**	noh ah-bloh ay-spahn-**yohl**
I speak a little Spanish.	**Hablo un poco de español.**	ah-bloh oon **poh**-koh day ay-spahn-**yohl**
What is this in Spanish?	¿Cómo se dice esto en español?	**koh**-moh say **dee**-thay **ay**-stoh ayn ay-spahn-**yohl**
Repeat?	**Repita?**	ray-**pee**-tah
Slowly.	**Despacio.**	day-**spah**-thee-oh
Do you understand?	¿Comprende?	kohm-**prehn**-day
I understand.	**Comprendo.**	kohm-**prehn**-doh
I don't understand.	**No comprendo.**	noh kohm-**prehn**-doh
Write it?	¿Me lo escribe?	may loh ay-**skree**-bay
Who speaks English?	¿Quién habla inglés?	kee-**ehn** ah-blah een-**glays**

Common questions in Spanish:

How much?	¿Cuánto?	**kwahn**-toh
How many?	¿Cuánto?	**kwahn**-toh
How long...?	¿Cuánto tiempo...?	**kwahn**-toh tee-**ehm**-poh
...is the trip	...es el viaje	ays ehl bee-**ah**-_hay_
How far?	¿A qué distancia?	ah kay dees-**tahn**-thee-ah

How?	¿Cómo?	koh-moh
Is it possible?	¿Es posible?	ays poh-**see**-blay
Is it necessary?	¿Es necesario?	ays nay-thay-**sah**-ree-oh
Can you help me?	¿Me puede ayudar?	may **pway**-day ah-yoo-**dar**
What?	¿Qué?	kay
What Is that?	¿Qué es esto?	kay ays **ay**-stoh
What is better?	¿Qué es mejor?	kay ays may *hor*
When?	¿Cuándo?	**kwahn**-doh
What time Is it?	¿Qué hora es?	kay **oh**-rah ays
At what time?	¿A qué hora?	ah kay **oh**-rah
On time? Late?	¿Puntual? ¿Tarde?	poon-too-**ahl** / tar-day
What time does this...?	¿A qué hora...?	ah kay **oh**-rah
...open	...abren	**ah**-brehn
...close	...clerran	thee-**ay**-rahn
Do you have...?	¿Tiene...?	tee-**ehn**-ay
Where is...?	¿Dónde está...?	**dohn**-day ay-**stah**
Where are...?	¿Dónde están...?	**dohn**-day ay-**stahn**
Where can I find...?	¿Dónde puedo encontrar...?	**dohn**-day **pway**-doh ayn-kohn-**trar**
Who?	¿Quién?	kee-**ehn**
Why?	¿Por qué?	por kay
Why not?	¿Por qué no?	por kay noh
Yes or no?	¿Sí o no?	see oh noh

To prompt a simple answer, ask, "*¿Sí o no?*" (Yes or no?). To turn a word or sentence into a question, ask it in a questioning tone. A simple way to ask, "Where are the toilets?" is to say, "*¿Servicios?*"

El yin and yang:

cheap / expensive	**barato / caro**	bah-**rah**-toh / **kah**-roh
big / small	**grande / pequeño**	**grahn**-day / pay-**kayn**-yoh
hot / cold	**caliente / frío**	kahl-**yehn**-tay / **free**-oh
open / closed	**abierto / cerrado**	ah-bee-**yehr**-toh / thehr-**rah**-doh
entrance / exit	**entrada / salida**	ayn-**trah**-dah / sah-**lee**-dah
arrive / depart	**llegar / salir**	yay-**gar** / sah-**leer**
early / late	**temprano / tarde**	tehm-**prah**-noh / **tar**-day
soon / later	**pronto / más tarde**	**prohn**-toh / mahs **tar**-day
fast / slow	**rápido / despacio**	**rah**-pee-doh / day-**spah**-thee-oh
here / there	**aquí / allí**	ah-**kee** / ah-**yee**
near / far	**cerca / lejos**	**thehr**-kah / **lay**-*h*ohs
good / bad	**bueno / malo**	**bway**-noh / **mah**-loh
best / worst	**mejor / peor**	may-**hor** / pay-**or**
a little / lots	**un poco / mucho**	oon **poh**-koh / **moo**-choh
more / less	**más / menos**	mahs / **may**-nohs
mine / yours	**mío / suyo**	**mee**-oh / **soo**-yoh
easy / difficult	**fácil / difícil**	**fah**-theel / dee-**fee**-theel
left / right	**izquierda / derecha**	eeth-kee-**ehr**-dah / day-**ray**-chah
up / down	**arriba / abajo**	ah-**ree**-bah / ah-**bah**-*h*oh
young / old	**joven / viejo**	*h*oh-behn / bee-**ay**-*h*oh
new / old	**nuevo / viejo**	noo-**ay**-boh / bee-**ay**-*h*oh
heavy / light	**pesado / ligero**	pay-**sah**-doh / lee-**hehr**-oh
dark / light	**oscuro / claro**	oh-**skoo**-roh / **klah**-roh
beautiful / ugly	**bonito / feo**	boh-**nee**-toh / **fay**-oh

smart / stupid	**listo / estúpido**	**lee**-stoh / ay-**stoo**-pee-doh
vacant / occupied	**libre / ocupado**	**lee**-bray / oh-koo-**pah**-doh
with / without	**con / sin**	kohn / seen

Big little words in Spain:

I	**yo**	yoh
you (formal)	**usted**	oo-**stehd**
you (informal)	**tú**	too
we	**nosotros**	noh-**soh**-trohs
he / she	**él / ella**	ehl / **ay**-yah
they	**ellos / ellas**	**ay**-yohs / **ay**-yahs
and	**y**	ee
at	**a**	ah
because	**porque**	**por**-kay
but	**pero**	**pay**-roh
by (via)	**por**	por
for	**para**	**pah**-rah
from	**de**	day
here	**aquí**	ah-**kee**
in	**en**	ayn
not	**no**	noh
now	**ahora**	ah-**oh**-rah
only	**solo**	**soh**-loh
or	**o**	oh
this	**esto**	**ay**-stoh
to	**a**	ah
very	**muy**	**moo**-ee

Spanish names for places:

Spain	**España**	ay-**spahn**-yah
Madrid	**Madrid**	mah-**dreed**
Seville	**Sevilla**	seh-**vee**-yah
Gibraltar	**Gibraltar**	*h*ee-brahl-**tar**
Portugal	**Portugal**	por-too-**gahl**
Lisbon	**Lisboa**	lees-**boh**-ah
Austria	**Austria**	**ow**-stree-ah
France	**Francia**	**frahn**-thee-ah
Germany	**Alemania**	ah-lay-**mahn**-yah
Great Britain	**Gran Bretaña**	grahn bray-**tahn**-yah
Greece	**Grecia**	**gray**-thee-ah
Italy	**Italia**	ee-**tah**-lee-ah
Morocco	**Marruecos**	mar-**way**-kohs
Netherlands	**Paises Bajos**	p**ī**-says bah-*h*ohs
Russia	**Rusia**	**roo**-see-ah
Switzerland	**Suiza**	soo-**ee**-thah
Turkey	**Turquía**	toor-**kee**-ah
Africa	**Africa**	**ah**-free-kah
Europe	**Europa**	ay-**roh**-pah
United States	**Estados Unidos**	ay-**stah**-dohs oo-**nee**-dohs
Canada	**Canadá**	kah-nah-**dah**
Mexico	**Méjico**	**may**-*h*ee-koh
Central America	**América Central**	ah-**may**-ree-kah thayn-**trahl**
South America	**América del Sur**	ah-**may**-ree-kah dayl soor
the world	**el mundo**	ehl **moon**-doh

Numbers

1	**uno**	**oo**-noh
2	**dos**	dohs
3	**tres**	trays
4	**cuatro**	**kwah**-troh
5	**cinco**	**theen**-koh
6	**seis**	says
7	**siete**	see-**eh**-tay
8	**ocho**	**oh**-choh
9	**nueve**	**nway**-bay
10	**diez**	dee-**ayth**
11	**once**	**ohn**-thay
12	**doce**	**doh**-thay
13	**trece**	**tray**-thay
14	**catorce**	kah-**tor**-thay
15	**quince**	**keen**-thay
16	**dieciséis**	dee-ay-thee-**says**
17	**diecisiete**	dee-ay-thee-see-**eh**-tay
18	**dieciocho**	dee-ay-thee-**oh**-choh
19	**diecinueve**	dee-ay-thee-**nway**-bay
20	**veinte**	**bayn**-tay
21	**veintiuno**	bayn-tee-**oo**-noh
22	**veintidós**	bayn-tee-**dohs**
23	**veintitrés**	bayn-tee-**trays**
30	**treinta**	**trayn**-tah

31	**treinta y uno**	**trayn**-tah ee **oo**-noh
40	**cuarenta**	kwah-**rehn**-tah
41	**cuarenta y uno**	kwah-**rehn**-tah ee **oo**-noh
50	**cincuenta**	theen-**kwehn**-tah
60	**sesenta**	say-**sehn**-tah
70	**setenta**	say-**tehn**-tah
80	**ochenta**	oh-**chehn**-tah
90	**noventa**	noh-**behn**-tah
100	**cien**	thee-**ehn**
101	**ciento uno**	thee-**ehn**-toh **oo**-noh
102	**ciento dos**	thee-**ehn**-toh dohs
200	**doscientos**	dohs-thee-**ehn**-tohs
1000	**mil**	meel
1996	**mil novecientos** **noventa y seis**	meel noh-bay-thee-**ehn**-tohs noh-**behn**-tah ee says
2000	**dos mil**	dohs meel
10,000	**diez mil**	dee-**ayth** meel
million	**millón**	mee-**yohn**
billion	**mil millones**	meel mee-**yoh**-nays
first	**primero**	pree-**may**-roh
second	**segundo**	say-**goon**-doh
third	**tercero**	tehr-**thehr**-oh
half	**mitad**	mee-**tahd**
100%	**cien por cien**	the-**ehn** por thee-**ehn**
number one	**número uno**	**noo**-may-roh **oo**-noh

Money

Can you change dollars?	¿Me puede cambiar dólares?	may **pway**-day kahm-bee-**ar** doh-lah-rays
What is your exchange rate for dollars...?	¿A cuanto pagan el dólar...?	ah **kwahn**-toh **pah**-gahn ehl **doh**-lar
...in traveler's checks	...en cheques de viajero	ayn **chay**-kays day bee-ah-*hay*-roh
What is the commission?	¿Cuánto es la comisión?	**kwahn**-toh ays lah koh-mee-see-**ohn**
Any extra fee?	¿Tiene cuota extra?	tee-**ehn**-ay **kwoh**-tah **ayk**-strah
I would like...	Quería...	keh-**ree**-ah
...small bills.	...billetes pequeños.	bee-**yeh**-tays pay-**kayn**-yohs
...large bills.	...billetes grandes.	bee-**yeh**-tays **grahn**-days
...coins.	...monedas.	moh-**nay**-dahs
Is this a mistake?	¿Es esto un error?	ays **ay**-stoh oon ehr-**ror**
I'm rich / poor.	Soy rico[a] / pobre.	soy **ree**-koh / **poh**-bray
I'm broke.	No tengo dinero.	noh **tayn**-goh dee-**nay**-roh
55 pesetas	cincuenta y cinco pesetas	theen-**kwehn**-tah ee **theen**-koh peh-**say**-tahs

Key money words:

bank	banco	**bahn**-koh
money	dinero	dee-**nay**-roh
change money	cambio de moneda	**kahm**-bee-oh day moh-**nay**-dah

exchange	**cambio**	**kahm**-bee-oh
commission	**comisión**	koh-mee-see-**ohn**
traveler's check	**cheque de viajero**	**chay**-kay day bee-ah-**hay**-roh
credit card	**tarjeta de crédito**	tar-**hay**-tah day **kray**-dee-toh
cash advance	**adelanto de dinero**	ah-day-**lahn**-toh day dee-**nay**-roh
cash machine	**caja automática**	**kah**-hah ow-toh-**mah**-tee-kah
cashier	**cajero**	**kah**-hehr-oh
cash	**dinero**	dee-**nay**-roh
bills	**billetes**	bee-**yeh**-tays
coins	**monedas**	moh-**nay**-dahs
receipt	**recibo**	ray-**thee**-boh

Spain is ahead of many European countries in bank card money changing. It's usually a snap to get a cash advance on your Visa card or a pile of pesos with your ATM card. But don't rely entirely on plastic to finance your trip. Travelers' checks are still far more widely accepted at Spanish banks.

Banks are open 9:00-2:00 Monday through Friday. Commissions are steep (starting around $5). Big department stores like *El Corte Inglés* in Madrid exchange money at decent rates during their business hours. *Casas de cambio* (exchange offices) are open long hours, but you'll pay for the convenience with a lousy rate or sky-high commission.

Time

What time is it?	¿Qué hora es?	kay **oh**-rah ays
It's...	Son las...	sohn lahs
...8:00 in the morning.	...ocho de la mañana.	**oh**-choh day lah mahn-**yah**-nah
...16:00.	...dieciséis.	dee-ay-thee-**says**
...4:00 in the afternoon.	...4:00 de la tarde.	**kwah**-troh day lah **tar**-day
...10:30 (in the evening).	...diez y media (de la noche).	dee-**ayth** ee **may**-dee-ah (day lah **noh**-chay)
...a quarter past nine.	...nueve y cuarto.	**nway**-bay ee **kwar**-toh
...a quarter to eleven.	...once menos cuarto.	**ohn**-thay **may**-nohs **kwar**-toh
...noon.	...doce.	**doh**-thay
...midnight.	...doce de la noche.	**doh**-thay day lah **noh**-chay
It's...	Es...	ays
...sunrise.	...amanecer.	ah-mah-nay-**thehr**
...sunset.	...puesta de sol.	**pway**-stah day sohl
...early / late.	...temprano / tarde.	tehm-**prah**-noh / **tar**-day
...on time.	...puntual.	poon-too-**ahl**

In Spain, the 24-hour clock (military time) is used mainly for train, bus, and ferry schedules. Friends use the same "clock" we do. You'd meet a friend at 3:00 *de la tarde* (in the afternoon) to catch a train at 15:15. You'll hear people say *"Buenas tardes"* (Good afternoon/evening) starting about 2:00 p.m. You won't hear *"Buenas noches"* (Good night) until around 10 p.m.

Timely words:

minute	**minuto**	mee-**noo**-toh
hour	**hora**	**oh**-rah
in the morning	**por la mañana**	por lah mahn-**yah**-nah
in the afternoon	**por la tarde**	por lah **tar**-day
in the evening	**por la noche**	por lah **noh**-chay
night	**noche**	**noh**-chay
day	**día**	**dee**-ah
today	**hoy**	oy
yesterday	**ayer**	ah-**yehr**
tomorrow	**mañana**	mahn-**yah**-nah
tomorrow morning	**mañana por la mañana**	mahn-**yah**-nah por lah mahn-**yah**-nah
anytime	**a cualquier hora**	ah kwahl-kee-**ehr oh**-rah
immediately	**inmediatamente**	een-may-dee-ah-tah-**mehn**-tay
in one hour	**dentro de una hora**	**dehn**-troh day **oo**-nah **oh**-rah
every hour	**cada hora**	**kah**-dah **oh**-rah
every day	**cada día**	**kah**-dah **dee**-ah
last	**último**	**ool**-tee-moh
this	**este**	**ay**-stay
next	**próximo**	**prohk**-see-moh
May 15	**15 de mayo**	**keen**-thay day **mah**-yoh

week	**semana**	say-**mah**-nah
Monday	**lunes**	**loo**-nays
Tuesday	**martes**	**mar**-tays
Wednesday	**miércoles**	mee-**ehr**-koh-lays
Thursday	**jueves**	*h***way**-bays
Friday	**viernes**	bee-**ehr**-nays
Saturday	**sábado**	**sah**-bah-doh
Sunday	**domingo**	doh-**meen**-goh
month	**mes**	mays
January	**enero**	ay-**nay**-roh
February	**febrero**	fay-**bray**-roh
March	**marzo**	**mar**-thoh
April	**abril**	**ah**-breel
May	**mayo**	**mah**-yoh
June	**junio**	*h***oon**-yoh
July	**julio**	*h***ool**-yoh
August	**agosto**	ah-**goh**-stoh
September	**septiembre**	sehp-tee-**ehm**-bray
October	**octubre**	ohk-**too**-bray
November	**noviembre**	noh-bee-**ehm**-bray
December	**diciembre**	dee-thee-**ehm**-bray
year	**año**	**ahn**-yoh
spring	**primavera**	pree-mah-**bay**-rah
summer	**verano**	bay-**rah**-noh
fall	**otoño**	oh-**tohn**-yoh
winter	**invierno**	een-bee-**ehr**-noh

TIME

Spanish holidays and happy days:

holiday	**festivo**	fay-**stee**-boh
national holiday	**festivo nacional**	fay-**stee**-boh nah-thee-oh-**nahl**
religious holiday	**día religioso**	**dee**-ah ray-lee-*h*ee-oh-soh
Easter	**Pascuas**	**pahs**-kwahs
Merry Christmas!	**¡Feliz Navidad!**	fay-**leeth** nah-bee-**dahd**
Happy new year!	**¡Feliz Año Nuevo!**	fay-**leeth ahn**-yoh **nway**-boh
Happy anniversary!	**¡Feliz aniversario!**	fay-**leeth** ah-nee-behr-**sah**-ree-oh
Happy birthday!	**¡Feliz cumpleaños!**	fay-**leeth** koom-play-**ahn**-yohs

The Spanish sing "Happy birthday" to the same tune we do, but they don't fill in the person's name. Here are the words: *Cumpleaños feliz, cumpleaños feliz, te deseamos todos cumpleaños, cumpleaños feliz.*

Other happy days in Spain include *Semana Santa* (Holy Week), leading up to Easter. It's a festive time throughout Iberia, especially in Sevilla. *Corpus Christi* comes early in June, *Ascensión de Maria* on August 15th, and *Día de la Hispanidad*, Spain's national holiday, is on October 12th.

Transportation

Trains

Is this the line for...?	¿Es esta la fila para...?	ays **ay**-stah lah **fee**-lah **pah**-rah
...tickets	...billetes	bee-**yeh**-tays
...reservations	...reservas	ray-sehr-bahs
How much is a ticket to...?	¿Cuánto cuesta el billete a...?	**kwahn**-toh **kway**-stah ehl bee-**yeh**-tay ah
A ticket to ___.	Un billete para ___.	oon bee-**yeh**-tay **pah**-rah
When is the next train?	¿Cuándo es el siguiente tren?	**kwahn**-doh ays ehl seeg-ee-**ehn**-tay trayn
I'd like to leave...	Quería salir...	keh-**ree**-ah sah-**leer**
I'd like to arrive...	Quería llegar...	keh-**ree**-ah yay-**gar**
...by ___.	...a las ___.	ah lahs
...in the morning.	...por la mañana.	por lah mahn-**yah**-nah
...in the afternoon.	...por la tarde.	por lah **tar**-day
...in the evening.	...por la noche.	por lah **noh**-chay

Is there a...?	¿Hay un...?	Ī oon
...earlier train	...tren más temprano	trayn mahs tehm-**prah**-noh
...later train	...tren más tarde	trayn mahs **tar**-day
...overnight train	...tren nocturno	trayn nohk-**toor**-noh
...supplement	...suplemento	soo-play-**mehn**-toh
Is there a discount for...?	¿Tienen descuento para...?	tee-**ehn**-nehn days-**kwehn**-toh **pah**-rah
...youths	...jovenes	*h*oh-beh-nays
...seniors	...la tercera edad	lah tehr-**thay**-rah ay-**dahd**
Is a reservation required?	¿Se requiere reserva?	say ray-kee-**eh**-ray ray-**sehr**-bah
I'd like to reserve...	Quiero reservar...	kee-**ehr**-oh ray-sehr-**bar**
...a seat.	...un asiento.	oon ah-see-**ehn**-toh
...a berth.	...una litera.	oo-nah **lee**-tay-rah
Where does (the train) leave from?	¿De dónde sale?	day **dohn**-day **sah**-lay
What track?	¿Qué vía?	kay **bee**-ah
On time? Late?	¿Puntual? ¿Tarde?	poon-too-**ahl** / **tar**-day
When will it arrive?	¿Cuándo tiene su llegada?	**kwahn**-doh tee-**ehn**-ay soo yay-**gah**-dah
Is it direct?	¿Es directo?	ays dee-**rehk**-toh
Must I transfer?	¿Tengo que cambiar?	**tayn**-goh kay kahm-bee-**ar**
When? Where?	¿Cuándo? ¿Dónde?	**kwahn**-doh / **dohn**-day
Which train to...?	¿Qué tren para...?	kay trayn **pah**-rah
Which train car to...?	¿Qué vagón para...?	kay bah-**gohn pah**-rah
Is this (seat) free?	¿Está libre?	ay-**stah lee**-bray

Save my place?	¿Guardeme mi asiento?	**gwar**-day-may mee ah-see-**ehn**-toh
Where are you going?	¿A dónde va?	ah **dohn**-day vah
I'm going to...	Voy a...	boy ah
Tell me when to get off?	¿Dígame cuándo tengo que bajarme?	**dee**-gah-may **kwahn**-doh **tayn**-goh kay bah-*har*-may

Ticket talk:

ticket	billete	bee-**yeh**-tay
one way	de ida	day ee-dah
roundtrip	ida y vuelta	**ee**-dah ee **bwehl**-tah
first class	primera clase	pree-**may**-rah **klah**-say
second class	segunda clase	say-**goon**-dah **klah**-say
reduced fare	tarifa reducida	tah-**ree**-fah ray-doo-**thee**-dah
validate	válido	**vah**-lee-doh
schedule	horario	oh-**rah**-ree-oh
departure	salida	sah-**lee**-dah
direct	directo	dee-**rehk**-toh
connection	enlace	ayn-**lah**-thay
express service	expreso	ayk-**spray**-soh
reservation	reserva	ray-**sehr**-bah
non-smoking	no fumadores	noh foo-mah-**doh**-rays
seat...	asiento...	ah-see-**ehn**-toh
...by the window	...con ventana	kohn bayn-**tah**-nah
...on the aisle	...cerca pasillo	**thehr**-kah pah-**see**-yoh
berth...	litera...	**lee**-tay-rah
...upper	...superior	soo-peh-ree-**or**
...middle	...medio	**may**-thee-oh
...lower	...baja	bah-*hah*
refund	devolución	day-voh-loo-thee-**ohn**

TRANSPORTATION

At the train station:

Spanish Railways	**R.E.N.F.E.**	**rehn**-fay
train station	**estación de tren**	ay-stah-thee-**ohn** day trayn
train information	**información de trenes**	een-for-mah-thee-**ohn** day **tray**-nays
train	**tren**	trayn
high-speed train	**Talgo**	**tahl**-goh
arrival	**llegada**	yay-**gah**-dah
departure	**salida**	sah-**lee**-dah
delay	**retraso**	ray-**trah**-soh
waiting room	**sala de espera**	**sah**-lah day ay-**spay**-rah
lockers	**casilleros**	kah-see-**yay**-rohs
baggage check room	**oficina de equipaje**	oh-fee-**thee**-nah day ay-kee-**pah**-hay
lost and found office	**oficina de objetos perdidos**	oh-fee-**thee**-nah day ohb-**hay**-tohs pehr-**dee**-dohs
tourist information office	**Oficina de Turismo**	oh-fee-**thee**-nah day too-**rees**-moh
to the platforms	**en los andenes**	ayn lohs **ahn**-deh-nays
platform	**andén**	ahn-**dayn**
track	**vía**	**bee**-ah
train car	**vagón**	bah-**gohn**
dining car	**coche comedor**	**koh**-chay koh-may-**dor**
sleeper car	**coche cama**	**koh**-chay **kah**-mah
conductor	**conductor**	kohn-dook-**tor**

Reading Spanish train schedules and tickets:

a	to
con retraso	late
clase	class
coche	car
de	from
diario	daily
días	days
días de semana	weekdays
días laborales	workdays (Monday-Saturday)
domingo	Sunday
domingos y festivos	Sunday and holidays
excepto	except
fecha	date
festivos	holiday
hasta	until
hora salida	departure time
llegadas	arrivals
plaza	seat, place
sábado	Saturday
salidas	departures
solo	only
tipo de tren	type of train
todos	every
via	via
1-5, 6, 7	Monday-Friday, Saturday, Sunday

Spanish schedules use the 24-hour clock. It's like American time until noon. After that, subtract twelve and add p.m. So 13:00 is 1 p.m., 19:00 is 7 p.m., and midnight is 24:00. If your train is scheduled to depart at 00:01, it'll leave one minute after midnight.

Spanish trains require reservations for longer trips (even if you have a Eurailpass and the train is empty). When you arrive in a town, make your out-bound reservation right away. In bigger cities, the downtown RENFE (Spanish Railways) office is sometimes more efficient at making reservations than the train station.

Trains in Spain range in speed from glacial to gunshot. The *regional* and *correo* are milk runs—you'll curdle. The *cercania* is a commuter train for big-city workers. The *rapido, tranvia, semi-directo,* and *expreso* are not as rapido as they sound. The *Intercity* and *Electro* are faster. The comfortable *Talgo* is even speedier, but can't beat the *AVE,* Spain's new bullet train, connecting Madrid and Sevilla in just 3 hours (85% covered by Eurailpass).

Buses and subways:

How do I get to...?	¿Cómo llego a...?	koh-moh yay-goh ah
Which bus to...?	¿Qué autocar para...?	kay ow-toh-kar pah-rah
Does it stop at...?	¿Tiene parada en....?	tee-ehn-ay pah-rah-dah ayn
Which metro stop for...?	¿Qué parada de metro para...?	kay pah-rah-dah day may-troh pah-rah
Must I transfer?	¿Tengo que cambiar?	tayn-goh kay kahm-bee-ar
How much is a ticket?	¿Cuánto cuesta el billete?	kwahn-toh kway-stah ehl bee-yeh-tay
Where can I buy a ticket?	¿Dónde puedo comprar un billete?	dohn-day pway-doh kohm-prar oon bee-yeh-tay

When is the...?	¿Cuando sale...?	kwahn-doh sah-lay
...first	...primero	pree-may-roh
...next	...siguiente	seeg-ee-ehn-tay
...last	...último	ool-tee-moh
...bus / subway	...autobús / metro	ow-toh-boos / may-troh
What's the frequency per hour / day?	¿Qué frecuencia tiene por hora / día?	kay fray-kwayn-thee-ah tee-ehn-ay por oh-rah / dee-ah
I'm going to...	Voy a...	boy ah
Tell me when to get off?	¿Digame cuándo tengo que bajarme?	dee-gah-may kwahn-doh tayn-goh kay bah-har-may

TRANSPORTATION

Key bus and subway words:

ticket	billete	bee-yeh-lay
city bus	autobús	ow-toh-boos
long-distance bus	autocar	ow-toh-kar
bus stop	parada de autobus	pah-rah-dah day ow-toh-boos
bus station	estación de autobuses	ay-stah-thee-ohn day ow-toh-boo-says
subway	metro	may troh
entrance / exit	entrada / salida	ayn-trah-dah / sah-lee-dah
stop	parada	pah-rah-dah
map	mapa	mah-pah
schedule	horario	oh-rah-ree-oh
direct	directo	dee-rehk-toh

Buses (*autocars*) connect many smaller towns better and cheaper than trains. Tourist information offices have bus schedules. Subways are handy in Madrid and Barcelona.

Taxis:

Taxi!	¡Taxi!	**tahk**-see
Can you call a taxi?	¿Puede llamarme a un taxi?	**pway**-day yah-**mar**-may ah oon **tahk**-see
Where is a taxi stand?	¿Dónde está la parada de taxi?	**dohn**-day ay-**stah** lah pah-**rah**-dah day **tahk**-see
Are you free?	¿Está libre?	ay-**stah lee**-bray
Occupied.	Ocupado.	oh-koo-**pah**-doh
How much will it cost to go to...?	¿Cuánto me costará...?	**kwahn**-toh may koh-stah-**rah**
...the airport	...al aeropuerto	ahl ah-ay-roh-**pwehr**-toh
...the train station	...a la estación de trenes	ah lah ay-stah-thee-**ohn** day **tray**-nays
...this address	...a esta dirección	ah **ay**-stah dee-rehk-thee-**ohn**
Too much.	Demasiado.	day-mah-see-**ah**-doh
This is all I have.	Esto es todo lo que tengo.	**ay**-stoh ays **toh**-doh loh kay **tayn**-goh
Can you take ___ people?	¿Puede llevar a ___ personas?	**pway**-day yay-**bar** ah ___ pehr-**soh**-nahs
Any extra fee?	¿Tiene cuota extra?	tee-**ehn**-ay **kwoh**-tah **ayk**-strah
The meter, please.	El taxímetro, por favor.	ehl tahk-**see**-may-troh por fah-**bor**
The most direct route.	La ruta más directa.	lah **roo**-tah mahs dee-**rehk**-tah

Slow down.	Más despacio.	mahs day-**spah**-thee-oh
If you don't slow down, I'll throw up.	Si no va más despacio, voy a vomitar.	see noh bah mahs day-**spah**-thee-oh boy ah boh-mee-**tar**
Stop here.	Pare aquí.	**pah**-ray ah-**kee**
Can you wait?	¿Puede esperar?	**pway**-day ay-spay-**rar**
I'll never forget this ride.	Nunca me voy a olvidar de este recorrido.	**noon**-kah may boy ah ohl-bee-**dar** day **ay**-stay ray-koh-**ree**-doh
Where did you learn to drive?	¿Dónde aprendió a conducir?	**dohn**-day ah-prehn-dee-**oh** ah kohn-doo-**theer**
I'll only pay what's on the meter.	Solo voy a pagar lo que dice el taxímetro.	**soh**-loh boy ah pah-**gar** loh kay **dee**-thay ehl tahk-**see**-may-troh
My change, please.	Mí cambio, por favor.	mee **kahm**-bee-oh por fah-**bor**
Keep the change.	Quédese con el cambio.	**kay**-day-say kohn ehl **kahm**-bee-oh

Taxis in Spain are reasonable, except for going to and from airports (use local buses for these trips). Taxis usually take up to four people. If you have trouble flagging down a taxi, ask for directions to a *parada de taxi* (taxi stand). In Madrid and Barcelona, subways are cheap and efficient.

Rental wheels:

I'd like to rent...	**Quería alquilar...**	keh-**ree**-ah ahl-kee-**lar**
...a car.	**...un coche.**	oon **koh**-chay
...a station wagon.	**...un coche familiar.**	oon **koh**-chay fah-mee-lee-**ar**
...a van.	**...una frugoneta.**	**oo**-nah froo-goh-**nay**-tah
...a motorcycle.	**...una moto.**	**oo**-nah **moh**-toh
...a motor scooter.	**...una motocicleta.**	**oo**-nah moh-toh-thee-**klay**-tah
...a bicycle.	**...una bicicleta.**	**oo**-nah bee-thee-**klay**-tah
How much per...?	**¿Cuánto es por...?**	**kwahn**-toh ays por
...hour	**...hora**	**oh**-rah
...day	**...día**	**dee**-ah
...week	**...semana**	say-**mah**-nah
Unlimited mileage?	**¿Sin límite de kilómetros?**	seen **lee**-mee-tay day kee-**loh**-may-trohs
I brake for bakeries.	**Paro en cada panadería.**	**pah**-roh ayn **kah**-dah pah-nah-deh-**ree**-ah
Is there...?	**¿Hay...?**	ī
...a helmet	**...un casco**	oon **kah**-skoh
...a discount	**...un descuento**	oon days-**kwehn**-toh
...a deposit	**...un depósito**	oon day-**poh**-see-toh
...insurance	**...seguro**	say-**goo**-roh
When do I bring it back?	**¿Cuándo lo traigo de vuelta?**	**kwahn**-doh loh **trī**-goh day boo-**ayl**-tah

Driving:

gas station	**gasolinera**	gah-soh-lee-**nay**-rah
The nearest gas station?	**¿La gasolinera más cercana?**	lah gah-soh-lee-**nay**-rah mahs thehr-**kah**-nah
Self-service?	**¿Auto-servicio?**	ow-toh-sehr-**bee**-thee-oh
Fill the tank.	**Llene el depósito.**	**yay**-nay ehl day-**poh**-see-toh
I need...	**Necesito...**	nay-thay-**see**-toh
...gas.	**...gasolina.**	gah-soh-**lee**-nah
...unleaded.	**...sin plomo.**	seen **ploh**-moh
...regular.	**...normal.**	nor-**mahl**
...super.	**...super.**	soo-**pehr**
...diesel.	**...diesel, gasoleo.**	**dee**-sehl, gah-**soh**-lee-oh
Check...	**Cheque...**	**chay**-kay
...the oil.	**...el aceite.**	ehl ah-**thay**-tay
...the air in the tires.	**...el aire en las ruedas.**	ehl **ah**-ray ayn lahs roo-**ay**-dahs
...the radiator.	**...el radiador.**	ehl rah-dee-ah-**dor**
...the battery.	**...la batería.**	lah bah-tay-**ree**-ah
...the fuses.	**...los fusibles.**	lohs foo-**see**-blays
...the fanbelt.	**...la correa del ventilador.**	lah koh-**ray**-ah dayl bayn-tee-lah-**dor**
...the brakes.	**...los frenos.**	lohs **fray**-nohs
...my pulse.	**...mi pulso.**	mee **pool**-soh

Rather than dollars and gallons, gas pumps in Spain read pesetas and liters. Gas costs roughly $1 per liter (about 4 liters in a gallon). In parts of Spain, diesel is called *gasoleo*.

Car trouble:

accident	**accidente**	ahk-thee-**dehn**-tay
breakdown	**averiado**	ah-bay-ree-**ah**-doh
funny noise	**ruido extraño**	roo-**ee**-doh ayk-**strahn**-yoh
electrical problem	**problema eléctrico**	proh-**blay**-mah ay-**lehk**-tree-koh
flat tire	**rueda pinchada**	roo-**ay**-dah peen-**chah**-dah
My car won't start.	**Mi coche no enciende.**	mee **koh**-chay noh ayn-thee-**ehn**-day
This doesn't work.	**Esto no funciona.**	**ay**-stoh noh foonk-thee-**oh**-nah
It's overheating.	**Está caliente.**	ay-**stah** kahl-**yehn**-tay
I need...	**Necesito...**	nay-thay-**see**-toh
...a tow truck.	**...una grúa.**	**oo**-nah **groo**-ah
...a mechanic.	**...un mecánico.**	oon may-**kah**-nee-koh
...a stiff drink.	**...un trago.**	oon **trah**-goh

For help with repair, look up "Repair" under Shopping.

Parking:

parking garage	**estacionamiento**	ay-stah-thee-oh-nah-mee-**ehn**-toh
Where can I park?	**¿Dónde puedo aparcar?**	**dohn**-day **pway**-doh ah-par-**kar**
Is parking nearby?	**¿Hay un estacionamiento cercano?**	ī oon ay-stah-thee-oh-nah-mee-**ehn**-toh thehr-**kahn**-noh

Can I park here?	¿Puedo aparcar aquí?	pway-doh ah-par-**kar** ah-**kee**
How long can I park here?	¿Por cuánto tiempo puedo aparcar aquí?	por **kwahn**-toh tee-**ehm**-poh **pway**-doh ah-par-**kar** ah-**kee**
Must I pay to park here?	¿Tengo que pagar por aparcar aquí?	**tayn**-goh kay pah-**gar** por ah-par-**kar** ah-**kee**
Is this a safe place to park?	¿Es este un sitio seguro para aparcar?	ays **ay**-stay oon **see**-tee-oh say-**goo**-roh **pah**-rah ah-par-**kar**

TRANSPORTATION

Parking in Spain can be hazardous. Park legally. Many towns require parking permits, sold at tobacco shops. To give your car a local profile, cover the rental decal and put a local newspaper inside the back window. Leave the car empty and, some would advise, unlocked overnight. If it's a hatchback, remove the shelf behind the back seat to show thieves you have *nada* in the trunk. Get safe parking tips from your hotel.

Finding your way:

I'm going to...	**Voy a...**	boy ah
How do I get to...?	**¿Cómo llego a...?**	**koh**-moh **yay**-goh ah
Is there a map?	**¿Hay un mapa?**	Ī oon **mah**-pah
How many minutes...?	**¿Cuántos minutos...?**	**kwahn**-tohs mee-**noo**-tohs
How many hours...?	**¿Cuántos horas...?**	**kwahn**-tohs oh-rahs
...on foot	**...a pié**	ah pee-**ay**
...by bicycle	**...en bicicleta**	ayn bee-thee-**klay**-tah
...by car	**...en coche**	ayn **koh**-chay
How many kilometers to...?	**¿Cuántos kilómetros a...?**	**kwahn**-tohs kee-**loh**-may-trohs ah
What's the... route to Madrid?	**¿Cuál es el... camino para Madrid?**	kwahl ays ehl... kah-**mee**-noh **pah**-rah mah-**dreed**
...best	**...mejor**	may-*hor*
...fastest	**...más rápido**	mahs **rah**-pee-doh
...most interesting	**...más interesante**	mahs een-tay-ray-**sahn**-tay
Point it out?	**¿Señálelo?**	sayn-**yah**-lay-loh
I'm lost.	**Estoy perdido[a].**	ay-**stoy** pehr-**dee**-doh
Where am I?	**¿Dónde estoy?**	**dohn**-day ay-**stoy**
Who am I?	**¿Quién soy?**	kee-**ehn** soy
Where is...?	**¿Dónde está...?**	**dohn**-day ay-**stah**
The nearest ...?	**¿El más cercano...?**	ehl mahs thehr-**kah**-noh
Where is this address?	**¿Dónde se encuentra esta dirección?**	**dohn**-day say ayn-**kwehn**-trah **ay**-stah dee-rehk-thee-**ohn**

Key route-finding words:

city map	**mapa de la ciudad**	**mah**-pah day lah thee-oo-**dahd**
road map	**mapa de carretera**	**mah**-pah day kah-ray-**tay**-rah
straight	**derecho**	day-**ray**-choh
left	**izquierda**	eeth-kee-**ehr**-dah
right	**derecha**	day-**ray**-chah
first	**primero**	pree-**may**-roh
next	**siguiente**	seeg-ee-**ehn**-tay
intersection	**intersección**	een-tehr-sehk-thee-**ohn**
stoplight	**semáforo**	say-**mah**-foh-roh
(main) square	**plaza (principal)**	**plah**-thah (preen-thee-**pahl**)
street	**calle**	**kah**-yay
bridge	**puente**	**pwehn**-tay
tunnel	**túnel**	**too**-nehl
highway	**carretera**	kah-ray-**tay**-rah
freeway	**autopista**	ow-toh-**pee**-stah
north	**norte**	**nor**-tay
south	**sur**	soor
east	**este**	**ay**-stay
west	**oeste**	oh-**ay**-stay

Reading road signs:

ceda el paso	yield
centro de la ciudad	to the center of town
cuidado	caution
despacio	slow
desvío	detour
dirección única	one-way street
entrada	entrance
estacionamiento prohibido	no parking
obras	workers ahead
salida	exit
peage	toll road
peatones	pedestrians
stop	stop

Here are the standard symbols you'll see.

DUH — NO ENTRY FOR CARS — ALL VEHICLES PROHIBITED — NO ENTRY — SPEED LIMIT (IN KM) — YIELD — NO PASSING — DANGER — PARKING

In any country, the flashing lights of a patrol car are a sure sign that someone's in trouble. If it's you, say, *"Lo siento, soy un turista."* (Sorry, I'm a tourist.) Or, for the adventurous: *"Si no le gusta como conduzco, sácate de la acera."* (If you don't like how I drive, stay off the sidewalk.)

Other signs you may bump into:

abierto	open
abierto de... a...	open from... to...
agua no potable	undrinkable water
alquilo	for rent
averiado	out of service
caballeros	men
camas	vacancy
cerrado	closed
cerrado por vacaciones	closed for vacation
cerrado por obras	closed for restoration
completo	no vacancy
entrada libre	free admission
habitaciones	vacancy
hay...	we have...
no fumar	no smoking
no tocar	do not touch
ocupado	occupied
paso prohibido	no entry
peligro	danger
prohibido	forbidden
salida de emergencia	emergency exit
señoras	women
servicios	toilets
Turismo	tourist information office
vendo	for sale

Sleeping

Places to stay:

hotel	**hotel**	oh-**tehl**
small, family-run hotel	**pensión**	payn-see-**ohn**
room in private home	**habitación**	ah-bee-tah-thee-**ohn**
youth hostel	**albergue de juventud**	ahl-**behr**-gay day hoo-behn-**tood**
vacancy sign (literally "rooms," "beds")	**habitaciones, camas**	ah-bee-tah-thee-**oh**-nays, **kah**-mahs
no vacancy	**completo**	kohm-**play**-toh

Spanish hotels come with a handy government-regulated classification system. Look for a blue and white plaque by the hotel door indicating the category.

Hotel (H) and **Hostales (Hs):** The most comfortable and expensive (rated with stars).

Hotel-Residencia (HR) and **Hostal-Residencia (HsR):** Basically hotels without restaurants. Don't confuse hostales with youth hostels.

Pensión (P), Casa de Huéspedes (CH), & Fonda (F): Cheaper, usually family-run places. If you're on a tight budget, these can be a good value.

Parador: Government-run hotels, often in refurbished castles or palaces. They can be a good value, but most feature snooty staff, snooty clientele, and rooms costing well over $100 per double.

Reserving a room:

A good time to call to reserve a room is the morning of the day you plan to arrive. If you want to reserve by fax from the U.S.A, use the nifty form in the appendix.

Hello.	Hola.	oh-lah
Do you speak English?	¿Habla usted Inglés?	ah-blah oo-**stehd** een-**glays**
Do you have a room...?	¿Tiene una habitación libre...?	tee-**ehn**-ay oo-nah ah-bee-tah-thee-**ohn** lee-bray
...for one person	...para una persona	pah-rah oo-nah pehr-**soh**-nah
...for two people	...para dos personas	pah-rah dohs pehr-**soh**-nahs
...for tonight	...para hoy	pah-rah oy
...for two nights	...para dos noches	pah-rah dohs noh-chays
...for this Friday	...para este viernes	pah-rah ay-stay bee-ehr-nays
...for June 21	...para 21 de Junio	pah-rah bayn-tee-oo-noh day hoon-yoh
Yes or no?	¿Sí o no?	see oh noh
I'd like...	Quería...	keh-**ree**-ah
...a private bathroom.	...un baño privado.	**bahn**-yoh pree-**vah**-doh
...your cheapest room.	...su habitación más barata.	soo ah-bee-tah-thee-**ohn** mahs bah-**rah**-tah
...___ bed(s) for ___ people in ___ room(s).	...___ cama(s) para ___ personas en ___ habitación(es).	**kah**-mah(s) **pah**-rah ___ pehr-**soh**-nahs ayn ___ ah-bee-tah-thee-**ohn**(ays)
How much is it?	¿Cuánto cuesta?	**kwahn**-toh **kway**-stah
Anything cheaper?	¿Nada más barato?	nah-dah mahs bah-**rah**-toh

I'll take it.	**La quiero.**	lah kee-**ehr**-oh
My name is...	**Me llamo...**	may **yah**-moh
I'll stay...	**Quedaré...**	kay-dah-**ray**
We'll stay...	**Quedaremos...**	kay-dah-**ray**-mohs
...for __ night(s).	**...para __ noche(s).**	**pah**-rah __ **noh**-chay(s)
I'll come...	**Vendré...**	bayn-**dray**
We'll come...	**Vendremos...**	bayn-**dray**-mohs
...in one hour.	**...en una hora.**	ayn **oo**-nah **oh**-rah
...before 4:00 in the afternoon.	**...antes de las cuatro de la tarde.**	**ahn**-tays day lahs **kwah**-troh day lah **tar**-day
...Friday before 6 p.m.	**...viernes antes de las 6:00 de la tarde.**	bee-**ehr**-nays **ahn**-tays day lahs says day lah **tar**-day
Thank you.	**Gracias.**	**grah**-thee-ahs

Getting specific:

I'd like a room...	**Quería una habitación...**	keh-**ree**-ah **oo**-nah ah-bee-tah-thee-**ohn**
...with / without / and	**...con / sin / y**	kohn / seen / ee
...toilet.	**...aseo.**	ah-**say**-oh
...shower.	**...ducha.**	**doo**-chah
...shower down the hall.	**...ducha al fondo del pasillo.**	**doo**-chah ahl **fohn**-doh dayl pah-**see**-yoh
...bathtub.	**...bañera.**	bahn-**yay**-rah
...double bed.	**...cama de matrimonio.**	**kah**-mah day mah-tree-**moh**-nee-oh
...twin beds.	**...camas gemelas.**	**kah**-mahs *hay*-**may**-lahs

...balcony.	...balcón.	bahl-**kohn**
...view.	...vista.	bee-**stah**
...with only a sink.	...solo con lavabo.	**soh**-loh kohn lah-**bah**-boh
...on the ground floor.	...en el piso bajo.	ayn ehl **pee**-soh **bah**-hoh
Is there an elevator?	¿Hay un ascensor?	ī oon ahs-thehn-**sor**
We arrive Monday, depart Wednesday.	Llegamos el lunes, salimos el miércoles.	yay-**gah**-mohs ehl **loo**-nays, sah-**lee**-mohs ehl mee-**ehr**-koh-lays
I have a reservation.	Tengo la reserva hecha.	**tayn**-goh lah ray-**sehr**-bah ay-chah
Confirm my reservation?	Confirme mi reserva?	kohn-**feer**-may mee ray-**sehr**-bah
I'll sleep anywhere. I'm desperate.	Puedo dormir en cualquier sitio. Estoy desesperado[a].	**pway**-doh **dor**-meer ayn kwahl-kee-**ehr see**-tee-oh. ay-**stoy** day-say-spay-**rah**-doh
I have a sleeping bag.	Tengo un saco de dormir.	**tayn**-goh oon **sah**-koh day dor-**meer**

Nailing down the price

How much is...?	¿Cuánto cuesta...?	**kwahn**-toh **kway**-stah
...a room for ___ people	...una habitación para ___ personas	oo-nah ah-bee-tah-thee-**ohn** pah-rah ___ pehr-**soh**-nahs
...your cheapest room	...su habitación más barata	soo ah-bee-tah-thee-**ohn** mahs bah-**rah**-tah
Is breakfast included?	¿El desayuno está incluido?	ehl day-sah-**yoo**-noh ay-**stah** een-kloo-**ee**-doh

Is breakfast required?	¿Se requiere desayuno?	say ray-kee-**ay**-ray day-sah-**yoo**-noh
How much without breakfast?	¿Cuánto cuesta sin el desayuno?	**kwahn**-toh **kway**-stah seen ehl day-sah-**yoo**-noh
Complete price?	¿El precio completo?	ehl **pray**-thee-oh kohm-**play**-toh
Is it cheaper if I stay ___ nights?	¿Es más barato si quedo ___ noches?	ays mahs bah-**rah**-toh see **kay**-doh ___ **noh**-chays
I will stay ___ nights.	Me quedaré ___ noches.	may kay-dah-**ray** ___ **noh**-chays

Choosing a room:

Can I see the room?	¿Puedo ver la habitación?	**pway**-doh behr lah ah-bee-tah-thee-**ohn**
Show me another room?	¿Enséñeme otra habitación?	ayn-**sayn**-yay-may **oh**-trah ah-bee-tah-thee-**ohn**
Do you have something...?	¿Tiene algo...?	tee-**ehn**-ay **ahl**-goh
...larger / smaller	...más grande / más pequeño	mahs **grahn**-day / mahs pay-**kayn**-yoh
...better / cheaper	...mejor / más barato	may-**hor** / mahs bah-**rah**-toh
...brighter	...con más claridad	kohn mahs klah-ree-**dahd**
...in the back	...en la parte de atrás	ayn lah **par**-tay day ah-**trahs**
...quieter	...más tranquillo	mahs trahn-**kee**-yoh
I'll take it.	La quiero.	lah kee-**ehr**-oh

My key, please.	Mi llave, por favor.	mee **yah**-bay por fah-**bor**
Sleep well.	Que duerma bien.	kay **dwehr**-mah bee-**yehn**
Good night.	Buenas noches.	**bway**-nahs **noh**-chays

In Spain, views often come with street noise (a Spanish specialty). You can ask for a room *"con vista"* or *"tranquillo."* If sleep is a priority, go with the latter.

Hotel help:

I'd like...	Quería...	keh-**ree**-ah
...a / another	...un / otro	oon / **oh**-troh
...towel.	...toalla.	toh-**ah**-yah
...pillow.	...almohada.	ahl-moh-**ah**-dah
...clean sheets.	...sábanas limpias.	**sah**-bah-nahs **leem**-pee-ahs
...blanket.	...manta.	**mahn**-tah
...glass.	...vaso.	**bah**-soh
...sink stopper.	...tapon.	tah-**pohn**
...soap.	...jabón.	*h*ah-**bohn**
...toilet paper.	...papel higiénico.	pah-**pehl** ee-*h*ee-**ay**-nee-koh
...crib.	...cuna.	**koo**-nah
...extra roll-away bed.	...cama plegable extra.	**kah**-mah play-**gah**-blay **ayk**-strah
...different room.	...habitación diferente	ah-bee-tah-thee-**ohn** dee-fay-**rehn**-tay
...silence.	...silencio.	see-**lehn**-thee-oh

Where can I wash / hang my laundry?	¿Dónde puedo lavar / tender mi ropa?	**dohn**-day **pway**-doh lah-**bar** / tehn-**dehr** mee **roh**-pah
I'd like to stay another night.	**Quería quedarme otra noche.**	keh-**ree**-ah kay-**dar**-may **oh**-trah **noh**-chay
Where can I park?	**¿Dónde puedo aparcar?**	**dohn**-day **pway**-doh ah-par-**kar**
What time do you lock up?	**¿A qué hora cierran la puerta?**	ah kay **oh**-rah thee-**ay**-rahn lah **pwehr**-tah
What time is breakfast?	**¿A qué hora es el desayuno?**	ah kay **oh**-rah ays ehl day-sah-**yoo**-noh
Please wake me at 7:00.	**Despiérteme a las 7:00, por favor.**	days-pee-**ehr**-tay-may ah lahs see-**eh**-tay por fah-**bor**

Hotel hassles:

Come with me.	**Venga conmigo.**	**vayn**-gah kohn-**mee**-goh
I have a problem in my room.	**Tengo un problema en mi habitación.**	**tayn**-goh oon proh-**blay**-mah ayn mee ah-bee-tah-thee-**ohn**
It smells bad.	**Huele mal.**	**way**-lay mahl
bugs	**moscas**	**moh**-skahs
cockroaches	**cucarachas**	koo-kah-**rah**-chahs
mice	**ratones**	rah-**toh**-nays
prostitutes	**prostitutas**	proh-stee-**too**-tahs
The bed is too soft / hard.	**La cama es muy blanda / dura.**	lah **kah**-mah ays **moo**-ee **blahn**-dah / **doo**-rah

Lamp...	**Lámpara...**	**lahm**-pah-rah
Lightbulb...	**Bombilla...**	bohm-**bee**-yah
Key...	**Llave...**	**yah**-bay
Lock...	**Cerradura...**	thehr-rah-**doo**-rah
Window...	**Ventana...**	bayn-**tah**-nah
Faucet...	**Grifo...**	**gree**-foh
Sink...	**Lavabo...**	lah-**bah**-boh
Toilet...	**Aseo...**	ah-**say**-oh
Shower...	**Ducha...**	**doo**-chah
...dooen't work.	**...no funciona.**	noh foonk-thee-**oh**-nah
There is no hot water.	**No hay agua caliente.**	noh ī ah-gwah kahl-**yehn**-tay
When is the water hot?	**¿Cuándo hay agua caliente?**	**kwahn**-doh ī ah-gwah kahl-**yehn**-tay

If the management treats you like a *cucaracha* (cockroach), ask to see the hotel's *libro de reclamaciones* (the government-required complaint book). Your problems will generally get solved in a jiffy.

Checking out:

I'll leave...	**Me iré...**	may ee-**ray**
We'll leave...	**Nos iremos...**	nohs ee-**ray**-mohs
...today / tomorrow.	**...hoy / mañana.**	oy / mahn-**yah**-nah
...very early.	**...muy temprano.**	**moo**-ee tehm-**prah**-noh
When is check-out time?	**¿Cuándo es la hora de salida?**	**kwahn**-doh ays lah **oh**-rah day sah-**lee**-dah

Can I pay now?	¿Le pago ahora?	lay **pah**-goh ah-**oh**-rah
The bill, please.	La cuenta, por favor.	lah **kwayn**-tah por fah-**bor**
Credit card O.K.?	¿Tarjeta de crédito O.K.?	tar-**hay**-tah day **kray**-dee-toh "O.K."
I slept like a log. (Sleep grabbed me.)	Dormí de un tirón.	dor-**mee** day oon tee-**rohn**
Everything was great.	Todo estuvo muy bien.	**toh**-doh ay-**stoo**-boh **moo**-ee bee-**yehn**
Will you call my next hotel for me?	Puede llamar a mí próximo hotel?	**pway**-day yah-**mar** ah mee **prohk**-see-moh oh-**tehl**
Can I...?	¿Puedo...?	**pway**-doh
Can we...?	¿Podemos...?	poh-**day**-mohs
...leave baggage here until ___	...guardar aquí las maletas hasta ___	gwar-**dar** ah-**kee** lahs mah-**lay**-tahs **ah**-stah

Camping:

tent	tienda	tee-**ayn**-dah
camping	camping	**kahm**-peeng
The nearest campground?	¿El camping más cercano?	ehl **kahm**-peeng mahs thehr-**kah**-noh
Can I...?	¿Puedo...?	**pway**-doh
Can we...?	¿Podemos...?	poh-**day**-mohs
...camp here for one night	...acampar aquí por una noche	ah-kahm-**par** ah-**kee** por **oo**-nah **noh**-chay
Do showers cost extra?	¿Cuestan extra las duchas?	**kway**-stahn **ayk**-strah lahs **doo**-chahs

Eating

EATING

Finding a restaurant:

Where's a good... restaurant?	¿Dónde hay un buen restaurante...?	**dohn**-day ī oon bwayn ray-stoh-**rahn**-tay
...cheap	...barato	bah-**rah**-toh
...local-style	...regional	ray-*h*ee-oh-**nahl**
...untouristy	...que no sea un sitio de turistas	kay noh **say**-ah oon **see**-tee-oh day too-**ree**-stahs
...Chinese	...chino	**chee**-noh
...fast food	...comida rápida	koh-**mee**-dah **rah**-pee-dah
...cafeteria	...cafeteria	kah-fay-**tay**-ree-ah
with a salad bar	con ensaladas	kohn ayn-sah-**lah**-dahs

Getting a table and menu:

Waiter.	Camarero.	kah-mah-**ray**-roh
Waitress.	Camarera.	kah-mah-**ray**-rah
I'd like...	Quería...	keh-**ree**-ah
...a table for one / two.	...una mesa para uno / dos.	**oo**-nah **may**-sah **pah**-rah **oo**-noh / dohs
...non-smoking.	...no fumadores.	noh foo-mah-**doh**-rays
...just a drink.	...solo para una bebida.	**soh**-loh **pah**-rah **oo**-nah bay-**bee**-dah
...a snack.	...un pincho.	oon **peen**-choh
...to see the menu.	...ver el menú.	behr ehl may-**noo**
...to order a meal.	...ordenar la comida.	or-day-**nar** lah koh-**mee**-dah
...to eat.	...comer.	koh-**mehr**

...to pay.	...pagar.	pah-**gar**
...to throw up.	...vomitar.	boh-mee-**tar**
What do you recommend?	¿Qué es lo que me recomienda?	kay ays loh kay may ray-kohm-**yehn**-dah
What's your favorite?	¿Cuál es su preferida?	kwahl ays soo pray-fay-**ree**-dah
Is it...?	¿Es esto...?	ays **ay**-stoh
...tasty	...sabroso	sah-**broh**-soh
...expensive	...caro	**kah**-roh
...light	...ligero	lee-*hay*-roh
Is it filling?	¿Esto le llena?	**ay**-stoh lay **yay**-nah
What is...?	¿Qué es...?	kay ays
...that	...esto	**ay**-stoh
...local	...típico	**tee**-pee-koh
...fast	...lo más rápido	loh mahs **rah**-pee-doh
...cheap and filling	...lo que llena y es barato	loh kay **yay**-nah ee ays bah-**rah**-toh
Do you have...?	¿Tiene...?	tee-**ehn**-ay
...an English menu	...un menú en Inglés	oon may-**noo** ayn een-**glays**
...children's portions	...raciónes para niños	rah-thee-**oh**-nays **pah**-rah **neen**-yohs

The Spanish eat late, and so will you if you'll be dining in restaurants. No self-respecting restaurant serves dinner before 8 p.m. To eat early, well, and within even the tightest budget, duck into a bar, where you can stab toothpicks into local munchies (see *Tapas* on page 60).

The menu:

menu	**menú**	may-**noo**
menu of the day	**menú del día**	may-**noo** dayl **dee**-ah
tourist menu	**menú de turista**	meh-**noo** day too-**ree**-stah
combination plate	**plato combinado**	**plah**-toh kohm-bee-**nah**-doh
special of the day	**especial del día**	ay-spay-thee-**ahl** dayl **dee**-ah
specialty of the house	**especialidad de la casa**	ay-spay-thee-ah-lee-**dahd** day lah **kah**-sah
breakfast	**desayuno**	day-sah-**yoo**-noh
lunch	**almuerzo**	ahlm-**wehr**-thoh
dinner	**cena**	**thay**-nah
appetizers	**aperitivos**	ah-pay-ree-**tee**-bohs
bread	**pan**	pahn
salad	**ensalada**	ayn-sah-**lah**-dah
soup	**sopa**	**soh**-pah
first course	**primer plato**	pree-**mehr plah**-toh
main course	**segundo plato**	say-**goon**-doh **plah**-toh
meat	**carne**	**kar**-nay
poultry	**aves**	**ah**-bays
seafood	**marisco**	mah-**ree**-skoh
egg dishes	**tortillas**	tor-**tee**-yahs
side dishes	**a parte**	ah **par**-tay
vegetables	**verduras**	behr-**doo**-rahs
cheese	**queso**	**kay**-soh
dessert	**postres**	**poh**-strays

beverages	**bebidas**	bay-**bee**-dahs
beer	**cerveza**	thehr-**bay**-thah
wine	**vino**	**bee**-noh
cover charge	**precio de entrada**	**pray**-thee-oh day ayn-**trah**-dah
service (not) included	**servicio (no) incluido**	sehr-**bee**-thee-oh (noh) een-kloo-**ee**-doh
with / without	**con / sin**	kohn / seen
and / or	**y / o**	ee / oh

Dietary restrictions:

I'm allergic to...	**Soy alérgico[a] a...**	soy ah-**lehr**-hee-koh ah
I cannot eat...	**No puedo comer...**	noh **pway**-doh koh-**mehr**
...dairy products.	**...productos lácteos.**	proh-**dook**-tohs lahk-tay-ohs
...meat / pork.	**...carne / cerdo.**	kar nay / **thehr**-doh
...salt / sugar.	**...sal / azúcar.**	sahl / ah-**thoo**-kar
I'm diabetic.	**Soy diabético[a].**	soy dee-ah-**bay**-tee-koh
Low cholesterol?	**¿Bajo en colesterol?**	**bah**-hoh ayn koh-lay-stay-**rohl**
No caffeine.	**No cafeína.**	noh kah-**fay**-nah
No alcohol.	**No alcohol.**	noh ahl-**kohl**
I'm a...	**Soy...**	soy
...vegetarian.	**...vegetariano[a].**	bay-hay-tah-ree-**ah**-noh
...strict vegetarian.	**...estricto[a] vegetariano[a].**	ay-**streek**-toh bay-hay-tah-ree-**ah**-noh
...carnivore.	**...carnívoro[a].**	kar-**nee**-boh-roh

Tableware and condiments:

plate	**plato**	**plah**-toh
napkin	**servilleta**	sehr-vee-**yay**-tah
knife	**cuchillo**	koo-**chee**-yoh
fork	**tenedor**	tay-nay-**dor**
spoon	**cuchara**	koo-**chah**-rah
cup	**taza**	**tah**-thah
glass	**vaso**	**bah**-soh
carafe	**garrafa**	gah-**rah**-fah
water	**agua**	**ah**-gwah
bread	**pan**	pahn
butter	**mantequilla**	mahn-tay-**kee**-yah
margarine	**margarina**	mar-gah-**ree**-nah
salt / pepper	**sal / pimienta**	sahl / pee-mee-**ehn**-tah
sugar	**azúcar**	ah-**thoo**-kar
artifical sweetener	**edulcorante**	ay-dool-koh-**rahn**-tay
honey	**miel**	mee-**ehl**
mustard	**mostaza**	moh-**stah**-thah
mayonnaise	**mayonesa**	mah-yoh-**nay**-sah

Restaurant requests and regrets:

A little. / More.	**Un poco. / Más.**	oon **poh**-koh / mahs
Another.	**Otro.**	**oh**-troh
The same.	**El mismo.**	ehl **mees**-moh
I did not order this.	**No ordené esto.**	noh or-day-**nay ay**-stoh
Is this included with the meal?	**¿Está esto incluido con la comida?**	ay-**stah ay**-stoh een-kloo-**ee**-doh kohn lah koh-**mee**-dah

English	Spanish	Pronunciation
I'm in a hurry.	Estoy en un apuro.	ay-**stoy** ayn oon ah-**poo**-roh
I must leave by...	Tengo que salir a...	**tayn**-goh kay sah-**leer** ah
When will the food be ready?	¿Cuando estará la comida lista?	**kwahn**-doh ay-stah-**rah** lah koh-**mee**-dah **lee**-stah
I've changed my mind.	Cambié de idea.	kahm-bee-**ay** day ee-**day**-ah
Can I get it "to go"?	¿Me lo empaqueta para llevar?	may loh aym-pah-**kay**-tah **pah**-rah yay-**bar**
This is...	Esto es...	**ay**-stoh ays
...dirty.	...sucio.	**soo**-thee-oh
...greasy.	...grasiento.	grah-see-**ehn**-toh
...salty.	...salado.	sah-**lah**-doh
...undercooked.	...crudo.	**kroo**-doh
...overcooked.	...muy hecho.	**moo**-ee ay-**choh**
...inedible.	...incomible.	een-koh-**mee**-blay
...cold.	...frío.	**free**-oh
Can you heat this up?	¿Me puede calentar esto?	may **pway**-day kah-lehn-**tar** **ay**-stoh
Enjoy your meal!	¡Qué aproveche!	kay ah-proh-**vay**-chay
Enough.	Suficiente.	soo-fee-thee-**ehn**-tay
Finished.	Terminado.	tehr-mee-**nah**-doh
Do your customers return?	¿Sus clientes vuelven?	soos klee-**ehn**-tays **bwehl**-behn
Yuck!	¡Que asco!	kay **ah**-skoh
Delicious!	¡Delicioso!	day-lee-thee-**oh**-soh
I'm stuffed! (I put on my boots!)	¡Me he puesto las botas!	may ay **pway**-stoh lahs **boh**-tahs

EATING

Paying for your meal:

Waiter.	Camarero.	kah-mah-**ray**-roh
Waitress.	Camarera.	kah-mah-**ray**-rah
The bill, please.	La cuenta, por favor.	lah **kwayn**-tah por fah-**bor**
Together.	Junto.	**hoon**-toh
Separate checks.	En cheques separados.	ayn **chay**-kays say-pah-**rah**-dohs
Credit card O.K.?	¿Tarjeta de crédito O.K.?	tar-**hay**-tah day **kray**-dee-toh "O.K."
Service included?	¿Servicio incluido?	sehr-**bee**-thee-oh een-kloo-**ee**-doh
This is not correct.	Esto no es correcto.	**ay**-stoh noh ays koh-**rehk**-toh
Can you explain this?	¿Me puede expliqar esto?	may **pway**-day ayk-splee-**kar ay**-stoh
What if I wash the dishes?	¿Qué le parece si lavo los platos?	kay lay pah-**ray**-thay see **lah**-boh lohs **plah**-tohs
Keep the change.	Quédese con el cambio.	**kay**-day-say kohn ehl **kahm**-bee-oh
This is for you.	Esto es para usted.	**ay**-stoh ays **pah**-rah oo-**stehd**

If the menu says *servicio incluido*, it means just that. While it's good style to leave the coins, there's no need to tip beyond what's already been tacked on to your bill. If the menu says *servicio no incluido*, leave about 10 to 15 percent for a tip.

Breakfast:

breakfast	**desayuno**	day-sah-**yoo**-noh
bread	**pan**	pahn
roll	**panecillo**	pah-nay-**thee**-yoh
toast	**tostadas**	toh-**stah**-dahs
butter	**mantequilla**	mahn-tay-**kee**-yah
jelly	**gelatina**	*h*ay-lah-**tee**-nah
pastry	**pasteles**	pah-**stay**-lays
fritters	**churros**	**choo** rohs
omelet	**tortilla**	tor-**tee**-yah
potato omelet	**tortilla española**	tor-**tee**-yah ay-spahn-**yoh**-lah
eggs...	**huevos...**	**way**-bohs
...fried	**...fritos**	**free**-tohs
...scrambled	**...revueltos**	ray-**bwehl**-tohs
boiled egg...	**huevo cocido...**	**way**-boh koh-**thee**-doh
...hard	**...duro**	**doo**-roh
...soft	**...pasado por agua**	pah-**sah**-doh por ah-**gwah**
ham	**jamón**	*h*ah-**mohn**
cheese	**queso**	**kay**-soh
yogurt	**yogur**	yoh-**goor**
cereal	**cereales**	thay-ray-**ah**-lays
milk	**leche**	**lay**-chay
hot cocoa	**chocolate caliente**	choh-koh-**lah**-tay kahl-**yehn**-tay
fruit juice	**zumo de fruta**	**thoo**-moh day **froo**-tah

orange juice	**zumo de naranja**	**thoo**-moh day nah-**rahn**-hah
coffee / tea (see Drinking)	**café / té**	kah-**fay** / tay
Is breakfast included (in the room cost)?	**¿El desayuno está incluido?**	ehl day-sah-**yoo**-noh ay-**stah** een-kloo-**ee**-doh

The traditional Spanish breakfast is *churros con chocolate*—greasy, cigar-shaped fritters or doughnuts that you dip in pudding-like chocolate. Try these at least once. For a more solid breakfast I prefer a slice of *tortilla española,* the hearty potato omelet that most cafés serve every morning. Add a little bread and *café con leche,* and you've got a cheap, filling meal.

Tapas:

Bars called *tascas* or *tabernas* offer delicious appetizers called *tapas* during "normal" American-style eating hours when Spanish restaurants are still closed. If you want a cheap, quick, tasty meal before the sun sets, do the "Tapa Tango." Just point to the food you want and say, *"un pincho"* for a bite-sized serving, *"una tapa"* for a larger serving, *"una ración"* for a generous serving, or *"un bocadillo"* for an appetizer sandwich. Be careful. While veggies are cheap, seafood can be very expensive.

aceitunas rellenas	stuffed olives
albóndigas	spiced meatballs with sauce
almejas a la marinera	clams in paprika sauce
bacalao	cod

calamares a la Romana	rings of deep-fried squid
callos	chickpeas with tripe and sauce
caña	glass of draft beer
chorizo	spicy Spanish sausage
empanadillas	pastries stuffed with meat or seafood
gambas a la plancha	grilled prawns
gambas de ajillos	prawns cooked in garlic and olive oil
garbanzos	marinated chickpeas
jamón serrano	cured ham
judías verdes	green beans
mixto	mixed, assorted
orejas	pigs' ears
patatas bravas	fried potatoes with hot sauce
pinchos de queso	pieces of cheese
pan	bread
pescaditos fritos	assorted fried fish
pinchos morunos	skewer of pork flavored with paprika
pulpo gallego	octopus
queso manchego	sheep cheese
salmón ahumado	smoked salmon
setas	mushrooms
tortilla	omelet (usually made with potatoes)

EATING

Soups and salads:

soup	**sopa**	**soh**-pah
soup of the day	**sopa del día**	**soh**-pah dayl **dee**-ah
broth...	**caldo...**	**kahl**-doh
...chicken	**...pollo**	**poh**-yoh
...meat	**...carne**	**kar**-nay
...fish	**...de pescado**	day pay-**skah**-doh
...with noodles	**...con tallarines**	kohn tah-yah-**ree**-nays
...with rice	**...con arroz**	kohn ah-**rohth**
thick vegetable soup	**puré de vegetales**	poo-**ray** day bay-*hay*-**tah**-lays
seafood soup	**sopa de mariscos**	**soh**-pah day mah-**ree**-skohs
chilled soup	**gazpacho**	gahth-**pah**-choh
green salad	**ensalada verde**	ayn-sah-**lah**-dah **behr**-day
chef's salad...	**ensalada de la casa...**	ayn-sah-**lah**-dah day lah **kah**-sah
...with ham and cheese	**...con queso y jamón**	kohn **kay**-soh ee *h*ah-mohn
...with egg	**...con huevo**	kohn **way**-boh
lettuce	**lechuga**	lay-**choo**-gah
tomatoes	**tomates**	toh-**mah**-tays
cucumbers	**pepinos**	pay-**pee**-nohs
oil / vinegar	**aceite / vinagre**	ah-**thay**-tay / bee-**nah**-gray
What is in this salad?	**¿Que tiene esta ensalada?**	kay tee-**ehn**-ay **ay**-stah ayn-sah-**lah**-dah

In Spanish restaurants, salad dressing is normally just the oil and vinegar at the table.

Seafood:

seafood	**marisco**	mah-**ree**-skoh
assorted seafood	**marisco variado**	mah-**ree**-skoh bah-ree-**ah**-doh
fish	**pescado**	pay-**skah**-doh
cod	**bacalao**	bah-kahl-**ow**
salmon	**salmón**	sahl-**mohn**
trout	**trucha**	**troo**-chah
tuna	**atún**	ah-**toon**
herring	**arenque**	ah-**rayn**-kay
sardines	**sardinas**	sar-**dee**-nahs
anchovies	**anchoas**	ahn-**choh**-ahs
clams	**almejas**	ahl-**may**-hahs
mussels	**mejillones**	may-hee-**yoh**-nays
oysters	**ostras**	**oh**-strahs
prawns	**gambas**	**gahm**-bahs
large prawns	**langostinos**	lahn-goh-**stee**-nohs
crab	**cangrejo**	kahn-**greh**-hoh
lobster	**langosta**	lahn-**goh**-stah
octopus	**pulpo**	**pool**-poh
squid	**calamares**	kah-lah-**mah**-rays
Where did this live?	**¿Dónde vivía este?**	**dohn**-day bee-**bee**-ah ay-stay
Just the head, please.	**Solo la cabeza, por favor.**	**soh**-loh lah kah-**bay**-thah por fah-**bor**

EATING

Poultry and meat:

poultry	**aves**	**ah**-bays
chicken	**pollo**	**poh**-yoh
turkey	**pavo**	**pah**-boh
duck	**pato**	**pah**-toh
meat	**carne**	**kar**-nay
beef	**carne de vaca**	**kar**-nay day **bah**-kah
roast beef	**carne asada**	**kar**-nay ah-**sah**-dah
beef steak	**biftec**	**beef**-tayk
hamburger	**hamburguesa**	ahm-boor-**gay**-sah
sausage	**chorizo,**	choh-**ree**-thoh,
	salchichon	sahl-chee-**chon**
veal	**ternera**	tehr-**nay**-rah
cutlet	**chuleta**	choo-**lay**-tah
pork	**cerdo**	**thehr**-doh
ham	**jamón**	*h*ah-**mohn**
lamb	**carnero**	kar-**nay**-roh
a wee goat	**cabrito**	kah-**bree**-toh
bunny	**conejo**	koh-**nay**-*h*oh
brains	**sesos**	**say**-sohs
tongue	**lengua**	**lehn**-gwah
liver	**hígado**	**ee**-gah-doh
kidney	**riñones**	reen-**yoh**-nays
tripe	**tripa**	**tree**-pah
horse	**caballo**	kah-**bah**-yoh
How long has this been dead?	**¿Cuánto tiempo hace que lo mataron?**	kwahn-toh tee-**ehm**-poh **ah**-thay kay loh mah-tah-**rohn**

How it's prepared:

hot	**caliente**	kahl-**yehn**-tay
cold	**frío**	**free**-oh
raw	**crudo**	**kroo**-doh
cooked	**cocinado**	koh-thee-**nah**-doh
baked	**asado**	ah-**sah**-doh
boiled	**cocido**	koh-**thee**-doh
fillet	**filete**	fee-**lay**-tay
fresh	**fresco**	**fray**-skoh
fried	**frito**	**free**-toh
grilled	**a la plancha**	ah lah **plahn**-chah
homemade	**hecho en casa**	**ay**-choh ayn **kah**-sah
medium	**medio**	**may**-dee-oh
microwave	**microondas**	mee-kroh-**ohn**-dahs
mild	**templado**	tehm-**plah**-doh
poached	**escalfado**	ay-skahl-**fah**-doh
rare	**poco hecho**	**poh**-koh ay-choh
roasted	**asado**	ah-**sah**-doh
smoked	**ahumado**	ah-oo-**mah**-doh
spicy hot	**picante**	pee-**kahn**-tay
steamed	**hervido**	ehr-**bee**-doh
stuffed	**rellenos**	ray-**yay**-nohs
sweet	**dulce**	**dool**-thay
well-done	**muy hecho**	**moo**-ee **ay**-choh

EATING

Spanish specialties:

cochinillo asado	roasted suckling pig marinated in herbs, oil, and white wine (Segovia & Toledo)
empanada gallega	a pizza-like pie of beef, pork or seafood with onions, tomatoes, and bell peppers
fabada asturiana	beans, pork, and paprika stew
gazpacho	chilled soup of tomatoes, cucumber, onions, and bell peppers
horchata	refreshing almond-flavored drink served at outdoor food and drink stalls
paella	saffron-flavored rice dish with seafood, chicken, and/or sausage
pimientos a la riojana	sweet peppers stuffed with minced meat
pisto	vegetarian stew of zucchini, tomatoes, and bell peppers
riñones al jerez	kidneys in a sherry sauce
sopa castellana	soup with egg, garlic, and bread

Veggies, pasta, beans, and rice:

vegetables	**verduras**	behr-**doo**-rahs
artichoke	**alcachofa**	ahl-kah-**choh**-fah
asparagus	**espárragos**	ay-**spah**-rah-gohs
beans	**judías**	*h*oo-**dee**-ahs
beets	**remolachas**	ray-moh-**lah**-chahs
broccoli	**brécol**	**bray**-kohl
cabbage	**repollo**	ray-**poh**-yoh
carrots	**zanahorias**	thah-nah-oh-**ree**-ahs

cauliflower	coliflor	koh-lee-**flor**
corn	maíz	mah-**eeth**
cucumber	pepino	pay-**pee**-noh
eggplant	berenjena	bay-rehn-**hay**-nah
French fries	patatas fritas	pah-**tah**-tahs **free**-tahs
garlic	ajo	**ah**-hoh
green beans	judías verdes	hoo-**dee**-ahs **behr**-days
lentils	lentajas	layn-**tah**-hahs
mushrooms	setas	**say**-tahs
olives	aceitunas	ah-thay-**too**-nahs
onions	cebollas	thay-**boh**-yahs
pasta	pasta	**pah**-stah
peas	guisantes	gee-**sahn**-tays
pepper...	pimiento...	pee-mee-**ehn**-toh
...green / red	...verde / rojo	**behr**-day / **roh**-hoh
...hot	...picante	pee-**kahn**-tay
pickles	pepinillos	pay-pee-**nee**-yohs
potatoes	patatas	pah-**tah**-tahs
rice	arroz	ah-**rohth**
spaghetti	espaguetis	ay-spah-**geh**-tees
spinach	espinacas	ay-spee-**nah**-kahs
tomatoes	tomates	toh-**mah**-tays
zucchini	calabacín	kah-lah-bah-**theen**

Fruits and nuts:

almond	**almendra**	ahl-**mayn**-drah
apple	**manzana**	mahn-**thah**-nah
apricot	**albaricoque**	ahl-bah-ree-**koh**-kay
banana	**plátano**	**plah**-tah-noh
canteloupe	**melón**	may-**lohn**
cherry	**cereza**	thay-**ray**-thah
chestnut	**castaña**	kah-**stahn**-yah
coconut	**coco**	**koh**-koh
date	**dátile**	**dah**-tee-lay
fig	**higo**	**ee**-goh
fruit	**fruta**	**froo**-tah
grapefruit	**pomelo**	poh-**may**-loh
grapes	**uvas**	**oo**-bahs
hazelnut	**avellana**	ah-bay-**yah**-nah
lemon	**limón**	lee-**mohn**
orange	**naranja**	nah-**rahn**-*h*ah
peach	**melocotón**	may-loh-koh-**tohn**
peanut	**cacahuete**	kah-kah-**way**-tay
pear	**pera**	**pay**-rah
pineapple	**piña**	**peen**-yah
pistachio	**pistacho**	pee-**stah**-choh
plum	**ciruela**	theer-**way**-lah
prune	**ciruela seca**	theer-**way**-lah **say**-kah
raspberry	**frambuesa**	frahm-**bway**-sah
strawberry	**fresa**	**fray**-sah
tangerine	**mandarina**	mahn-dah-**ree**-nah
walnut	**nuez**	noo-**ayth**
watermelon	**sandía**	sahn-**dee**-ah

Just desserts:

dessert	**postres**	**poh**-strays
caramel custard	**flan**	flahn
cake	**bizcocho**	beeth-**koh**-choh
ice cream cake	**tarta helada**	**tar**-tah ay-**lah**-dah
fruit cup	**variado de fruta**	bah-ree-**ah**-doh day **froo**-tah
tart	**tarta**	**tar**-tah
whipped cream	**nata montada**	**nah**-tah mohn-**tah**-dah
chocolate mousse	**mousse**	moos
pudding	**pudín**	poo-**deen**
pastry	**pasteles**	pah-**stay**-lays
cookies	**galletas, pastas**	gah-**yay**-tahs, **pah**-stahs
candy	**caramelo**	kah-rah-**may**-loh
low calorie	**bajo en calorías**	**bah**-*h*oh ayn kah-loh-**ree**-ahs
homemade	**hecho en casa**	**ay**-choh ayn **kah**-sah
Superb!	**¡Riquísimo!**	ree-**kee-see**-moh
Exquisite!	**¡Exquisito!**	ayks-kee-**see**-toh

Ice cream:

ice cream	**helado**	ay-**lah**-doh
sherbet	**sorbete**	sor-**bay**-tay
cone	**cucurucho**	koo-koo-**roo**-choh
cup	**tarrina**	tah-**ree**-nah
vanilla	**vainilla**	bī-**nee**-yah
chocolate	**chocolate**	choh-koh-**lah**-tay
strawberry	**fresa**	**fray**-sah
lemon	**limón**	lee-**mohn**

Drinking

Water, milk, and juice:

mineral water	**agua mineral**	**ah**-gwah mee-nay-**rahl**
with / without...	**con / sin...**	kohn / seen
...carbonation	**...burbujas**	boor-**boo**-*h*ahs
tap water	**agua del grifo**	**ah**-gwah dayl **gree**-foh
milk...	**leche...**	**lay**-chay
...skim	**...desnatada**	days-nah-**tah**-dah
...fresh	**...fresca**	**fray**-skah
...hot	**...caliente**	kahl-**yehn**-tay
hot chocolate	**chocolate caliente**	choh-koh-**lah**-tay kahl-**yehn**-tay
juice...	**zumo...**	**thoo**-moh
...fruit	**...de fruta**	day **froo**-tah
...orange	**...de naranja**	day nah-**rahn**-*h*ah
...apple	**...de manzana**	day mahn-**thah**-nah
with / without...	**con / sin...**	kohn / seen
...ice / sugar	**...hielo / azúcar**	**yay**-loh / ah-**thoo**-kar
glass / cup	**vaso / taza**	**bah**-soh / **tah**-thah
bottle	**botella**	boh-**tay**-yah
small / large	**pequeña / grande**	pay-**kayn**-yah / **grahn**-day
Is the water safe to drink?	**¿Es el agua potable?**	ays ehl **ah**-gwah poh-**tah**-blay

Coffee and tea:

coffee...	**café...**	kah-**feh**
...espresso	**...espreso**	ay-**spreh**-soh
...black	**...solo**	**soh**-loh
...with a little milk	**...cortado**	kor-**tah**-doh
...with a lot of milk	**...con leche**	kohn **lay**-chay
...with sugar	**...con azúcar**	kohn ah-**thoo**-kar
...decaffeinated	**...descafeinado**	day-skah-fay-**nah**-doh
...instant	**...soluble**	soh-**loo**-blay
...iced	**...con hielo**	kohn **yay**-loh
...American-syle	**...americano**	ah-may-ree-**kah**-noh
hot water	**agua caliente**	**ah**-gwah kahl-**yehn**-tay
tea / lemon	**té / limón**	tay / lee-**mohn**
tea bag	**infusion de té**	een-foo-see-**ohn** day tay
iced tea	**té con hielo**	tay kohn **yay**-loh
small / large	**corto / largo**	**kor**-toh / **lar**-goh
small cup	**taza mediana**	**tah**-thah may-dee-**ah**-nah
large cup	**taza grande**	**tah** thah **grahn**-day
Another cup.	**Otra taza.**	**oh**-trah **tah**-thah
Same price if I sit or stand?	**¿El mismo precio si me siento o si estoy de pié?**	ehl **mees**-moh **pray**-thee-oh see may see-**ehn**-toh oh see ay-**stoy** day pee-**ay**

In bigger cities, bars have menu boards that clearly list three price levels: prices are cheapest at the *barra* (counter), higher at the *mesa* (table), and highest on the *terraza* (terrace).

Wine:

I would like...	**Quería...**	keh-**ree**-ah
We would like...	**Queríamos...**	keh-**ree**-ah-mohs
...a glass	**...un vaso**	oon **bah**-soh
...a carafe	**...una garrafa**	**oo**-nah gah-**rah**-fah
...a bottle	**...una botella**	**oo**-nah boh-**tay**-yah
...of red wine	**...de vino tinto**	day **bee**-noh **teen**-toh
...of white wine	**...de vino blanco**	day **bee**-noh **blahn**-koh
...the wine list	**...la lista de vinos**	lah **lee**-stah day **bee**-nohs

Wine words:

wine	**vino**	**bee**-noh
table wine	**vino de mesa**	**bee**-noh day **may**-sah
cheap house wine	**vino de la casa**	**bee**-noh day lah **kah**-sah
local	**local**	loh-**kahl**
red	**tinto**	**teen**-toh
white	**blanco**	**blahn**-koh
rosé	**rosado**	roh-**sah**-doh
sparkling	**cava**	**kah**-vah
sweet	**dulce**	**dool**-thay
medium	**semi-seco**	say-mee-**say**-koh
dry	**seco**	**say**-koh
very dry	**muy seco**	**moo**-ee **say**-koh
cork	**corcho**	**kor**-choh

A carafe of house wine with your meal is often very cheap.

Beer:

beer	**cerveza**	thehr-**bay**-thah
glass of draft beer	**caña**	**kahn**-yah
big glass of draft beer	**tubo**	**too**-boh
bottle	**botella**	boh-**tay**-yah
light / dark	**rubia / negra**	**roo**-bee-ah / **nay**-grah
local / imported	**local / importada**	loh-**kahl** / eem-por-**tah**-dah
small / large	**pequeña / grande**	pay-**kayn**-yah / **grahn**-day
alcohol-free	**sin-alcohol**	seen-ahl-**kohl**
low calorie	**light**	"light"
cold / colder	**fría / más fría**	**free**-ah / mahs **free**-ah

Bar talk:

What would you like?	**¿Qué quiere?**	kay kee-**ay**-ray
What is the local specialty?	**¿Cuál es la especialidad regional?**	kwahl ays lah ay-spay-thee-ah-lee-**dahd** ray-hee-oh-**nahl**
Straight.	**Solo.**	**soh**-loh
With / Without...	**Con / Sin...**	kohn / seen
...alcohol.	**...alcohol.**	ahl-**kohl**
...ice.	**...hielo.**	**yay**-loh
One more.	**Otro.**	**oh**-troh
Cheers!	**¡Salud!**	sah-**lood**

Let's make a toast to...!	¡Vamos a brindar por...!	**bah**-mohs ah breen-**dar** por
...you	...usted	oo-**stehd**
...Spain	...España	ay-**spahn**-yah
I'm feeling...	Me siento...	may see-**ehn**-toh
...a little drunk.	...un poco borracho[a].	oon **poh**-koh boh-**rah**-choh
...blitzed.	...borracho[a].	boh-**rah**-choh

In Spain, wine lovers will find delicious wines at reasonable prices. *Rioja* wines are excellent. The words *Reserva* and *Gran Reserva* on the label are signs of a better quality. Whites and reds from the *Penedés* region near Barcelona are a good value. *Valdepeñas* wines are usually cheap and forgettable.

Jerez (sherry), a fortified wine from the Jerez region, is an acquired taste. Types of sherry range from dry to sweet: *fino, manzanilla, amontillado, olovoso, cream.*

For a refreshing blend of red wine, seltzer, fruit, and fruit juice, try *Sangria. Chinchon* is an anise-flavored liqueur, and *cava* is Spanish champagne. ¡*Salud!*

Picnicking

At the market:

Self-service?	¿Auto-servicio?	ow-toh-sehr-bee-thee-oh
Ripe for today?	¿Maduro para hoy?	mah-doo-roh pah-rah oy
Does it need to be cooked?	¿Esto necesita cocinarse?	ay-stoh nay-thay-see-tah koh-thee-nar-say
May I taste a little?	¿Podría probarlo?	poh-dree-ah proh-bar-loh
Fifty grams.	Cincuenta gramos.	theen-kwehn-tah grah-mohs
One hundred grams.	Cien gramos.	thee-ehn grah-mohs
More. / Less.	Más. / Menos.	mahs / may-nohs
A piece.	Un trozo.	oon troh-thoh
A slice.	Una rodaja.	oo-nah roh-dah-hah
Sliced.	En rodajas.	ayn roh-dah-hahs
Will you make me a sandwich?	¿Me puede hacer un bocadillo?	may pway-day ah-thehr oon boh-kah-dee-yoh
To take out.	Para llevar.	pah-rah yay-bar
Is there a park nearby?	¿Hay un parque cerca de aquí?	T oon par kay thehr-kah day ah-kee
Okay to picnic here?	¿Se puede hacer picnic aquí?	say pway-day hah-thehr peek-neek ah-kee
Enjoy your meal!	¡Qué aproveche!	kay ah-proh-vay-chay

While you can opt for the one-stop *supermercado*, it's more fun to assemble your picnic and practice your Spanish visiting the small shops. A hundred grams of meat or cheese is about ¼ pound, enough for two sandwiches.

Picnic prose:

open air market	**mercado municipal**	mehr-**kah**-doh moo-nee-thee-**pahl**
supermarket	**supermercado**	soo-pehr-mehr-**kah**-doh
picnic	**picnic**	peek-**neek**
sandwich	**bocadillo**	boh-kah-**dee**-yoh
bread	**pan**	pahn
whole wheat bread	**pan de trigo**	pahn day **tree**-goh
roll	**panecillo**	pah-nay-**thee**-yoh
ham	**jamón**	*h*ah-**mohn**
smoked ham	**jamón serrano**	*h*ah-**mohn** say-**rah**-noh
sausage	**salchichón**	sahl-chee-**chohn**
cheese	**queso**	**kay**-soh
mild / sharp	**suave / fuerte**	**swah**-bay / **fwehr**-tay
mustard...	**mostaza...**	mohs-**tah**-thah
mayonnaise...	**mayonesa...**	mah-yoh-**nay**-sah
...in a tube	**...en tubo**	ayn **too**-boh
yogurt	**yogur**	yoh-**goor**
fruit	**fruta**	**froo**-tah
box of juice	**lata de zumo**	**lah**-tah day **thoo**-moh
cold drinks	**bebidas frías**	bay-**bee**-dahs **free**-ahs
spoon / fork...	**cuchara / tenedor...**	koo-**chah**-rah / tay-nay-**dor**
...made of plastic	**...de plástico**	day **plah**-stee-koh
cup / plate...	**vaso / plato...**	**bah**-soh / **plah**-toh
...made of paper	**...de papel**	day **pah**-pehl

Spanish-English Menu Decoder

This decoder won't unlock every word on the menu, but it'll get you *ostras* (oysters) instead of *orejas* (pigs' ears).

a parte   side dish
aceite   oil
aceitunas   olives
agua   water
ahumado   smoked
ajo   garlic
albaricoque   apricot
albóndigas   meat balls
alcachofa   artichoke
almejas   clams
almendra   almond
almuerzo   lunch
anchoas   anchovies
aperitivos   appetizers
arenque   herring
arroz   rice
asado   baked
atún   tuna
avellana   hazelnut
aves   poultry
azúcar   sugar
bacalao   cod
bebida   beverage
berenjena   eggplant
biftec   beef steak
bizcocho   cake
blanco   white

bocadillo   sandwich
botella   bottle
brécol   broccoli
burbujas   carbonation
caballo   horse
cabrito   a wee goat
cacahuete   peanut
café   coffee
calabacín   zucchini
calamares   squid
caldo   broth
caliente   hot (not cold)
cangrejo   crab
caña   draft beer
caramelo   candy
carne   meat
carne de vaca   beef
carnero   lamb
casa   house
castaña   chestnut
cebollas   onions
cena   dinner
cerdo   pork
cereales   cereal
cereza   cherry
cerveza   beer
chino   chinese

chorizo sausage
chuleta cutlet
churros fritters
ciruela plum
cochinillo suckling pig
cocido broiled
cocinado cooked
coco coconut
coliflor cauliflower
combinado combination
comida food
con with
conejo rabbit
cono cone
corto small
crudo raw
cuchara scoop, spoon
dátile date
delicioso delicious
del día of the day
desayuno breakfast
dulce sweet
duro hard
empanada meat pie
ensalada salad
escalfado poached
espaguetis spaghetti
espárragos asparagus
especial special
espinacas spinach
espumoso sparkling
filete fillet
flan caramel custard

frambuesa raspberry
fresa strawberry
fresco fresh
frío cold
fritos fried
fruta fruit
galletas cookies
gambas prawns
garrafa carafe
gazpacho chilled soup
gelatina jelly
grande large
guisantes peas
hamburguesa hamburger
hecho en casa homemade
helado ice cream
hervido steamed
hielo ice
hígado liver
higo fig
horchata almond drink
huevos eggs
importada imported
incluido included
jamón ham
judías beans
langosta lobster
langostinos large prawns
leche milk
lechuga lettuce
lengua tongue
lentajas lentils
ligero light

limón limon
maíz corn
mandarina tangerine
mantequilla butter
manzana apple
margarina margarine
marisco seafood
mayonesa mayonnaise
medio medium
mejillones mussels
melocotón peach
melón canteloupe
mesa table
microondas microwave
miel honey
mostaza mustard
naranja orange
negra dark
no not
no incluido not included
nuez walnut
o or
orejas pigs' ears
ostras oysters
paella saffron rice dish
pan bread
panecillo roll
para llevar to go
pastas cookies
pasteles pastries
patatas potatoes
patatas fritas French fries
pato duck

pavo turkey
pepinillos pickles
pepinos cucumber
pequeño small
pera pear
pescado fish
picante spicy hot
pimiento bell pepper
pincho snack
piña pineapple
pistacho pistachio
plancha grilled
plátano banana
plato plate
pollo chicken
pomelo grapefruit
postres desserts
primer first
pudín pudding
pulpo octopus
queso cheese
ración portion
rápido fast
rellenos stuffed
remolachas beets
repollo cabbage
revueltos scrambled
riñones kidney
rodaja slice
rojo red
rosado rosé
rubia light
sabroso tasty

sal salt
salchichón sausage
salmón salmon
sandía watermelon
sardinas sardines
seco dry
segundo second
servicio service
sesos brains
setas mushrooms
sin without
solo only
sopa soup
sorbete sherbet
tallarines noodles
tapas appetizers
tarrina cup
tarta tart
taza cup
té tea
templado mild
ternera veal
tinto red
típico typical

tomates tomatoes
tortilla omelet
tostadas toast
tripa tripe
trozo piece
trucha trout
tubo draft beer
turista tourist
uvas grapes
vainilla vanilla
variado assorted
vaso glass
vegetales vegetables
vegetariano vegetarian
verde green
verdura vegetable
vinagre vinegar
vino wine
y and
yogur yoghurt
zanahorias carrots
zumo juice

Sightseeing

Where is...?	¿Dónde está...?	dohn-day ay-stah
...the best view	...la mejor vista	lah may-hor bee-stah
...the main square	...la plaza principal	lah plah-thah preen-thee-pahl
...the old town center	...el casco viejo	ehl kah-skoh bee-ay-hoh
...the museum	...el museo	ehl moo-say-oh
...the castle	...el castillo	ehl kah-stee-yoh
...the palace	...el palacio	ehl pah-lah-thee-oh
...the ruins	...las ruinas	lahs rwee-nahs
...a festival	...un festival	oon fay-stee-vahl
...a fair	...una feria	oo-nah feh-ree-ah
...the tourist information office	...la Oficina de Turismo	lah oh-fee-thee-nah day too-rees-moh
Do you have...?	¿Tiene...?	tee-ehn-ay
...a map	...un mapa	oon mah-pah
...information	...información	een-for-mah-thee-ohn
...a guidebook	...una guía	oo-nah gee-ah
...a tour	...una visita	oo-nah bee-see-tah
...in English	...en inglés	ayn een-glays
When is the next tour in English?	¿Cuándo es la siguiente visita en inglés?	kwahn-doh ays lah seeg-ee-ehn-tay bee-see-tah ayn een-glays
Is it free?	¿Es gratis?	ays grah-tees
How much is it?	¿Cuánto cuesta?	kwahn-toh kway-stah

SIGHTSEEING

Is there a discount for...?	¿Tienen descuento para...?	tee-**eh**-nehn days-**kwehn**-toh **pah**-rah
...youth	...la juventud	lah *h*oo-behn-**tood**
...students	...estudiantes	ay-stoo-dee-**ahn**-tays
...seniors	...la tercera edad	lah tehr-**thay**-rah ay-**dahd**
Is (the ticket) good all day?	¿Es válido para todo el día?	ays **bah**-lee-doh **pah**-rah **toh**-doh ehl **dee**-ah
Can I get back in?	¿Puedo volver a entrar?	**pway**-doh bohl-**behr** ah ayn-**trar**
What time does this open / close?	¿A qué hora abren / cierran?	ah kay **oh**-rah **ah**-brehn / thee-**ay**-rahn
What time is the last entry?	¿A qué hora es la última entrada?	ah kay **oh**-rah ays lah **ool**-tee-mah ayn-**trah**-dah
PLEASE let me in.	POR FAVOR, déjeme entrar.	por fah-**bor** **day**-*h*ay-may ayn-**trar**
I've traveled all the way from...	He viajado desde...	ay bee-ah-*h*ah-doh **dehs**-day
I must leave tomorrow.	Tengo que irme mañana.	**tayn**-goh kay **eer**-may mahn-**yah**-nah
I promise I'll be fast.	Le prometo que vendré rápido.	lay proh-**may**-toh kay bayn-**dray rah**-pee-doh

At the bullring:

bullfight	corrida de toros	koh-**ree**-dah day **toh**-rohs
bullring	plaza del toros	**plah**-thah dayl **toh**-rohs
the bull	el toro	ehl **toh**-roh
kill	matar	mah-**tar**

| sunny / shady side | **sol / sombra** | sohl / **sohm**-brah |
| bull run | **encierro** | ayn-thee-**ay**-roh |

The bulls run through Pamplona (and some people) every July. Bullfights occur throughout April-October, usually on Sundays. In a Spanish bullfight, *el toro* (the bull) is killed by the *matador* and his assistants: *picadors* (guys on horseback) and *banderilleros* (acrobatic helpers). If you're squeamish, go to Portugal, where the bull lives to fight another day.

In the museum:

Where is...?	**¿Dónde está...?**	dohn-day ay-**stah**
I'd like to see...	**Quería ver...**	keh-**ree**-ah behr
Photo / Video O.K.?	**¿Foto / Vídeo O.K.?**	**foh**-toh / **bee**-day-oh "O.K."
No flash / tripod.	**No flash / trípode.**	noh flahsh / **tree**-poh-day
I like it.	**Me gusta.**	may **goo**-stah
It's so...	**Es tan...**	ays tahn
...beautiful.	**...bonito.**	boh-**nee**-toh
...ugly.	**...feo.**	**fay**-oh
...strange.	**...extraño.**	ayk-**strahn**-yoh
...boring.	**...aburrido.**	ah-boo-**ree**-doh
...interesting.	**...interesante.**	een-tay-ray-**sahn**-tay
Wow!	**¡Caray!**	kah-**rī**
My feet hurt!	**¡Me duelen los pies!**	may **dway**-lehn lohs pee-**ays**
I'm exhausted!	**¡Estoy cansadísimo[a]!**	ay-**stoy** kahn-sah-**dee**-see-moh

Art and architecture:

art	**arte**	**ar**-tay
artist	**artista**	ar-**tee**-stah
painting	**cuadro**	**kwah**-droh
self portrait	**autorretrato**	ow-toh-ray-**trah**-toh
sculptor	**escultor**	ay-skool-**tor**
sculpture	**escultura**	ay-skool-**too**-rah
architect	**arquitecto**	ar-kee-**tehk**-toh
architecture	**arquitectura**	ar-kee-tehk-**too**-rah
original	**original**	oh-ree-_h_ee-**nahl**
restored	**restaurado**	ray-stow-**rah**-doh
B.C.	**A.C.**	ah thay
A.D.	**D.C.**	day thay
century	**siglo**	**see**-gloh
style	**estilo**	ay-**stee**-loh
Abstract	**Abstracto**	ahb-**strahk**-toh
Ancient	**Antiguo**	ahn-**tee**-gwoh
Art Nouveau	**Modernista**	moh-dehr-**nee**-stah
Baroque	**Barroco**	bah-**roh**-koh
Classical	**Clásico**	**klah**-see-koh
Gothic	**Gótico**	**goh**-tee-koh
Impressionist	**Impresionismo**	eem-pray-see-oh-**nees**-moh
Medieval	**Medieval**	may-dee-ay-**vahl**
Modern	**Moderno**	moh-**dehr**-noh
Moorish	**Moros**	**moh**-rohs
Renaissance	**Renacimiento**	ray-nah-thee-mee-**ehn**-toh
Romanesque	**Románico**	roh-**mah**-nee-koh
Romantic	**Romanticismo**	roh-mahn-tee-**thees**-moh

Art terms unique to Spain:

Alcazaba: A Moorish castle.
Alcázar: A Moorish fortress or palace.
Azulejo: Blue tile.
Churrigueresque: Super-thick Spanish Baroque, named after a local artist.
Moriscos: The Islamic Arabs (Moors) who ruled much of Spain and Portugal from 711 to 1492. The Moorish culture left a deep mark on Iberia. An understanding of the Moorish occupation will help you better understand your sightseeing.
Mozarabs: Christians in Spain under Moorish rule.
Mudejar: The Gothic-Islamic style of the Moors in Spain after the Christian conquest.
Plateresque: The frilly late Gothic style of Spain.

Castles and palaces:

castle	**castillo**	kah-**stee**-yoh
palace	**palacio**	pah-**lah**-thee-oh
kitchen	**cocina**	koh-**thee**-nah
cellar	**bodega**	boh-**day**-gah
dungeon	**calabozo**	kah-lah-**boh**-thoh
moat	**foso**	**foh**-soh
fortified walls	**paredes fortificadas**	pah-**ray**-days for-tee-fee-**kah**-dahs
tower	**torre**	**toh**-ray
fountain	**fuente**	**fwehn**-tay
garden	**jardín**	har-**deen**

king	**rey**	ray
queen	**reina**	ray-**ee**-nah
knights	**caballería**	kah-bah-yay-**ree**-ah

Religious words:

cathedral	**catedral**	kah-tay-**drahl**
church	**iglesia**	ee-**glay**-see-ah
synagogue	**sinagoga**	see-nah-**goh**-gah
chapel	**capilla**	kah-**pee**-yah
cross	**cruz**	krooth
treasury	**tesoro**	tay-**soh**-roh
crypt	**cripta**	**kreep**-tah
dome	**cúpula**	**koo**-poo-lah
bells	**campanas**	kahm-**pah**-nahs
organ	**órgano**	**or**-gah-noh
choir	**coro**	**koh**-roh
relic	**reliquia**	ray-**lee**-kee-ah
saint	**santo[a]**	**sahn**-toh
God	**Dios**	**dee**-ohs
Jewish	**judío**	hoo-**dee**-oh
Moslem	**musulmán**	moo-sool-**mahn**
Protestant	**protestante**	proh-tay-**stahn**-tay
Catholic	**católico**	kah-**toh**-lee-koh
agnostic	**agnóstico**	ahg-**noh**-stee-koh
atheist	**ateo**	ah-**tay**-oh
When is the mass / service?	**¿A qué hora es la misa / servicio?**	ah kay **oh**-rah ays lah **mee**-sah / sehr-**bee**-thee-oh
Are there concerts in the church?	**¿Hay conciertos en la iglesia?**	ī kohn-thee-**ehr**-tohs ayn lah ee-**glay**-see-ah

Shopping

Names of shops:

antiques	**anticuarios**	ahn-tee-**kwah**-ree-ohs
art gallery	**galería de arte**	gah-lay-**ree**-ah day **ar**-tay
bakery	**panadería**	pah-nah-deh-**ree**-ah
barber shop	**barbería**	bar-beh-**ree**-ah
beauty salon	**peluquería**	pay-loo-keh-**ree**-ah
book shop	**librería**	lee-bray-**ree**-ah
camera shop	**tienda de fotos**	tee-**ehn**-dah day **foh**-tohs
department store	**grandes almacenes**	**grahn**-days ahl-mah-**thay**-nays
flea market	**rastro**	**rahs**-troh
flower market	**floristería**	floh-ree-steh-**ree**-ah
grocery store	**supermercado**	soo-pehr-mehr-**kah**-doh
hardware store	**ferretería**	fehr-ray-tay-**ree**-ah
jewelry shop	**joyería**	*h*oy-eh-**ree**-ah
laundromat	**lavandería**	lah-bahn-deh-**ree**-ah
newsstand	**kiosco**	kee-**oh**-skoh
open air market	**mercado municipal**	mehr-**kah**-doh moo-nee-thee-**pahl**
office supplies	**material de oficina**	mah-tay-ree-**ahl** day oh-fee-**thee**-nah
optician	**óptico[a]**	**ohp**-tee-koh
pharmacy	**farmacia**	far-mah-**thee**-ah
photocopy shop	**fotocopias**	foh-toh-**koh**-pee-ahs

shopping mall	**centro comercial**	**thehn**-troh koh-mehr-thee-**ahl**
souvenir shop	**tienda de souvenirs**	tee-**ehn**-dah day soo-bay-**neers**
supermarket	**supermercado**	soo-pehr-mehr-**kah**-doh
toy store	**tienda de juguetes**	tee-**ehn**-dah day hoo-**gay**-tays
travel agency	**agencia de viajes**	ah-*hayn*-thee-ah day bee-ah-*hays*
used bookstore	**tienda de libros usados**	tee-**ehn**-dah day **lee**-brohs oo-**sah**-dohs
wine shop	**tienda de vinos**	tee-**ehn**-dah day **bee**-nohs

Shop till you drop:

sale	**rebajas**	ray-**bah**-*h*ahs
How much is it?	**¿Cuánto cuesta?**	**kwahn**-toh **kway**-stah
I'm / We're...	**Estoy / Estamos...**	ay-**stoy** / ay-**stah**-mohs
...browsing.	**...mirando.**	mee-**rahn**-doh
I'd like...	**Quería...**	keh-**ree**-ah
Do you have...?	**¿Tiene usted...?**	tee-**ehn**-ay oo-**stehd**
...something cheaper	**...algo más barato**	**ahl**-goh mahs bah-**rah**-toh
...more	**...más**	mahs
Can I see...?	**¿Puedo ver...?**	**pway**-doh behr
This one.	**Este.**	**ay**-stay
Can I try it on?	**¿Puedo probarlo?**	**pway**-doh proh-**bar**-loh
Do you have a mirror?	**¿Tiene un espejo?**	tee-**ehn**-ay oon ay-**spay**-*h*oh

Too...	Muy...	moo-ee
...big.	...grande.	grahn-day
...small.	...pequeño.	pay-kayn-yoh
...expensive.	...caro.	kah-roh
Did you make this?	¿Hizo usted esto?	ee-thoh oo-stehd ay-stoh
What is this made of?	¿De qué está hecho esto?	day kay ay-stah ay-choh ay-stoh
Is it machine washable?	¿Se puede lavar en la lavadora?	say pway-day lah-bar ayn lah lah-bah-doh-rah
Will it shrink?	¿Esto encoge?	ay-stoh ayn-koh-hay
Credit card O.K.?	¿Tarjeta de crédito O.K.?	tar-hay-tah day kray-dee-toh "O.K."
Can you ship this?	¿Puede enviar esto?	pway-day ayn-bee-ar ay-stoh
Tax-free?	¿Libre de impuestos?	lee-bray day eem-pway-stohs
I'll think about it.	Voy a pensármelo.	boy ah payn-sar-may-loh
What time do you close?	¿A qué hora cierran?	ah kay oh-rah thee-ay-rahn
What time do you open tomorrow?	¿A qué hora abren mañana?	ah kay oh-rah ah-brehn mahn-yah-nah
Is that your best price?	¿Es éste su mejor precio?	ays ay-stay soo may-hor pray-thee-oh
My last offer.	Mi última oferta.	mee ool-tee-mah oh-fehr-tah
I'm nearly broke.	Casi no tengo dinero.	kah-see noh tayn-goh dee-nay-roh
My friend...	Mi amigo[a]...	mee ah-mee-goh
My husband...	Mi marido...	mee mah-ree-doh
My wife...	Mi mujer...	mee moo-hehr
...has the money.	...tiene el dinero.	tee-ehn-ay ehl dee-nay-roh

SHOPPING

In Spain, shops are closed for a long lunch from 13:30 until about 16:30, and all day on Sundays. Local souvenirs and postcards are cheapest in the big department stores. *El Corte Inglés* is Spain's ultimate department store, offering everything from cheap souvenirs, train and theater tickets, a money exchange office, to haircuts on Sundays. Madrid's is a block uphill from the *Puerta del Sol*. If you brake for garage sales, you'll pull a U-turn for Madrid's *El Rastro* flea market. Europe's best flea market sprawls for miles each Sunday.

You can find colors and types of fabrics listed in the dictionary near the end of this book.

Repair:

These handy lines can apply to any repair, whether it's a stuck zipper, broken leg, or dying car.

This is broken.	Esto está roto.	ay-stoh ay-stah roh-toh
Can you fix it?	¿Lo puede arreglar?	loh pway-day ah-ray-glar
Just do the essentials.	Haga solo lo esencial.	ah-gah soh-loh loh ay-sehn-thee-ahl
How much will it cost?	¿Cuánto costará?	kwahn-toh koh-stah-rah
When will it be ready?	¿Cuándo estará listo?	kwahn-doh ay-stah-rah lee-stoh
I need it by ___.	Lo necesito para ___.	loh nay-thay-thee-toh pah-rah

Entertainment

What's happening tonight?	¿Qué hay esta noche?	kay ī ay-stah noh-chay
Can you recommend something?	¿Me recomienda algo?	may ray-kohm-yehn-dah ahl-goh
Is it free?	¿Es gratis?	ays grah-tees
Where can I buy a ticket?	¿Dónde puedo comprar un billete?	dohn-day pway-doh kohm-prar oon bee-yeh-tay
When does it start?	¿Cuándo empieza esto?	kwahn-doh aym-pee-ay-thah ay-stoh
When does it end?	¿Cuándo acaba esto?	kwahn-doh ah-kah-bah ay-stoh
Will you go out with me?	¿Vendría conmigo?	bayn-dree-ah kohn-mee-goh
Where's the best place to dance nearby?	¿Dónde está el más cercano y mejor sitio para bailar?	dohn-day ay-stah ehl mahs thehr-kah-noh ee may-hor see-tee-oh pah-rah bī-lar
Do you want to dance?	¿Quiere bailar conmigo?	koo ay ray bī-lar kohn-mee-goh
Again?	¿Otra más?	oh-trah mahs
Where is the best place to stroll?	¿Dónde está el mejor paseo?	dohn-day ay-stah ehl may-hor pah-say-oh
It's been a wonderful night.	Ha sido una noche encantadora.	ah see-doh oo-nah noh-chay ayn-kahn-tah-doh-rah

Entertaining words:

movie...	película...	pay-**lee**-koo-lah
...original version	...versión original	behr-see-**ohn** oh-ree-*h*ee-**nahl**
...in English	...en inglés	ayn een-**glays**
...with subtitles	...con subtítulos	kohn soob-**tee**-too-lohs
...dubbed	...doblada	doh-**blah**-dah
music...	música...	**moo**-see-kah
...live	...en vivo	ayn **bee**-boh
...classical	...clásica	**klah**-see-kah
...folk	...folklórica	fohk-**loh**-ree-kah
rock	rock	rohk
jazz	jazz	"jazz"
blues	blues	"blues"
singer	cantante	kahn-**tahn**-tay
concert	concierto	kohn-thee-**ehr**-toh
show	espectáculo	ay-spehk-**tah**-koo-loh
dancing	baile	bī-lay
flamenco	flamenco	flah-**mayn**-koh
folk dancing	baile folklórico	bī-lay fohk-**loh**-ree-koh
disco	disco	**dee**-skoh
cover charge	entrada	ayn-**trah**-dah

For free, enjoyable entertainment, join the locals for a *paseo*, an evening stroll through town.

Phoning

The nearest phone?	¿El teléfono más cercano?	ehl tay-**lay**-foh-noh mahs thehr-**kah**-noh
Where is the telephone office?	¿Dónde está la Telefónica?	**dohn**-day ay-**stah** lah tay-lay-**foh**-nee-kah
I'd like to telephone...	Quería llamar...	keh-**ree**-ah yah-**mar**
...the United States.	...a los Estados Unidos.	ah lohs ay-**stah**-dohs oo-**nee**-dohs
How much per minute?	¿Cuánto es por minuto?	**kwahn**-toh ays por mee-**noo**-toh
I'd like to make a... call.	Quería hacer una llamada...	keh-**ree**-ah ah-**thehr** oo-nah yah-**mah**-dah
...local	...local.	loh-**kahl**
...collect	...a cobro revertido.	ah **koh**-broh ray-behr-**tee**-doh
...credit card	...con tarjeta.	kohn tar-**hay**-tah
...long distance (within Spain)	...nacional.	nah-thee-oh-**nahl**
...international	...internacional.	een-tehr-nah-thee-oh-**nahl**
It doesn't work.	No funciona.	noh foonk-thee-**oh**-nah
May I use your phone?	¿Puedo usar su teléfono?	**pway**-doh oo-**sar** soo tay-**lay**-foh-noh
Can you dial for me?	¿Puede marcarme el número?	**pway**-day mar-**kar**-may ehl **noo**-may-roh
Can you talk for me?	¿Puede hablar usted por mí?	**pway**-day ah-**blar** oo-**stehd** por mee
It's busy.	Está comunicando.	ay-**stah** koh-moo-nee-**kahn**-doh

Will you try again?	¿Llamará otra vez?	yay-mah-**rah oh**-trah bayth
Hello. (on phone)	**Diga.**	**dee**-gah
My name is...	**Me llamo...**	may **yah**-moh
My number is...	**Mi número es...**	mee **noo**-may-roh ays
Speak slowly and clearly.	**Hable despacio y claro.**	**ah**-blay day-**spah**-thee-oh ee **klah**-roh
Wait a moment.	**Un momento.**	oon moh-**mehn**-toh
Don't hang up.	**No cuelgue.**	noh **kwayl**-gay

Key telephone words:

telephone	**teléfono**	tay-**lay**-foh-noh
telephone card	**tarjeta telefónica**	tar-**hay**-tah tay-lay-**foh**-nee-kah
telephone office	**Telefónica**	tay-lay-**foh**-nee-kah
operator	**telefonista**	tay-lay-foh-**nee**-stah
international assistance	**asistencia internacional**	ah-see-**stehn**-thee-ah een-tehr-nah-thee-oh-**nahl**
country code	**prefijo del país**	pray-**fee**-hoh dayl pah-**ees**
area code	**prefijo**	pray-**fee**-hoh
telephone book	**guía de teléfonos**	**gee**-ah day tay-**lay**-foh-nohs
toll-free call	**llamada gratuita**	yah-**mah**-dah grah-**twee**-tah
out of service	**averiado**	ah-bay-ree-**ah**-doh

Buy a handy *tarjeta telefónica* (phone card) at a *tabacos* (tobacco) shop. Insert the card into a phone and call anywhere in the world. See "Let's Talk Telephones" near the end of this book for tips on making calls.

Mailing

Where is the post office?	¿Dónde está la oficina de correos?	**dohn**-day ay-**stah** lah oh-fee-**thee**-nah day koh-**ray**-ohs
Which window for...?	¿Cuál es la ventana para...?	kwahl ays lah bayn-**tah**-nah **pah**-rah
...stamps	...sellos	**say**-yohs
...packages	...paquetes	pah-**kay**-tays
To the United States...	Para los Estados Unidos...	**pah**-rah lohs ay-**stah**-dohs oo-**nee**-dohs
...by air mail.	...por avión.	por ah-bee-**ohn**
...slow and cheap.	...por barco.	por **bar**-koh
How much is it?	¿Cuánto cuesta?	**kwahn**-toh **kway**-stah
How many days will it take?	¿Cuántos días tardará?	**kwahn**-tohs **dee**-ahs tar-dah-**rah**

Handy postal words:

post office	oficina de correos	oh foo **thee** nah day koh-**ray**-ohs
stamp	sello	**say**-yoh
postcard	postal	poh-**stahl**
letter	carta	**kar**-tah
aerogram	aerograma	ah-ay-roh-**grah**-mah
envelope	sobre	**soh**-bray
package	paquete	pah-**kay**-tay
box	caja	**kah**-hah

string	**cordón**	kor-**dohn**
tape	**cinta adhesiva**	**theen**-tah ah-day-**see**-bah
mailbox	**buzón**	boo-**thohn**
air mail	**por avión**	por ah-bee-**ohn**
express	**rápido**	**rah**-pee-doh
surface mail (slow and cheap)	**por barco**	por **bar**-koh
book rate	**tarifa**	tah-**ree**-fah
weight limit	**peso máximo**	**pay**-soh **mahk**-see-moh
registered	**certificada**	thehr-tee-fee-**kah**-dah
insured	**asegurada**	ah-say-goo-**rah**-dah
fragile	**frágil**	frah-*h*eel
contents	**contenido**	kohn-teh-**nee**-doh
customs	**aduana**	ah-**dwah**-nah
to / from	**a / desde**	ah / **dehs**-day
address	**dirección**	dee-rehk-thee-**ohn**
zip code	**código postal**	**koh**-dee-goh poh-**stahl**
general delivery	**Lista de Correos**	**lee**-stah day koh-**ray**-ohs

In Spain, you can often get stamps at the corner *tabacos* (tobacco) shop. As long as you know which stamps you need, this is a great convenience.

Red Tape & Profanity

Filling out forms:

Sr. / Sra. / Srta.	Mr. / Mrs. / Miss
nombre	first name
apellido	last name
dirección	address
domicilio	address
calle	street
ciudad	city
estado	state
país	country
nacionalidad	nationality
origen / destino	origin / destination
edad	age
fecha de nacimiento	date of birth
lugar de nacimiento	place of birth
sexo	sex
masculino	male
femenino	female
casado / casada	married man / married woman
soltero / soltera	single man / single woman
profesión	profession
adulto	adult
niño / niña	boy / girl
niños	children
familia	family
firma	signature
fecha	date

RED TAPE

Spanish profanity:

In any country, red tape inspires profanity. In case you're wondering what the more colorful locals are saying...

Go to hell!	¡Vete al infierno!	**bay**-tay ahl een-fee-**ehr**-noh
Kiss my ass.	Bésame culo.	**bay**-sah-may **koo**-loh
bastard	bastardo	bah-**star**-doh
bitch	perra	**pehr**-rah
child of a whore	hijo[a] de puta	**ee**-*h*oh day **poo**-tah
breasts (colloq.)	tetas	**tay**-tahs
penis (colloq.)	polla, minga	**poh**-yah, **meen**-gah
shit	mierda	mee-**ehr**-dah
drunk	borracho[a]	boh-**rah**-choh
idiot	idiota	ee-dee-**oh**-tah
imbecile	imbécil	eem-**bay**-theel
jerk (horned sheep)	cabrón[a]	kah-**brohn**
stupid	estúpido[a]	ay-**stoo**-pee-doh
Did someone...?	¿Hizo alguien...?	**ee**-thoh **ahl**-gee-ehn
...fart	...un pedo	oon **pay**-doh
...burp	...un erupto	oon ay-**roop**-toh

Like most Mediterranean people, the Spanish employ some colorful gestures. For a run-down on these, see "Gestures" near the end of this book.

Help!

Help!	¡Ayuda!	ah-**yoo**-dah
Help me!	!Ayúdenme!	ah-**yoo**-dehn-may
Call a doctor!	¡Llamen a un médico!	**yah**-mehn ah oon **may**-dee-koh
ambulance	ambulancia	ahm-boo-**lahn**-thee-ah
accident	accidente	ahk-thee-**dehn**-tay
injured	herido	ay-**ree**-doh
emergency	emergencia	ay-mehr-**hayn**-thee-ah
fire	fuego	**fway**-goh
police	policía	poh-lee-**thee**-ah
thief	ladrón	lah-**drohn**
pick-pocket	carterista	kar-tay-**ree**-stah
I've been ripped off.	Me han robado.	may ahn roh-**bah**-doh
I've lost my...	He perdido mi...	ay pehr-**dee**-doh mee
...passport.	...pasaporte.	pah-sah-**por**-tay
...ticket.	...billete.	bee-**yeh**-tay
...baggage.	...equipaje.	ay-kee-**pah**-hay
...purse.	...bolso.	**bohl**-soh
...wallet.	...cartera.	kar-**tay**-rah
...faith in humankind.	...fe en los seres humanos.	fay ayn lohs **say**-rays oo-**mah**-nohs
I'm lost.	Estoy perdido[a].	ay-**stoy** pehr-**dee**-doh

HELP!

Help for women:

Leave me alone.	**Déjame sola.**	**day**-*h*ah-may **soh**-lah
I *vant* to be alone.	**Me gustaría estar sola.**	may goo-stah-**ree**-ah ay-**star** soh-lah
I'm not interested.	**No estoy interesada.**	noh ay-**stoy** een-tay-ray-**sah**-dah
I'm married.	**Estoy casada.**	ay-**stoy** kah-**sah**-dah
I'm a lesbian.	**Soy lesbiana.**	soy lehs-bee-**ah**-nah
I have a contagious disease.	**Tengo una enfermedad contagiosa.**	**tayn**-goh **oo**-nah ayn-fehr-may-**dahd** kohn-tah-*h*ee-**oh**-sah
Don't touch me.	**No me toque.**	noh may **toh**-kay
You're disgusting.	**Es asqueroso.**	ays ah-skay-**roh**-soh
Stop following me.	**No me siga.**	noh may **see**-gah
This man is bothering me.	**Este señor me está molestando.**	ay-**stay sayn**-yor may ay-**stah** moh-lay-**stahn**-doh
Enough!	**¡Basta!**	**bah**-stah
Get lost!	**¡Vete!**	**bay**-tay
Go to hell!	**¡Vete al infierno!**	**bay**-tay ahl een-fee-**ehr**-noh
I'll call the police!	**¡Voy a llamar a la policía!**	boy ah yah-**mar** ah lah poh-lee-**thee**-ah

Whenever macho males threaten to turn leering into a contact sport, local women stroll holding hands or arm-in-arm. Wearing conservative clothes and avoiding smiley eye contact also convey a "No way, José" message.

Health

I feel sick.	Estoy enfermo[a].	ay-**stoy** ayn-**fehr**-moh
I need a doctor...	Necesito un doctor...	nay-thay-**see**-toh oon dohk-**tor**
...who speaks English.	...que hable inglés.	kay **ah**-blay een-**glays**
It hurts here.	Me duele aquí.	may **dway**-lay ah-**kee**
I'm allergic to...	Soy alérgico[a] a...	soy ah-**lehr**-hee-koh ah
...penicillin.	...penicilina.	pay-nee-thee-**lee**-nah
I am diabetic.	Soy diabético[a].	soy dee-ah-**bay**-tee-koh
I've missed a period.	No me vino el periodo.	noh may **bee**-noh ehl pay-ree-**oh**-doh
My friend has...	Mi amigo[a] tiene...	mee ah-**mee**-goh tee-**ehn**-ay
I have...	Tengo...	**tayn**-goh
...a burn.	...una quemadura.	**oo**-nah kay-mah-**doo**-rah
...chest pains.	...dolor de pecho.	doh-**lor** day **pay**-choh
...a cold.	...un resfriado.	oon rays-free-**ah**-doh
...constipation.	...estreñimiento.	ay-strayn-yee-mee-**ehn**-toh
...a cough.	...catarro.	kah-**tah**-roh
...diarrhea.	...diarrea.	dee-ah-**ray**-ah
...dizziness.	...vértigo.	**behr**-tee-goh
...a fever.	...fiebre.	fee-**ay**-bray
...the flu.	...gripe.	**gree**-pay
...the giggles.	...la risa en la boca.	lah **ree**-sah ayn lah **boh**-kah
...a headache.	...dolor de cabeza.	doh-**lor** day kah-**bay**-thah
...hemorrhoids.	...hemorroides.	ay-moh-**roy**-days

...high blood pressure.	**...tensión alta.**	tayn-thee-**ohn** ahl-tah
...indigestion.	**...indigestión.**	een-dee-*h*ay-stee-**ohn**
...an infection.	**...una infección.**	**oo**-nah een-fehk-thee-**ohn**
...a migraine.	**...una jaqueca.**	**oo**-nah *h*ah-**kay**-kah
...nausea.	**...náuseas.**	**now**-see-ahs
...a rash.	**...erupción.**	ay-roop-thee-**ohn**
...a sore throat.	**...dolor de garganta.**	doh-**lor** day gar-**gahn**-tah
...a stomach ache.	**...dolor de estómago.**	doh-**lor** day ay-**stoh**-mah-goh
...a swelling.	**...un hinchazón.**	oon een-chah-**thohn**
...a toothache.	**...dolor de muelas.**	doh-**lor** day moo-ay-lahs
...a venereal disease.	**...una enfermedad venérea.**	**oo**-nah ayn-fehr-may-**dahd** vay-**nay**-ray-ah
...worms.	**...lombrices.**	lohm-**bree**-thays
I have body odor.	**Huelo a sudor.**	**way**-loh ah soo-**dor**
Is it serious?	**¿Es esto serio?**	ays **ay**-stoh **say**-ree-oh

Handy Spanish health words:

pain	**dolor**	doh-**lor**
dentist	**dentista**	dayn-**tee**-stah
doctor	**doctor[a]**	dohk-**tor**
nurse	**enfermera**	ayn-fehr-**may**-rah
health insurance	**seguro médico**	say-**goo**-roh **may**-dee-koh
hospital	**hospital**	oh-spee-**tahl**
bandage	**venda**	**bayn**-dah
medicine	**medicina**	may-dee-**thee**-nah

pharmacy	**farmacia**	far-mah-**thee**-ah
prescription	**receta**	ray-**thay**-tah
pill	**píldora**	**peel**-doh-rah
aspirin	**aspirina**	ah-spee-**ree**-nah
non-aspirin substitute	**Nolotil**	**noh**-loh-teel
antibiotic	**antibiótico**	ahn-tee-bee-**oh**-tee-koh
cold medicine	**medicina para el resfriado**	may-dee-**thee**-nah **pah**-rah ehl rays-free-**ah**-doh
cough drops	**pastilles de tós**	pah-**stee**-yahs day tohs
pain killer	**analgésico**	ah-nahl-**hay**-see-koh
Preparation H	**Preparación H**	pray-pah-rah-thee-**ohn ah**-chay
vitamins	**vitaminas**	bee-tah-**mee**-nahs

Contacts and glasses:

glasses	**gafas**	**gah**-fahs
sunglasses	**gafas de sol**	**gah**-fahs day sohl
prescription	**prescripción**	pray-skreep-thee-**ohn**
contact lenses...	**lentillas...**	layn-**tee**-yahs
...soft / hard	**...blandas / de cristal**	blahn daho / day kree-**stahl**
solution...	**solución...**	soh-loo-thee-**ohn**
...cleaning	**...limpiadora**	leemp-yah-**doh**-rah
...soaking	**...de jabón**	day *hah*-bohn
I've lost / swallowed a contact lens.	**Tengo perder / tragar una lentilla.**	tayn-goh pehr-**dehr** / trah-**gar oo**-nah layn-**tee**-yah

HEALTH

Toiletries:

comb	**peine**	**pay**-nay
conditioner	**acondicionador**	ah-kohn-dee-thee-oh-nah-**dor**
condoms	**preservativos**	pray-sehr-bah-**tee**-bohs
dental floss	**seda dental**	**say**-dah dayn-**tahl**
deodorant	**desodorante**	day-soh-doh-**rahn**-tay
hairbrush	**cepillo del pelo**	thay-**pee**-yoh dayl **pay**-loh
hand lotion	**crema de manos**	**kray**-mah day **mah**-nohs
lip salve	**cacao de labios**	kah-**kah**-oh day **lah**-bee-ohs
nail clipper	**corta uñas**	**kor**-tah **oon**-yahs
razor	**maquinilla de afeitar**	mah-kee-**nee**-yah day ah-fay-**tar**
sanitary napkins	**compresas**	kohm-**pray**-sahs
shampoo	**champú**	**chahm**-poo
shaving cream	**espuma de afeitar**	**ay**-spoo-mah day ah-fay-**tar**
soap	**jabón**	*h*ah-bohn
sunscreen	**protección de sol**	proh-tehk-thee-**ohn** day sohl
tampons	**tampones**	tahm-**poh**-nays
tissues	**pañuelos de papel**	pahn-yoo-**ay**-lohs day pah-**pehl**
toilet paper	**papel higiénico**	pah-**pehl** ee-*h*ee-**ay**-nee-koh
toothbrush	**cepillo de dientes**	thay-**pee**-yoh day dee-**ehn**-tays
toothpaste	**pasta de dientes**	**pah**-stah day dee-**ehn**-tays
tweezers	**pinzas**	**peen**-thahs

Chatting

My name is...	Me llamo...	may **yah**-moh
What's your name?	¿Cómo se llama?	**koh**-moh say **yah**-mah
How are you?	¿Cómo está?	**koh**-moh ay-**stah**
Fine, thanks.	Bien, gracias.	bee-**yehn grah**-thee-ahs
Where are you from?	¿De dónde es?	day **dohn**-day ays
What city?	¿Qué ciudad?	kay thee-oo-**dahd**
What country?	¿Qué país?	kay pah-**ees**
What planet?	¿Qué planeta?	kay plah-**nay**-tah
I'm...	Soy...	soy
...American.	...americano[a].	ah-may-ree-**kah**-noh
...Canadian.	...canadiense.	kah-nah-dee-**ehn**-say

Nothing more than feelings:

I am / You are...	Estoy / Está...	ay-**stoy** / ay-**stah**
...happy.	...contento[a].	kohn-**tehn**-toh
...sad.	...triste.	**tree**-slay
...tired.	...cansado[a].	kahn-**sah**-doh
...thirsty.	...sediento[a].	say-dee-**ehn**-toh
I am / You are...	Tengo / Tiene...	**tayn**-goh / tee-**ehn**-ay
...hungry.	...hambre.	**ahm**-bray
...cold / hot.	...frío / calor.	**free**-oh / kah-**lor**
...homesick.	...morriña.	moh-**reen**-yah
...lucky.	...suerte.	**swehr**-tay

CHATTING

Who's who:

My...	Mi...	mee
...male friend / female friend.	...amigo / amiga.	ah-**mee**-goh / ah-**mee**-gah
...boyfriend / girlfriend.	...novio / novia.	**noh**-bee-oh / **noh**-bee-ah
...husband / wife.	...marido / esposa.	mah-**ree**-doh / ay-**spoh**-sah
...son / daughter.	...hijo / hija.	ee-*h*oh / ee-*h*ah
...brother / sister.	...hermano / hermana.	ehr-**mah**-noh / ehr-**mah**-nah
...father / mother.	...padre / madre.	**pah**-dray / **mah**-dray
...uncle / aunt.	...tío / tía.	**tee**-oh / **tee**-ah
...nephew / niece.	...sobrino / sobrina.	soh-**bree**-noh / soh-**bree**-nah
...male / female cousin.	...primo / prima.	**pree**-moh / **pree**-mah
...grandpa / grandma.	...abuelo / abuela.	ah-**bway**-loh / ah-**bway**-lah
...grandson / granddaughter.	...nieto / nieta.	nee-**ay**-toh / nee-**ay**-tah

Family, school, and work:

Are you married? (asked of a man)	¿Está casado?	ay-**stah** kah-**sah**-doh
Are you married? (asked of a woman)	¿Está casada?	ay-**stah** kah-**sah**-dah
Do you have children?	¿Tiene hijos?	tee-**ehn**-ay ee-*h*ohs
How many boys / girls?	¿Cuántos niños / niñas?	**kwahn**-tohs **neen**-yohs / **neen**-yahs
Do you have photos?	¿Tiene fotos?	tee-**ehn**-ay **foh**-tohs

How old is your child?	¿Cuántos años tiene su hijo[a]?	kwahn-tohs ahn-yohs tee-ehn-ay soo ee-hoh
Beautiful child!	¡Qué niño[a] más guapo[a]!	kay neen-yoh mahs gwah-poh
Beautiful children!	¡Qué niños[as] más guapos[as]!	kay neen-yohs mahs gwah-pohs
What are you studying?	¿Qué está estudiando?	kay ay-stah ay-stoo-dee-ahn-doh
I'm studying...	Estoy estudiando...	ay-stoy ay-stoo-dee-ahn-doh
I'm... years old.	Tengo... años.	tayn-goh... ahn-yohs
How old are you?	¿Cuántos años tiene?	kwahn-tohs ahn-yohs tee-ehn-ay
Do you have brothers and sisters?	¿Tiene hermanos y hermanas?	tee-ehn-ay ehr-mah-nohs ee ehr-mah-nahs
Will you teach me a simple Spanish song?	¿Me enseñaría una canción simple en español?	may ayn-sayn-yah-ree-ah oo-nah kahn-thee-ohn seem-play ayn ay-spahn-yohl
I'm a...	Soy...	soy
...student.	...estudiante.	ay-stoo-dee-ahn-tay
...teacher.	...profesor[a].	proh-fay-sor
...worker.	...trabajador[a].	trah-bah-hah-dor
...bureaucrat.	...burocrático[a].	boo-roo-krah-tee-koh
...professional traveler.	...viajante de profesión.	bee-ah-hahn-tay day proh-fay-see-ohn
What is your job?	¿En qué trabaja?	ayn kay trah-bah-hah
Do you like your work?	¿Le gusta su trabajo?	lay goo-stah soo trah-bah-hoh

Travel talk:

I am / Are you...?	**Estoy / ¿Está...?**	ay-**stoy** / ay-**stah**
...on vacation	**...de vacaciones**	day bah-kah-thee-**oh**-nays
...on business	**...de negocios**	day nay-**goh**-thee-ohs
How long have you been traveling?	**¿Cuánto tiempo hace que están viajando?**	**kwahn**-toh tee-**ehm**-poh **ah**-thay kay ay-**stahn** bee-ah-**hahn**-doh
day / week	**día / semana**	**dee**-ah / say-**mah**-nah
month / year	**mes / año**	mays / **ahn**-yoh
When are you going home?	**¿Cuándo va para casa?**	**kwahn**-doh bah **pah**-rah **kah**-sah
This is my first time in...	**Esta es mi primera vez en...**	**ay**-stah ays mee pree-**may**-rah bayth ayn
It is (not) a tourist trap.	**(No) es un timo turistica.**	(noh) ays oon **tee**-moh too-**ree**-stee-kah
Today / Tomorrow I'll go to...	**Hoy / Mañana iré a...**	oy / mahn-**yah**-nah ee-**ray** ah
I'm happy here.	**Estoy contento[a] aquí.**	ay-**stoy** kohn-**tehn**-toh ah-**kee**
The Spanish are friendly.	**Los españoles son amables.**	lohs ay-spahn-**yoh**-lays sohn ah-**mah**-blays
Spain is wonderful.	**España es preciosa.**	ay-**spahn**-yah ays pray-thee-**oh**-sah
To travel is to live.	**Viajar es vivir.**	bee-ah-**har** ays bee-**beer**
Have a good trip!	**¡Buen viaje!**	bwayn bee-**ah**-hay

Map talk:

You can use these phrases, along with the maps of Iberia, Europe, and the U.S.A. near the end of this book, to delve into family history and explore travel dreams.

I live here.	Vivo aquí.	bee-boh ah-kee
I was born here.	Nací aquí.	nah-thee ah-kee
My ancestors came from...	Mis familiares son de...	mee fah-mee-lee-ah-rays sohn day
I've traveled to...	He viajado a...	ay bee-ah-hah-doh ah
Next I'll go to...	Después iré a...	days-pways ee-ray ah
Where do you live?	¿Dónde vive?	dohn-day bee-bay
Where were you born?	¿Dónde ha nacido?	dohn-day ah nah-thee-doh
Where did your ancestors come from?	¿De dónde son sus familiares?	day dohn-day sohn soos fah-mee-lee-ah-rays
Where have you traveled?	¿Adónde ha viajado?	ah-dohn-day ah bee-ah-hah-doh
Where are you going?	¿Adónde va?	ah-dohn-day bah
Where would you like to go?	¿Adónde le gustaría ir?	ah-dohn-day lay goo-stah-ree-ah eer

CHATTING

Favorite things:

What's your favorite...?	¿Cuál es su... favorito?	kwahl ays soo... fah-voh-**ree**-toh
...art	...arte	**ar**-tay
...book	...libro	**lee**-broh
...hobby	...pasatiempo	pah-sah-tee-**ehm**-poh
...ice cream	...helado	ay-**lah**-doh
...male singer	...cantante	kahn-**tahn**-tay
...male author	...autor	ow-**tor**
...male movie star	...actor	ahk-**tor**
...sport	...deporte	day-**por**-tay
...vice	...vicio	**bee**-thee-oh
What's your favorite...?	¿Cuál es su... favorita?	kwahl ays soo... fah-voh-**ree**-tah
...food	...comida	koh-**mee**-dah
...music	...música	**moo**-see-kah
...female singer	...cantante	kahn-**tahn**-tay
...female author	...autora	ow-**toh**-rah
...female movie star	...actriz	ahk-**treeth**
...movie	...película	pay-**lee**-koo-lah

Responses for all occasions:

I like that.	Eso me gusta.	**ay**-soh may **goo**-stah
I like you.	Me cae bien.	may kī bee-**yehn**
That's great!	¡Qué bien!	kay bee-**yehn**
Wow!	¡Caray!	kah-**rī**
Perfect.	Perfecto.	pehr-**fehk**-toh
Funny.	Divertido.	dee-behr-**tee**-doh
Interesting.	Interesante.	een-tay-ray-**sahn**-tay
I don't smoke.	No fumo.	noh **foo** moh
Really?	¿De verdad?	day behr-**dahd**
Congratulations!	¡Felicidades!	fay-lee-thee-**dah**-days
Well done!	¡Bien hecho!	bee-**ehn** ay-choh
You're welcome.	De nada.	day **nah**-dah
Bless you! (after sneeze)	¡Salud!	sah-**lood**
Excuse me.	Perdóneme.	pehr-**doh**-nay-may
What a pity!	¡Qué lastima!	kay lah-**stee**-mah
That's life.	Así es la vida.	ah-**see** ays lah bee-dah
No problem.	No hay problema.	noh ī proh-**blay**-mah
O.K.	De acuerdo.	day ah-**kwehr**-doh
This is the good life!	¡Esto si que es vida!	**ay**-stoh see kay ays bee-dah
Good luck!	¡Buena suerte!	**bway**-nah **swehr**-tay
Let's go!	¡Vamos!	**bah**-mohs

CHATTING

Thanks a million:

Thank you very much.	**Muchas gracias.**	**moo**-chahs **grah**-thee-ahs
You are...	**Usted es...**	oo-**stehd** ays
...kind.	**...amable.**	ah-**mah**-blay
...generous.	**...generoso[a].**	*h*eh-nay-**roh**-soh
...hairy.	**...peludo[a].**	pay-**loo**-doh
This is / You are...	**Esto es / Usted es...**	**ay**-stoh ays / oo-**stehd** ays
...wonderful.	**...maravilloso[a].**	mah-rah-bee-**yoh**-soh
...great fun.	**...muy divertido.**	**moo**-ee dee-behr-**tee**-doh
You've been a tremendous help.	**Me ha ayudado mucho.**	may ah ah-yoo-**dah**-doh **moo**-choh
I will remember you...	**Le recordaré...**	lay ray-kor-dah-**ray**
...always.	**...siempre.**	see-**aym**-pray
...till Tuesday.	**...hasta el martes.**	**ah**-stah ehl **mar**-tays

Weather:

What will the weather be like tomorrow?	**¿Qué tiempo va a hacer mañana?**	kay tee-ehm-poh bah ah ah-**thehr** mahn-**yah**-nah
sunny / cloudy	**asoleado / nublado**	ah-soh-lay-**ah**-doh / noo-**blah**-doh
hot / cold	**caluroso / frío**	kah-loo-**roh**-soh / **free**-oh
muggy / windy	**húmedo / viento**	**oo**-may-doh / bee-**ehn**-toh
rain / snow	**lluvia / nieve**	**yoov**-yah / nee-**ay**-bay

Create Your Own Conversation

You can mix and match these words into a conversation.
Make it as deep or silly as you want.

Who:

I / you	yo / usted	yoh / oo-**stehd**
he / she	él / ella	ehl / **ay**-yah
we / they	nosotros / ellos	noh-**soh**-trohs / **ay**-ohs
my / your...	mi / su...	mee / soo
...parents / children	...padres / niños	**pah**-drays / **neen**-yohs
men / women	hombres / mujeres	**ohm**-brays / moo-**heh**-rays
rich / poor	ricos / pobres	**ree**-kohs / **poh**-brays
politicians	políticos	poh-**lee**-tee-kohs
big business	gran negocio	grahn nay-**goh**-thee-oh
mafia	mafia	**mah**-fee-ah
military	militar	mee-lee-**tar**
Spanish	españoles	ay-spahn-**yoh**-lays
Portuguese	portugueses	por-too-**gay**-says
French	franceses	frahn-**thay**-says
Germans	alemanes	ah-lay-**mah**-nays
Americans	americanos	ah-may-ree-**kah**-nohs
liberals	liberales	lee-bay-**rah**-lays
conservatives	conservativos	kohn-sehr-bah-**tee**-bohs
radicals	radicales	rah-dee-**kah**-lays
travelers	viajantes	bee-ah-**hahn**-tays
everyone	todo la gente	**toh**-doh lah **hehn**-tay
God	Dios	**dee**-ohs

What:

want	**querer**	keh-**rehr**
need	**necesitar**	nay-thay-see-**tar**
take / give	**coger / dar**	koh-*h*ehr / dar
love / hate	**amar / odiar**	ah-**mar** / oh-dee-**ar**
work / play	**trabajar / jugar**	trah-bah-**har** / *h*oo-**gar**
have / lack	**tener / carecer de**	tay-**nehr** / kah-ray-**thehr** day
learn / fear	**aprender / temer**	ah-prehn-**dehr** / tay-**mehr**
help / abuse	**ayudar / abusar de**	ah-yoo-**dar** / ah-boo-**sar** day
prosper / suffer	**prosperar / sufrir**	proh-spay-**rar** / soof-**reer**
buy / sell	**comprar / vender**	kohm-**prar** / vayn-**dehr**

Why:

love / sex	**amor / sexo**	ah-**mor** / **sex**-oh
money / power	**dinero / poder**	dee-**nay**-roh / poh-**dehr**
work / food	**trabajo / comida**	trah-**bah**-*h*oh / koh-**mee**-dah
family	**familia**	fah-**meel**-yah
health	**salud**	sah-**lood**
hope	**esperanza**	ay-spay-**rahn**-thah
education	**educación**	ay-doo-kah-thee-**ohn**
guns	**pistolas**	pee-**stoh**-lahs
religion	**religión**	ray-lee-*h*ee-**ohn**
happiness	**alegría**	ah-lay-**gree**-ah
marijuana	**marijuana**	mah-ree-*h*wah-nah
democracy	**democracia**	day-moh-krah-**thee**-ah
taxes	**impuestos**	eem-**pway**-stohs
lies	**mentiras**	mayn-**tee**-rahs

corruption	**corrupción**	koh-roop-thee-**ohn**
pollution	**polución**	poh-loo-thee-**ohn**
television	**televisión**	tay-lay-vee-thee-**ohn**
relaxation	**relajación**	ray-lah-hah-thee-**ohn**
violence	**violencia**	bee-oh-**layn**-thee-ah
respect	**respecto**	ray-**spehk**-toh
racism	**racismo**	rah-**thees**-moh
war / peace	**guerra / paz**	**gehr**-rah / pahth
global perspective	**perspectiva global**	pehr-spehk-**tee**-vah gloh-**bahl**

You be the judge:

(no) problem	**(no hay) problema**	(noh ī) proh-**blay**-mah
(not) good	**(no es) bueno**	(noh ays) **bway**-noh
(not) dangerous	**(no es) peligroso**	(noh ays) pay-lee-**groh**-soh
(not) fair	**(no es) justo**	(noh ays) *hoo*-stoh
(not) guilty	**(no es) culpable**	(noh ays) kool-**pah**-blay
(not) powerful	**(no es) poderoso**	(noh ays) poh-day-**roh**-soh
(not) stupid	**(no es) estúpido**	(noh ays) ay-**stoo**-pee-doh
(not) happy	**(no es) feliz**	(noh ays) fay-**leeth**
because / for	**porque / para**	**por**-kay / **pah**-rah
and / or / from	**y / o / de**	ee / oh / day
too much	**demasiado**	day-mah-see-**ah**-doh
(never) enough	**(nunca) suficiente**	(**noon**-kah) soo-fee-thee-**ehn**-tay
same / better / worse	**igual / mejor / peor**	ee-**gwahl** / may-*hor* / pay-**or**
here	**aquí**	ah-**kee**
everywhere	**en todas partes**	ayn **toh**-dahs **par**-tays

Assorted beginnings and endings:

I like...	**Me gusta...**	may **goo**-stah
I don't like...	**No me gusta...**	noh may **goo**-stah
Do you like...?	**¿Le gusta...?**	lay **goo**-stah
When I was young...	**Cuando era más joven...**	kwahn-doh **ay**-rah mahs *h*oh-behn
I am / Are you...?	**Soy / ¿Es...?**	soy / ays
...optimistic / pessimistic	**...optimista / pesimista**	ohp-tee-**mee**-stah / pay-see-**mee**-stah
I (don't) believe...	**Yo (no) creo...**	yoh (noh) **kray**-oh
Do you believe in...?	**¿Cree usted en...?**	**kray**-yay oo-**stehd** ayn
..God	**...Dios**	**dee**-ohs
..life after death	**...la vida después de la muerte**	lah **bee**-dah days-**pways** day lah **mwehr**-tay
...extraterrestrial life	**...la vida extraterreste**	lah **bee**-dah ayk-strah-tay-**rehs**-tay
...Santa Claus	**...Papá Noel**	pah-**pah** noh-**ehl**
Yes. / No.	**Sí. / No.**	see / noh
Maybe. / I don't know.	**Tal vez. / No sé.**	tahl bayth / noh say
What is most important in life?	**¿Qué es lo más importante en la vida?**	kay ays loh mahs eem-por-**tahn**-tay ayn lah **bee**-dah

The problem is...	**El problema es...**	ehl proh-**blay**-mah ays
The answer is...	**La respuesta es...**	lah rehs-**pway**-stah ays
We have solved the world's problems.	**Nosotros hemos resuelto los problemas del mundo.**	noh-**soh**-trohs ay-mohs ray-**swayl**-toh lohs proh-**blay**-mahs dayl **moon**-doh

Political words relevant to Spain:

Basque ETA: Separatist Basque terrorist group.
Guerra Civil: The 1936-1939 Civil War, which ended with Franco's Nationalists (fascists aided by Hitler) overthrowing the Spanish Republican government (aided by the USSR and Hemingway).
Falange: Franco's fascist party.
Franco: Spain's fascist dictator from 1939 to 1975.
Gonzalez: Spain's current Socialist Prime Minister.
Guernica: Basque town destroyed by Franco during the Civil War, immortalized by a Picasso painting (now in Madrid).
Juan Carlos: Democratic king who succeeded Franco.
OTAN: NATO
Republicanos: Supporters of Spain's democratically elected government, overthrown by Franco's fascists.
Nacionalistas: Supporters of Franco during the Civil War.

CHATTING

A Spanish Romance

Words of love:

I / me / you	**yo / mi / tú**	yoh / mee / too
flirt	**coquetear**	koh-kay-tay-**ar**
kiss	**beso**	**bay**-soh
hug	**abrazo**	ah-**brah**-thoh
love	**amor**	ah-**mor**
make love	**hacer el amor**	ah-**thehr** ehl ah-**mor**
condom	**preservativo**	pray-sehr-bah-**tee**-boh
contraceptive	**contraceptivo**	kohn-trah-thehp-**tee**-boh
safe sex	**sexo sin peligro**	**sex**-oh seen pay-**lee**-groh
sexy	**sexy**	"sexy"
romantic	**romántico**	roh-**mahn**-tee-koh
honey	**cariño[a]**	kah-**reen**-yoh
my angel	**mi ángel**	mee **ahn**-hayl
my love	**mi amor**	mee ah-**mor**
my heaven	**mi cielo**	mee thee-**ay**-loh

Ah, amor:

What's the matter?	**¿Qué le pasa?**	kay lay **pah**-sah
Nothing.	**Nada.**	**nah**-dah
I am / Are you...?	**Estoy / ¿Eres...?**	ay-**stoy** / **ay**-rays
...straight	**...heterosexual**	ay-tay-roh-sehk-soo-**ahl**
...gay	**...homosexual**	oh-moh-sehk-soo-**ahl**

...undecided	...indeciso[a]	een-day-**thee**-soh
...prudish	...prudente	proo-**dehn**-tay
...horny	...caliente	kahl-**yehn**-tay
We are on our honeymoon.	Estamos de luna de miel.	ay-**stah**-mohs day loo-nah day mee-**ehl**
I have...	Tengo...	**tayn**-goh
...a boyfriend.	...un novio.	oon noh-bee-oh
...a girlfriend.	...una novia.	**oo**-nah noh-bee-ah
I'm married.	Estoy casado[a].	ay-**stoy** kah-**sah**-doh
I'm not married.	No estoy casado[a].	noh ay-**stoy** kah-**sah**-doh
I'm rich and single.	Soy rico[a] y soltero[a].	soy **ree**-koh ee sohl-**tay**-roh
I'm lonely.	Estoy solo[a].	ay-**stoy** soh-loh
I have no diseases.	No tengo enfermedades.	noh **tayn**-goh ayn-fehr-may-**dah**-days
I have many diseases.	Tengo muchas enfermedades.	**tayn**-goh **moo**-chahs ayn-fehr-may-**dah**-days
Can I see you again?	¿Te puedo volver a ver?	tay **pway**-doh bohl-**behr** ah behr
You are my most beautiful souvenir.	Tú eres mi mejor recuerdo.	too ay-rays mee may-*hor* ray-**kwehr**-doh
Kiss me more.	Bésame mucho.	**bay**-sah-may **moo**-choh
Is this an aphrodisiac?	¿Es esto un afrodisíaco?	ays ay-stoh oon ah-froh-dee-**see**-ah-koh
This is (not) my first time.	Esta (no) es mi primera vez.	**ay**-stah (noh) ays mee pree-**may**-rah bayth
Do you do this often?	¿Haces esto muy a menudo?	**ah**-thays **ay**-stoh **moo**-ee ah may-**noo**-doh

How's my breath?	¿Me huele el aliento?	may **way**-lay ehl ahl-**yehn**-toh
Let's just be friends.	**Vamos a dejarlo como amigos.**	**bah**-mohs ah day-*har*-loh **koh**-moh ah-**mee**-gohs
I'll pay for my share.	**Pagaré mi parte.**	pah-gah-**ray** mee **par**-tay
Would you like a massage...?	¿**Te gustaría un masaje...?**	tay goo-stah-**ree**-ah oon mah-**sah**-*h*ay
...for your back	...**para tu espalda**	**pah**-rah too ay-**spahl**-dah
...for your feet	...**por tus pies**	por toos pee-**ays**
Why not?	¿**Por qué no?**	por kay noh
Try it.	**Pruébalo.**	proo-**ay**-bah-loh
It tickles.	**Esto me hace cosquillas.**	**ay**-stoh may **ah**-thay koh-**skee**-yahs
Oh my God!	¡**Dios mío!**	**dee**-ohs **mee**-oh
I love you.	**Te quiero.**	tay kee-**ehr**-oh
Darling, will you marry me?	¿**Querida, te casarás conmigo?**	kay-**ree**-dah tay kah-sah-**rahs** kohn-**mee**-goh

Conversing with Spanish animals:

rooster / cock-a-doodle-doo	**gallo / cacarea**	**gah**-yoh / kah-kah-**ray**-ah
bird / tweet tweet	**pajaro / pío pío**	pah-*hah*-roh / **pee**-oh **pee**-oh
cat / meow	**gato / miau**	**gah**-toh / **mee**-ow
dog / woof woof	**perro / guao guao**	**pehr**-roh / gwow gwow
duck / quack quack	**pato / cua cua**	**pah**-toh / kwah kwah
cow / moo	**vaca / muh**	**bah**-kah / moo
pig / oink oink	**cerdo / (just snort)**	**thehr**-doh / (just snort)

PORTUGUESE

Getting Started

Portuguese

...is your passport to Europe's bargain basement. And for its wonderful pricetag, you'll enjoy piles of fresh seafood, brilliant sunshine, and local character that has yet to notice the 1990's. With its old world charm comes a bigger language barrier than you'll find elsewhere in Europe. A phrase book is of greater value here than anywhere else in western Europe.

Here are a few tips on pronouncing Portuguese words:

C usually sounds like C in cat.
But *C* followed by *E* or *I* sounds like S in sun.
Ç sounds like S in sun.
CH sounds like SH in shine.
G usually sounds like G in go.
But *G* followed by *E* or *I* sounds like S in treasure.
H is silent.
J sounds like S in treasure.
LH sounds like LI in billion.
NH sounds like NI in onion.
R is trrrilled.
S usually sounds like SH in shine.
But between vowels, *S* sounds like Z in zoo.
SS sounds like S in sun.

Portuguese vowels:

A can sound like A in father or A in sang.
E can sound like E in get, AY in play, or I in wish.
É sounds like E in get.
Ê sounds like AY in play.
I sounds like EE in seed.
O can sound like O in note, AW in raw, or OO in
   moon.
Ô and *OU* sound like O in note.
U sounds like OO in moon.

As with any Romance language, sex is important. A man is *simpático* (friendly), a woman is *simpática*. In this book, we show bi-sexual words like this: *simpático[a]*. If you're speaking of a woman (which includes women speaking about themselves), use the *a* ending. It's always pronounced "ah." A word that ends in *r*, such as *cantor* (singer), will appear like this: *cantor[a]*. A *cantora* is a female singer. A word ending in *e*, such as *interessante* (interesting), applies to either sex.

Adjectives agree with the noun. A clean room is a *quarto limpo*, a clean towel is a *toalha limpa*. You'll be quizzed on this later.

If a word ends in a vowel, the Portuguese usually stress the second-to-last syllable. Words ending in a consonant are stressed on the last syllable. To override these rules, the Portuguese add an accent mark (such as ´, ˜, or ^) to the syllable that should be stressed, like this: *rápido* (fast) is pronounced **rah**-pee-doo.

Just like French, its linguistic buddy, Portuguese has nasal sounds. A vowel followed by either *n* or *m* or topped with a ˜ (such as *ã* or *õ*) is usually nasalized. In the phonetics, nasalized vowels are indicated by an underlined <u>n</u> or <u>w</u>. As you say the vowel, let its sound come through your nose as well as your mouth.

Here are the phonetics for nasal vowels:

ay<u>n</u>	nasalize the AY in day.
oh<u>n</u>	nasalize the O in bone.
oo<u>n</u>	nazalize the O in moon.
o<u>w</u>	nasalize the OW in now.

Some words have only a slight nasal sound. To help you pronounce these words, we add an *ng* or *n* in the phonetics: *sim* (yes) is pronounced **seeng**, and *muito* (very) like **mween**-too.

Here's a quick guide to the rest of the phonetics used in this book:

a	like A in sang.
ah	like A in father.
aw	like AW in raw.
ay	like AY in play.
ee	like EE in seed.
eh	like E in get.
chr	sounds like "air."
g	like G in go.
i	like I in hit.
ī	like I in light.
oh	like O in note.
oo	like OO in moon.
or	like OR in core.
ow	like OW in now.
oy	like OY in toy.
s	like S in sun.
zh	like S in treasure.

Too often, tourists insist on speaking Spanish to the Portuguese. Your attempts at Portuguese will endear you to the locals. And if you throw in *"por favor"* (please) whenever you can, you'll eat better, sleep easier, and make friends faster.

Portuguese Basics

Greeting and meeting the Portuguese:

Hello.	**Olá.**	oh-**lah**
Good morning.	**Bom-dia.**	boh<u>n</u>-**dee**-ah
Good afternoon.	**Boa-tarde.**	boh-ah-**tar**-deh
Good evening.	**Boa-noite.**	boh-ah-**noy**-teh
Good night.	**Boa-noite.**	boh-ah-**noy**-teh
Mr. / Mrs.	**Senhor / Senhora**	sin-**yor** / sin-**yoh**-rah
Miss	**Menina**	meh-**nee**-nah
How are you?	**Como está?**	koh-moo ish-**tah**
Very well.	**Muito bem.**	**mween**-too bay<u>n</u>
Thank you. (said by a male)	**Obrigado.**	oh-bree-**gah**-doo
Thank you. (said by a female)	**Obrigada.**	oh-bree-**gah**-dah
And you?	**E você?**	ee voh-**say**
My name is...	**Chamo-me...**	**shah**-moo-meh
What's your name?	**Como se chama?**	**koh**-moo seh **shah**-mah
Pleased to meet you.	**Prazer em conhecer.**	prah-**zehr** ay<u>n</u> kohn-yeh-**sehr**
Where are you from?	**De onde é que você é?**	deh oh<u>n</u>-deh eh keh voh-**say** eh
So long!	**Até logo!**	ah-**teh law**-goo
Goodbye.	**Adeus.**	ah-**deh**-oosh
Good luck!	**Boa sorte!**	**boh**-ah **sor**-teh
Have a good trip!	**Boa-viagem!**	boh-ah-vee-**ah**-zhay<u>n</u>

BASICS

Survival phrases

In 1917, according to legend, the Virgin Mary visited Fatima using only these phrases. They're repeated on your tear-out cheat sheet near the end of this book.

The essentials:

Hello.	**Olá.**	oh-**lah**
Do you speak English?	**Fala inglês?**	**fah**-lah een-**glaysh**
Yes. / No.	**Sim. / Não.**	seeng / now
I don't speak Portuguese.	**Não falo português.**	now **fah**-loo poor-too-**gaysh**
I'm sorry.	**Desculpe.**	dish-**kool**-peh
Please.	**Por favor.**	poor fah-**vor**
Thank you.	**Obrigado[a].**	oh-bree-**gah**-doo
It's (not) a problem.	**(Não) á problema.**	(now) ah proo-**blay**-mah
Very good.	**Muito bem.**	**mween**-too bayn
You are very kind.	**É muito simpático[a].**	eh **mween**-too seeng-**pah**-tee-koo
Goodbye.	**Adeus.**	ah-**deh**-oosh

Where?

Where is...?	**Onde é que é...?**	**ohn**-deh eh keh eh
...a hotel	**...um hotel**	oon oh-**tehl**
...a youth hostel	**...uma pousada de juventude**	**oo**-mah poh-**zah**-dah deh zhoo-vayn-**too**-deh
...a restaurant	**...um restaurante**	oon rish-toh-**rahn**-teh

...a supermarket	...**um supermercado**	oon soo-pehr-mehr-**kah**-doo
...a pharmacy	...**uma farmácia**	oo-mah far-**mah**-see-ah
...a bank	...**um banco**	oon **bang**-koo
...the train station	...**a estação de comboio**	ah ish-tah-**sow** deh kohn-**boy**-yoo
...tourist information	...**a informação turística**	ah een-for-mah-**sow** too-reesh-tee-kah
...the toilet	...**a casa de banho**	ah **kah**-zah deh **bahn**-yoo
men / women	**homens / mulheres**	aw-maynsh / mool-**yeh**-rish

How much?

How much is it?	**Quanto custa?**	kwahn-too koosh-tah
Write it?	**Escreva?**	ish-**kray**-vah
Cheap(er).	**(Mais) barato.**	(mīsh) bah-**rah**-too
Cheapest.	**O mais barato.**	oo mīsh bah-**rah**-too
Is it free?	**É grátis?**	eh **grah**-teesh
Is it included?	**Está incluido?**	ish-**tah** een-kloo-**ee**-doo
Do you have...?	**Tem...?**	tayn
I would like...	**Gostaria...**	goosh-tah-**ree**-ah
We would like...	**Gostaríamos...**	goosh-tah-**ree**-ah-moosh
...this.	...**isto.**	**eesh**-too
...just a little.	...**só um bocadinho.**	saw oon boo-kah-**deen**-yoo
...more.	...**mais.**	mīsh
...a ticket.	...**um bilhete.**	oon beel-**yeh**-teh
...a room.	...**um quarto.**	oon **kwar**-too
...the bill.	...**a conta.**	ah **kohn**-tah

How many?

one	**um**	oon
two	**dois**	doysh
three	**três**	traysh
four	**quatro**	**kwah**-troo
five	**cinco**	**seeng**-koo
six	**seis**	saysh
seven	**sete**	**seh**-teh
eight	**oito**	**oy**-too
nine	**nove**	**naw**-veh
ten	**dez**	dehsh

You'll find more to count on in the Numbers chapter.

When?

At what time?	**A que horas?**	ah keh **aw**-rahsh
Just a moment.	**Um momento.**	oon moo-**mayn**-too
Now.	**Agora.**	ah-**goh**-rah
Soon.	**Em breve.**	ayn **bray**-veh
Later.	**Mais tarde.**	mish **tar**-deh
Today.	**Hoje.**	**oh**-zheh
Tomorrow.	**Amanhã.**	ah-ming-**yah**

Mix and match these survival phrases to say: "Two tickets,"
or "Yes, thanks," or "Where is a cheap restaurant?" or "The
bill, please."

Struggling with Portuguese:

Do you speak English?	**Fala inglês?**	**fah**-lah een-**glaysh**
A teeny weeny bit?	**Um pouquinho?**	oo<u>n</u> poh-**keen**-yoo
Please speak English.	**Por favor fale inglês.**	poor fah-**vor fah**-leh een-**glaysh**
You speak English well.	**Fala bem inglês.**	**fah**-lah bay<u>n</u> een-**glaysh**
I don't speak Portuguese.	**Não falo português.**	no<u>w</u> **fah**-loo poor-too-**gaysh**
I speak a little Portuguese.	**Falo um pouco em português.**	**fah**-loo oo<u>n</u> **poh**-koo ay<u>n</u> poor-too-**gaysh**
What is this in Portuguese?	**O que é isto em português?**	oo keh eh **eesh**-too ay<u>n</u> poor-too-**gaysh**
Repeat?	**Repita?**	ray-**pee**-tah
Slowly.	**Devagar.**	deh-vah-**gar**
Do you understand?	**Compreende?**	koh<u>n</u>-pree-**ayn**-deh
I understand.	**Compreendo.**	koh<u>n</u>-pree-**ayn**-doo
I don't understand.	**Não compreendo.**	no<u>w</u> koh<u>n</u>-pree-**ayn**-doo
Write it?	**Escreva?**	ish-**kray**-vah
Who speaks English?	**Quem fala inglês?**	kay<u>n</u> **fah**-lah een-**glaysh**

In Portugal, a woman who looks over 35 years old is addressed as *senhora*, younger than 35 as *menina*. Good luck...

Common questions in Portuguese:

How much?	Quanto custa?	kwahn-too koosh-tah
How many?	Quantos?	kwahn-toosh
How long...?	Quanto tempo...?	kwahn-too tayn-poo
...is the trip	...é a viagem	eh ah vee-ah-zhayn
How far?	A que distância?	ah keh deesh-tahn-see-ah
How?	Como?	koh-moo
Is it possible?	É possível?	eh poo-see-vehl
Is it necessary?	É necessário?	eh neh-seh-sah-ree-oo
Can you help me?	Pode me ajudar?	paw-deh meh ah-zhoo-dar
What?	O quê?	oo kay
What is that?	O que é isso?	oo keh eh ee-soo
What is better?	O que é melhor?	oo keh eh mil-yor
When?	Quando?	kwahn-doo
What time is it?	Que horas são?	keh aw-rahsh sow
At what time?	A que horas?	ah keh aw-rahsh
On time?	Pontual?	pohn-too-ahl
Late?	Atrasado?	ah-trah-zah-doo
What time does this...?	A que horas é que...?	ah keh aw-rahsh eh keh
...open	...abre	ah-breh
...close	...fecha	fay-shah
Do you have...?	Tem...?	tayn
Where is...?	Onde é...?	ohn-deh eh
Where are...?	Onde estão...?	ohn-deh ish-tow
Where can I find...?	A onde posso encontrar...?	ah ohn-deh paw-soo ayn-kohn-trar

Who?	**Quem?**	kay<u>n</u>
Why?	**Porquê?**	poor-**kay**
Why not?	**Porquê não?**	poor-**kay** no<u>w</u>
Yes or no?	**Sim ou não?**	seeng oh no<u>w</u>

You can turn a word or sentence into a question by asking it in a questioning tone. *"Isso é bom"* (It's good) becomes *"Isso é bom?"* (Is it good?).

Yin and yang:

cheap / expensive	**barato / caro**	bah-**rah**-too / **kah**-roo
big / small	**grande / pequeno**	**grahn**-deh / pay-**kay**-noo
hot / cold	**quente / frio**	**kayn**-teh / **free**-oo
open / closed	**aberto / fechado**	ah-**behr**-too / feh-**shah**-doo
entrance / exit	**entrada / saída**	ayn-**trah**-dah / sah-**ee**-dah
arrive / depart	**chegar / partir**	shay-**gar** / par-**teer**
early / late	**cedo / tarde**	**say**-doo / **tar**-deh
soon / later	**em breve /** **mais tarde**	ay<u>n</u> **bray**-veh / mīsh **tar**-deh
fast / slow	**rápido / lento**	**rah**-pee-doo / **layn**-too
here / there	**aqui / ali**	ah-**kee** / ah-**lee**
near / far	**perto / longe**	**pehr**-too / **lohn**-zheh
good / bad	**bom / mau**	boh<u>n</u> / mow
best / worst	**melhor / pior**	mil-**yor** / pee-**yor**
a little / lots	**um pouco / muito**	oo<u>n</u> **poh**-koo / **mween**-too
more / less	**mais / menos**	mīsh / **may**-noosh
mine / yours	**meu / vosso**	**meh**-oo / **vaw**-soo

easy / difficult	**fácil / difícil**	fah-seel / dee-**fee**-seel
left / right	**esquerda / direita**	ish-**kehr**-dah / dee-**ray**-tah
up / down	**cima / baixo**	**see**-mah / bī-shoo
young / old	**jovem / velho**	zhaw-vay<u>n</u> / **vehl**-yoo
new / old	**novo / velho**	**noh**-voo / **vehl**-yoo
heavy / light	**pesado / leve**	peh-**zah**-doo / **leh**-veh
dark / light	**escuro / claro**	ish-**koo**-roo / **klah**-roo
beautiful / ugly	**lindo / feio**	**leen**-doo / **fay**-oo
smart / stupid	**esperto / estúpido**	ish-**pehr**-too / ich **too**-pee-doo
vacant / occupied	**livre / ocupado**	**lee**-vreh / oo-koo-**pah**-doo
with / without	**com / sem**	koh<u>n</u> / say<u>n</u>

Big little words in Portugal:

I	**eu**	**eh**-oo
you (formal)	**você**	voh-**say**
you (informal)	**tu**	too
we	**nós**	nawsh
he	**ele**	**eh**-leh
she	**ela**	**eh**-lah
they	**eles**	**eh**-lish
and	**e**	ee
at	**á**	ah
because	**porque**	**poor**-keh
but	**mas**	mahsh
by (via)	**via**	**vee**-ah
for	**para**	**pah**-rah
from	**de**	deh

here	**aqui**	ah-**kee**
in	**em**	ay<u>n</u>
not	**não**	no<u>w</u>
now	**agora**	ah-**goh**-rah
only	**só**	saw
or	**ou**	oh
that	**aquilo**	ah-**kee**-loo
this	**isto**	**eesh**-too
to	**para**	**pah**-rah
very	**muito**	**mween**-too

Portuguese names for places:

Portugal	**Portugal**	poor-too-**gahl**
Lisbon	**Lisboa**	leezh-**boh**-ah
Spain	**Espanha**	ish-**pahn**-yah
Morocco	**Marrocos**	mah-**raw**-koosh
France	**França**	**frahn**-sah
Germany	**Alemanha**	ah-leh-**mahn**-yah
Switzerland	**Suiça**	**swee**-sah
Italy	**Italia**	ee-**tahl**-yah
Great Britain	**Inglaterra**	eeng-glah-**tehr**-rah
Europe	**Europa**	eh-oo-**roh**-pah
United States	**Estados Unidos**	ish-**tah**-doosh oo-**nee**-doosh
Canada	**Canadá**	kah-nah-**dah**
world	**o mundo**	oo **moo<u>n</u>**-doo

Numbers

1	**um**	oo<u>n</u>
2	**dois**	doysh
3	**três**	traysh
4	**quatro**	**kwah**-troo
5	**cinco**	**seeng**-koo
6	**seis**	saysh
7	**sete**	**seh**-teh
8	**oito**	**oy**-too
9	**nove**	**naw**-veh
10	**dez**	dehsh
11	**onze**	**ohn**-zeh
12	**doze**	**doh**-zeh
13	**treze**	**tray**-zeh
14	**catorze**	kah-**tor**-zeh
15	**quinze**	**keen**-zeh
16	**dezasseis**	deh-zah-**saysh**
17	**dezassete**	deh-zah-**seh**-teh
18	**dezoito**	deh-**zoy**-too
19	**dezanove**	deh-zah-**naw**-veh
20	**vinte**	**veen**-teh
21	**vinte e um**	**veen**-teh ee oo<u>n</u>
22	**vinte e dois**	**veen**-teh ee doysh
23	**vinte e três**	**veen**-teh ee traysh
30	**trinta**	**treen**-tah
31	**trinta e um**	**treen**-tah ee oo<u>n</u>

40	**quarenta**	kwah-**rayn**-tah
41	**quarenta e um**	kwah-**rayn**-tah ee oon
50	**cinquenta**	seeng-**kwayn**-tah
60	**sessenta**	seh-**sayn**-tah
70	**setenta**	seh-**tayn**-tah
80	**oitenta**	oy-**tayn**-tah
90	**noventa**	noh-**vayn**-tah
100	**cem**	sayn
101	**cento e um**	**sayn**-too ee oon
102	**cento e dois**	**sayn**-too ee doysh
200	**duzentos**	doo-**zayn**-toosh
1000	**mil**	meel
1996	**mil novecentos**	meel naw-veh-**sayn**-toosh
	e noventa e seis	ee noo-**vayn**-tah ee saysh
2000	**dois mil**	doysh meel
million	**milhão**	mil-**yow**
billion	**bilhão**	bil-**yow**
first	**primeiro**	pree-**may**-roo
second	**segundo**	seh-**goon**-doo
third	**terceiro**	tehr-**say**-roo
half	**metade**	meh-**tah**-deh
100%	**cem per cento**	sayn pehr **sayn**-too
number one	**número um**	**noo**-meh-roo oon

Money

Can you change dollars?	**Pode trocar dollares?**	**paw**-deh troo-**kar daw**-lah-rish
What is your exchange rate for dollars...?	**Qual é a taxa de câmbio para o dollar...?**	kwahl eh ah **tah**-shah deh **kahm**-bee-oo **pah**-rah oo **daw**-lar
...in traveler's checks	**...em cheque de viagem**	ayn **sheh**-keh deh vee-**ah**-zhayn
What is the commission?	**O que é a comissao?**	oo keh eh ah koo-mee-**sow**
Any extra fee?	**À taxa extra?**	ah **tah**-shah Ish-trah
I would like...	**Gostaria...**	goosh-teh-**ree**-ah
...small bills.	**...notas pequenas.**	**naw**-tahsh peh-**kay**-nahsh
...large bills.	**...notas grandes.**	**naw**-tahsh **grahn**-dish
...coins.	**...moedas.**	moo-**eh**-dahsh
Is this a mistake?	**Isto é um erro?**	**eesh**-too eh oon **eh**-roo
I'm rich.	**Sou rico[a].**	soh **ree**-koo
I'm poor.	**Sou pobre.**	soh **paw**-broh
I'm broke.	**Estou teso[a].**	ish-**toh** tay-zoo
$50	**cinquenta escudos**	seeng-**kwayn**-tah ish-**koo**-doosh

Key money words:

bank	**banco**	**bang**-koo
money	**dinheiro**	deen-**yay**-roo
change money	**troca de dinheiro**	**troo**-kah deh deen-**yay**-roo
exchange	**troca**	**troo**-kah
commission	**comissão**	koo-mee-**sow**
traveler's check	**cheques de viagem**	**sheh**-keh deh vee-**ah**-zhayn
credit card	**cartão de crédito**	kar-**tow** deh **kreh**-dee-too
cash advance	**avanço de dinheiro**	ah-**van**-soo deh deen-**yay**-roo
cash machine	**caixa automática**	**kī**-shah ow-toh-**mah**-tee-kah
cashier	**caixa**	**kī**-shah
cash	**dinheiro**	deen-**yay**-roo
bills	**notas**	**naw**-tahsh
coins	**moedas**	moo-**eh**-dahsh
receipt	**recibo**	reh-**see**-boo

Commissions for changing money vary wildly in Portugal. Shop around. In airports and on big city streets, you'll see easy-to-use change machines that take your American cash (or any other major currency) and give you *escudos* in exchange. They usually give a decent rate, charge no fee, and are "open" 24 hours a day.

Time

What time is it?	**Que horas são?**	keh **aw**-rahsh sow
It's...	**São...**	sow
...8:00 in the morning.	**...oito horas da manhã.**	**oy**-too **aw**-rahsh dah ming-**yah**
...16:00.	**...dezasseis horas.**	deh-zah-**saysh aw**-rahsh
...4:00 in the afternoon.	**...das quarto da tarde.**	dahsh **kwar**-too dah **tar**-deh
...10:30 (in the evening).	**...dez horas e meia (da noite).**	dehsh **aw**-rahsh ee **may**-ah (dah **noy**-teh)
...a quarter past nine.	**...nove e um quarto.**	**naw**-veh ee oon **kwar**-too
...a quarter to eleven.	**...um quarto para as onze.**	oon **kwar**-too **pah**-rah ahsh **ohn**-zeh
...noon.	**...meio-dia.**	may-oo-**dee**-ah
...midnight.	**...meia-noite.**	may-ah-**noy**-teh
...sunrise.	**...nascer do sol.**	**nahsh sehr** doo sohl
...sunset.	**...por do sol.**	poor doo sohl
...early / late.	**...cedo / tarde.**	**say**-doo / **tar**-deh
...on time.	**...pontual.**	pohn-too-**ahl**

In Portugal, the 24-hour clock (or military time) is used mainly for train, bus, and ferry schedules. Informally, the Portuguese use the same "12-hour clock" we do.

Timely words:

minute	**minuto**	mee-**noo**-too
hour	**hora**	**aw**-rah
in the morning	**da manhã**	dah ming-**yah**
in the afternoon	**da tarde**	dah **tar**-deh
in the evening	**da noite**	dah **noy**-teh
night	**noite**	**noy**-teh
day	**dia**	**dee**-ah
today	**hoje**	**oh**-zheh
yesterday	**ontem**	**ohn**-tayn
tomorrow	**amanhã**	ah-ming-**yah**
tomorrow morning	**amanhã de manhã**	ah-ming-**yah** deh ming-**yah**
anytime	**a qualquer hora**	ah kwahl-**kehr aw**-rah
immediately	**imediatamente**	ee-meh-dee-ah-tah-**mayn**-teh
in one hour	**em uma hora**	ayn oo-mah **aw**-rah
every hour	**todas as horas**	**toh**-dahss ahsh **aw**-rahsh
every day	**todos os dias**	**toh**-doosh oosh **dee**-ahsh
last	**último**	**ool**-tee-moo
this	**este**	**aysh**-teh
next	**próximo**	**praw**-see-moo
May 15	**quinze de Maio**	**keen**-zeh deh **mah**-yoo

The Portuguese say *"Bom-dia"* (Good morning) until noon, *"Boa-tarde"* (Good afternoon) until dark, and *"Bom-noite"* (Good evening) after dark.

week	semana	seh-**mah**-nah
Monday	segunda-feira	seh-goon-dah-**fay**-rah
Tuesday	terça-feira	tehr-sah-**fay**-rah
Wednesday	quarta-feira	kwar-tah-**fay**-rah
Thursday	quinta-feira	keen-tah-**fay**-rah
Friday	sexta-feira	saysh-tah-**fay**-rah
Saturday	sábado	**sah**-bah-doo
Sunday	domingo	doo-**meeng**-goo
month	mês	maysh
January	Janeiro	zhah-**nay**-roo
February	Fevereiro	feh-veh-**ray**-roo
March	Março	**mar**-soo
April	Abril	ah-**breel**
May	Maio	**mah**-yoo
June	Junho	**zhoon**-yoo
July	Julho	**zhool**-yoo
August	Agosto	ah-**gohsh**-too
September	Setembro	seh-**tayn**-broo
October	Outubro	oh-**too**-broo
November	Novembro	noo-**vayn**-broo
December	Dezembro	deh-**zayn**-broo
year	ano	**ah**-noo
spring	primavera	pree-mah-**veh**-rah
summer	verão	veh-**row**
fall	outono	oh-**toh**-noo
winter	inverno	een-**vehr**-noo

Holidays and happy days:

holiday	**feriado**	feh-ree-**ah**-doo
national holiday	**feriado nacional**	feh-ree-**ah**-doo nah-see-oo-**nahl**
religious holiday	**feriado religioso**	feh-ree-**ah**-doo ray-lee-zhee-**oh**-zoo
Merry Christmas!	**Feliz Natal!**	feh-**leesh** nah-**tahl**
Happy New Year!	**Feliz Ano Novo!**	feh-**leesh** ah-noo **noh**-voo
Happy wedding anniversary!	**Feliz aniversário de casamento!**	feh-**leesh** ah-nee-vehr-**sah**-ree-oo deh kah-zah-**mayn**-too
Happy birthday!	**Feliz aniversário!**	feh-**leesh** ah-nee-vehr-**sah**-ree-oo

The Portuguese sing "Happy birthday" to the same tune we do, but they sing it twice. Here are the words: *Parabéns a você, nesta data querida, muitas felecidades, muitos anos de vida. Hoje é dia de festa, cantam as nossas almas, para* (fill in name), *uma salva de palmas!* Whew!

Portugal celebrates its independence day on December 1st. Other major holidays include Easter week, *Dia de Camões* (June 10th, in honor of the Portuguese poet Luis de Camões), *Ascenção de Maria* (August 15th), and *Dia da República* (October 5th).

Transportation

TRANSPORTATION

Trains:

Is this the line for...?	Esta é a fila para...?	ehsh-tah eh ah fee-lah pah-rah
...tickets	...bilhetes	beel-yeh-tish
...reservations	...reservas	reh-zehr-vahsh
How much is a ticket to...?	Quanto custa o bilhete para...?	kwahn-too koosh-tah oo beel-yeh-teh pah-rah
A ticket to ___.	Um bilhete para ___.	oon beel-yeh-teh pah-rah
When is the next train?	Quando é o próximo comboio?	kwahn-doo eh oo praw-see-moo kohn-boy-oo
I'd like to leave...	Gostaria de ir embora...	goosh-tah-ree-ah deh eer ayn-boh-rah
I'd like to arrive...	Gostaria de chegar...	goosh-tah-ree-ah deh shay-gar
...by ___.	...por ___.	poor
...in the morning.	...de manhã.	deh ming-yah
...in the afternoon.	...do tarde.	deh tar-deh

...in the evening.	**...ao anoitecer.**	ow ah-noy-teh-**sehr**
Is there a...?	**Será que á um...?**	seh-**rah** keh ah oo<u>n</u>
...earlier train	**...comboio mais cedo**	koh<u>n</u>-**boy**-oo mīsh **say**-doo
...later train	**...comboio mais tarde**	koh<u>n</u>-**boy**-oo mīsh **tar**-deh
...overnight train	**...comboio durante a noite**	koh<u>n</u>-**boy**-oo doo-**rayn**-teh ah **noy**-teh
...supplement	**...suplemento**	soo-pleh-**mayn**-too
Is there a discount for...?	**Tem desconto para...?**	tay<u>n</u> dish-**kohn**-too **pah**-rah
...youth	**...jovens**	**zhaw**-vay<u>n</u>sh
...seniors	**...pessoas de terceira idade**	peh-**soh**-ahsh deh tehr-**say**-rah ee-**dah**-deh
Is a reservation required?	**É preciso reservar?**	eh preh-**see**-zoo reh-zehr-**var**
I'd like to reserve a...	**Gostaria de reservar um...**	goosh-tah-**ree**-ah deh reh-zehr-**var** oo<u>n</u>
...seat.	**...assento.**	ah-**sayn**-too
...berth.	**...beliche.**	beh-**lee**-sheh
Where does (the train) leave from?	**De onde é que parte?**	deh oh<u>n</u>-deh eh keh **par**-teh
What track?	**Que linha?**	keh **leen**-yah
On time?	**Pontual?**	poh<u>n</u>-too-**ahl**
Late?	**Atrasado?**	ah-trah-**zah**-doo
When will it arrive?	**Quando é que vai chegar?**	**kwahn**-doo eh keh vī shay-**gar**
Is it direct?	**É directo?**	eh dee-**reh**-too
Must I transfer?	**É preciso mudar?**	eh preh-**see**-zoo moo-**dar**

When? Where?	**Quando? Onde?**	kwahn-doo / ohn-deh
Which train to...?	**Que comboio para...?**	keh kohn-boy-yoo pah-rah
Which train car for...?	**Que carruagem para...?**	keh kar-wah-zhayn pah-rah
Is this (seat) free?	**Está livre?**	ish-tah lee-vreh
That's my seat.	**Este é o meu lugar.**	aysh-teh eh oo meh-oo loo-gar
Save my place?	**Guarde o meu lugar?**	gwar-deh oo meh-oo loo-gar
Where are you going?	**Onde é que vai?**	ohn-deh eh keh vī
I'm going to...	**Vou para...**	voh pah-rah
Tell me when to get off?	**Diga-me quando vou sair?**	dee-gah-meh kwahn-doo voh sah-eer

TRANSPORTATION

Ticket talk:

ticket	**bilhete**	beel-yeh-teh
one way	**uma ida**	oo-mah ee-dah
roundtrip	**ida e volta**	ee-dah oo vohl-tah
first class	**primeira classe**	pree-may-rah klah-seh
second class	**segunda classe**	seh-goon-dah klah-seh
validate	**validade**	vah-lee-dah-deh
schedule	**horário**	aw-rah-ree-oo
departure	**partida**	par-tee-dah
direct	**directo**	dee-reh-too
connection	**conexão**	koo-nehk-sow
reservation	**reserva**	ray-zehr-vah

non-smoking	**não fumador**	no<u>w</u> foo-mah-**dor**
seat...	**assento...**	ah-**say<u>n</u>**-too
...by the window	**...à janela**	ah zhah-**neh**-lah
...on the aisle	**...sobre corredor**	**soh**-breh koo-ray-**dor**
berth	**beliche**	beh-**lee**-sheh
refund	**reembolso**	reh-ay<u>n</u>-**bohl**-soo

At the train station:

Portuguese State Railways	**Caminhos de Ferro**	kah-**meen**-yoosh deh **fehr**-roo
train station	**estação de comboio**	ish-tah-**sow** deh koh<u>n</u>-**boy**-yoo
train information	**informação sobre comboios**	een-for-mah-**sow soh**-breh koh<u>n</u>-**boy**-yoosh
train	**comboio**	koh<u>n</u>-**boy**-yoo
high-speed train	**expresso**	ish-**preh**-soo
arrival	**chegada**	shay-**gah**-dah
departure	**partida**	par-**tee**-dah
delay	**atrazo**	ah-**trah**-zoo
waiting room	**sala de espera**	**sah**-lah deh ish-**peh**-rah
lockers	**depósito de bagagem automático**	deh-**paw**-zee-too deh bah-**gah**-zhay<u>n</u> ow-too-**mah**-tee-koo
baggage check room	**despacho de bagagem**	dish-**pah**-shoo deh bah-**gah**-zhay<u>n</u>
lost and found office	**perdidos e achados**	pehr-**dee**-doosh ee ah-**shah**-doosh

tourist information	**informação turistica**	een-for-mah-**sow** too-**reesh**-tee-kah
to the platforms	**acesso ão cais**	ah-**seh**-soo ow kīsh
platform	**cais**	kīsh
track	**linha**	**leen**-yah
train car	**carruagem**	kar-**wah**-zhayn
dining car	**carruagem restaurante**	kar-**wah**-zhayn rish-toh-**rahn**-teh
sleeper car	**carruagem cama**	kar-**wah**-zhayn **kah**-mah
conductor	**condutor**	kohn-doo-**tor**

TRANSPORTATION

Reading Portuguese train and bus schedules:

até	until
atrasado	late
chegada	arrival
de	from
diário	daily
dias	days
dias de semana	weekdays
domingos e feriados	Sundays and holidays
excepto	except
para	to
partida	departure
sabádo	Saturday
só	only
todo	every
1-5, 6, 7	Monday-Friday, Saturday, Sunday

Buses and subways:

How do I get to..?	**Como é que vou para...?**	**koh**-moo eh keh voh **pah**-rah
Which bus to...?	**Que autocarro para...?**	keh ow-too-**kah**-roo **pah**-rah
Does it stop at...?	**Para em...?**	**pah**-rah ayn
Which metro stop for...?	**Qual é a paragem para...?**	kwahl eh ah pah-**rah**-zhayn **pah**-rah
Must I transfer?	**É preciso mudar?**	eh preh-**see**-zoo moo-**dar**
How much is a ticket?	**Quanto custa um bilhete?**	**kwahn**-too **koosh**-tah oon beel-**yeh**-teh
Where can I buy a ticket?	**A onde posso comprar um bilhete?**	ah **ohn**-deh **paw**-soo kohn-**prar** oon beel-**yeh**-teh
When does the... leave?	**Quando é que... parte?**	**kwahn**-doo eh keh... **par**-teh
...first	**...primeiro**	pree-**may**-roo
...next	**...próximo**	**praw**-see-moo
...last	**...último**	**ool**-tee-moo
...bus / subway	**...autocarro / metro**	ow-too-**kah**-roo / **meh**-troo
What's the frequency per hour / day?	**Qual é a frequência por hora / dia?**	kwahl eh ah freh-**kayn**-see-ah poor **aw**-rah / **dee**-ah
I'm going to...	**Vou para...**	voh **pah**-rah
Tell me when to get off?	**Diga-me quando vou sair?**	**dee**-gah-meh **kwahn**-doo voh sah-**eer**

Handy bus and subway words:

ticket	**bilhete**	beel-**yeh**-teh
city bus	**autocarro**	ow-too-**kah**-roo
long-distance bus	**camioneta**	kahm-yoo-**neh**-tah
bus stop	**paragem de autocarro**	pah-**rah**-zhayn deh ow-too-**kah**-roo
bus station	**terminal das camionetas**	tehr-mee-**nahl** dahsh kahm-yoo-**neh**-tahsh
subway	**metro**	**meh**-troo
subway station	**estação de metro**	ish-tah-**sow** deh **meh**-troo
direct	**directo**	dee-**reh**-too
connection	**conexão**	koo-nehk-**sow**

Taxis:

Taxi!	**Táxi!**	**tahk**-see
Can you call a taxi?	**Pode chamar um táxi?**	**paw**-deh shah-**mar** oon **tahk**-see
Where can I get a taxi?	**Onde posso apanhar um táxi?**	**ohn**-deh **paw**-soo ah-pahn-**yar** oon **tahk**-see
Are you free?	**Está livre?**	ish-**tah** **lee**-vreh
Occupied.	**Ocupado.**	oo-koo-**pah**-doo
How much will it cost to go to...?	**Quanto é que custa a viagem para...?**	**kwahn**-too eh keh **koosh**-tah ah vee-**ah**-zhayn **pah**-rah
...the airport	**...o aeroporto**	oo ah-roh-**por**-too
...the train station	**...estação do comboio**	ish-tah-**sow** doo kohn-**boy**-oo
...this address	**...este endereço**	**aysh**-teh ayn-deh-**ray**-soo

Too much.	É muito caro.	eh **mween**-too **kah**-roo
This is all I have.	Isto é só o que tenho.	**eesh**-too eh saw oo keh **tayn**-yoo
Can you take ___ people?	Pode levar ___ pessoas?	**paw**-deh leh-**var** ___ peh-**soh**-ahsh
Any extra fee?	À taxa extra?	ah **tah**-shah **ish**-trah
The meter, please.	O medidor, por favor.	oo may-dee-**dor** poor fah-**vor**
The most direct route.	O caminho mais direto.	oo kah-**meen**-yoo mīsh dee-**reh**-too
Slow down.	Mais devagar.	mīsh deh-vah-**gar**
If you don't slow down, I'll throw up.	Se não for mais devagar, vou vomitar.	seh no<u>w</u> for mīsh day-vah-**gar** voh voo-mee-**tar**
Stop here.	Pare aqui.	**pah**-rah ah-**kee**
Can you wait?	Pode esperar?	**paw**-deh ish-peh-**rar**
I'll never forget this ride.	Nunca vou esquecer esta viagem.	**noon**-kah voh ish-keh-**sehr** **ehsh**-tah vee-**ah**-zhay<u>n</u>
Where did you learn to drive?	Onde é que aprendeu a conduzir?	**oh**<u>n</u>-deh eh keh ah-**prayn**-doo ah koh<u>n</u>-doo-**zeer**
I'll only pay what's on the meter.	Só pago o que o medidor diz.	saw **pah**-goo oo keh oo may-dee-**dor** deesh
My change, please.	O meu troco, por favor.	oo **meh**-oo **troh**-koo poor fah-**vor**
Keep the change.	Fique com o troco.	**fee**-keh koh<u>n</u> oo **troh**-koo

Rental wheels:

I'd like to rent...	**Gostaria de alugar...**	goosh-tah-**ree**-ah deh ah-loo-**gar**
...a car.	**...um carro.**	oon **kah**-roo
...a station wagon.	**...uma carrinha.**	**oo**-mah kah-**reen**-yah
...a van.	**...uma furgoneta.**	**oo**-mah foor-goo-**nay**-tah
...a motorcycle.	**...uma mota.**	**oo**-mah **moh**-tah
...a motor scooter.	**...uma motocicleta.**	**oo**-mah moh-toh-see-**kleh**-tah
...a bicycle.	**...uma bicicleta.**	**oo**-mah bee-see-**kleh**-tah
How much...?	**Quanto custa...?**	**kwahn**-too **koosh**-tah
...per hour	**...á hora**	ah **aw**-rah
...per day	**...ao dia**	ow **dee**-ah
...per week	**...á semana**	ah seh-**mah**-nah
Unlimited mileage?	**Quilómetragem ilimitada?**	kee-**loh**-meh-trah-zhayn ee-loo-mee-**tah**-dah
I brake for bakeries.	**Paro em todas as padarias.**	**pah**-roo ayn **toh**-dahsh ahsh pah-dah-**ree**-ahsh
Is there...?	**Á...?**	ah
...a helmet	**...um capacete**	oon kah-pah-**say**-teh
...a discount	**...um desconto**	oon dish-**kohn**-too
...a deposit	**...um deposito**	oon deh-**poh**-zee-too
...insurance	**...seguro**	say-**goo**-roo
When do I bring it back?	**Quando devolvo para traz?**	**kwahn**-doo deh-**vohl**-voo **pah**-rah trahsh

Driving:

gas station	**bomba de gasolina**	**bohn**-bah deh gah-zoo-**lee**-nah
The nearest gas station?	**A próxima bomba de gasolina?**	ah **praw**-see-mah **bohn**-bah deh gah-zoo-**lee**-nah
Is it self-service?	**É self-service?**	eh "self-service"
Fill the tank.	**Abastecer o carro.**	ah-bahsh-teh-**sehr** oo **kah**-roo
I need...	**Preciso...**	preh-**see**-zoo
...gas.	**...gasolina.**	gah-zoo-**lee**-nah
...unleaded.	**...sem chumbo.**	sayn **shoon**-boo
...regular.	**...normal.**	nor-**mahl**
...super.	**...super.**	soo-**pehr**
...diesel.	**...diesel.**	dee-**zehl**
Check...	**Verificar...**	veh-ree-fee-**kar**
...the oil.	**...o óleo.**	oo **awl**-yoo
...the air in the tires.	**...o ar nos pneus.**	oo ar noosh **pehn**-yoosh
...the radiator.	**...o radiador.**	oo rah-dee-ah-**dor**
...the battery.	**...a bateria.**	ah bah-teh-**ree**-ah
...the brakes.	**...os travões.**	oosh trah-**vohnsh**
...my pulse.	**...a minha pulsação.**	ah **meen**-yah pool-sah-**sow**

Rather than dollars and gallons, gas pumps in Portugal will read escudos and liters (basically 4 liters in a gallon). Drive carefully. Statistically, Portugal's roads are the most dangerous in Europe.

Car trouble:

accident	**acidente**	ah-see-**dayn**-teh
breakdown	**parado**	pah-**rah**-doo
funny noise	**barulho estranho**	bah-**rool**-yoo ish-**trahn**-yoo
electrical problem	**problema elétrico**	proo-**blay**-mah eh-**leh**-tree-koo
flat tire	**pneu furado**	**pehn**-yoo foo-**rah**-doo
My car won't start.	**O meu carro não arranca.**	oo meh-oo kah-roo now ah-rang-kah
This doesn't work.	**Isto não trabalha.**	eesh-too now trah-**bahl**-yah
It's overheating.	**Está muito quente.**	ish-tah mween-too **kayn**-teh
I need...	**Preciso...**	preh-**see**-zoo
...a tow truck.	**...um reboque.**	oon reh-**baw**-keh
...a mechanic.	**...um mecânico.**	oon meh-**kahn**-nee-koo
...a stiff drink.	**...whiskey.**	"whiskey"

For help with repair, look up "Repair" under Shopping.

Parking:

parking garage	**garagem**	gah-**rah**-zhayn
Where can I park?	**Onde é que posso estacionar?**	ohn-deh eh keh **paw**-soo ish-tah-see-oo-**nar**
Is parking nearby?	**É perto do estacionamento?**	eh **pehr**-too doo ish-tah-see-oo-nah-**mayn**-too

TRANSPO

Can I park here?	**Posso fazer parking aqui?**	**paw**-soo fah-**zehr** par-**keeng** ah-**kee**
How long can I park here?	**Quanto tempo posso estacionar aqui?**	**kwahn**-too **tayn**-poo **paw**-soo ish-tah-see-oo-**nar** ah-**kee**
Must I pay to park here?	**É preciso pagar para estacionar aqui?**	eh preh-**see**-zoo pah-**gar** **pah**-rah ish-tah-see-oo-**nar** ah-**kee**
Is this a safe place to park?	**É seguro estacionar aqui?**	eh say-**goo**-roo ish-tah-see-oo-**nar** ah-**kee**

Finding your way:

I'm going to...	**Vou para...**	voh **pah**-rah
How do I get to...?	**Como é que vou para...?**	**koh**-moo eh keh voh **pah**-rah
Do you have a map?	**Tem um mapa?**	tayn oon **mah**-pah
How many minutes / hours...?	**Quantos minutos / horas...?**	**kwahn**-toosh mee-**noo**-toosh / **aw**-rahsh
...on foot	**...a pé**	ah peh
...on bicycle	**...de bicicleta**	deh bee-see-**kleh**-tah
...by car	**...de carro**	deh **kah**-roo
How many kilometers to...?	**Quantos kilómetros para...?**	**kwahn**-toosh kee-**law**-meh-troosh **pah**-rah
What's the... route to Lisbon?	**Qual é... estrada para Lisboa?**	kwahl eh... ish-**trah**-dah **pah**-rah leezh-**boh**-ah
...best	**...a melhor**	ah mil-**yor**
...fastest	**...a mais rápida**	ah mīsh **rah**-pee-dah

...most interesting	...a mais interessante	ah mīsh een-teh-reh-**sahn**-teh
Point it out?	**Aponte?**	ah-**pohn**-teh
I'm lost.	**Estou perdido[a].**	ish-**toh** pehr-**dee**-doo
Where am I?	**Onde é que estou?**	**ohn**-deh eh keh ish-**toh**
Who am I?	**Quem é que sou?**	kayn eh keh soh
Where is...?	**Onde é que é...?**	**ohn**-deh eh keh eh
The nearest...?	**O próximo...?**	oo **praw**-see-moo
Where is this address?	**Onde é este endereço?**	**ohn**-deh eh aysh-toh ayn-deh-**ray**-soo

Key route-finding words:

map	**mapa**	**mah**-pah
straight ahead	**em frente**	ayn **frayn**-teh
left	**esquerda**	ish-**kehr**-dah
right	**direita**	dee-**ray**-tah
first	**primeira**	pree-**may**-rah
next	**próximo**	**praw**-see-moo
intersection	**cruzamento**	kroo-zah-**mayn**-too
stoplight	**sinal de luz**	soo-nahl doh loosh
square	**praça**	**prah**-sah
street	**rua**	**roo**-ah
bridge	**ponte**	**pohn**-teh
tunnel	**túnel**	**too**-nehl
highway	**autoestrada**	ow-too-ish-**trah**-dah
north	**norte**	**nor**-teh
south	**sul**	sool
east	**este**	**ehsh**-teh
west	**oeste**	**wehsh**-teh

Reading road signs:

abrandar	yield
baixa	to the center of town
construção na estrada	workers ahead
cuidado	caution
desvio	detour
devagar	slow
entrada	entrance
estacionamento proibido	no parking
pare	stop
peões	pedestrians
saída	exit
sentido único	one-way street

Other signs you may bump into:

aberto das... ás...	open from... to...
água não potável	undrinkable water
casa de banho, WC	toilet
fechado para férias	closed for vacation
fechado para restauração	closed for restoration
homens	men
ocupado	occupied
mulheres	women
para alugar / venda	for rent / sale
perigo	danger
proibido	forbidden
proíbida a entrada	no entry
proibido fumar	no smoking
saída de emergência	emergency exit
Turismo	tourist information office

Sleeping

Places to stay:

hotel	**hotel**	oh-**tehl**
family-run hotel	**pensão,** **residência**	payn-**sow,** reh-zee-**dayn**-see-ah
fancy historic hotel	**pousada**	poh-**zah**-dah
room in private home	**quarto**	**kwar**-too
youth hostel	**pousada de** **juventude**	poh-**zah**-dah deh zhoo-vayn-**too**-deh
vacancy sign (literally "rooms")	**quartos**	**kwar**-toosh

Reserving a room:

A good time to reserve a room by phone is the morning of the day you plan to arrive. To reserve from the U.S. by fax, use the handy form in the appendix.

Hello.	**Olá.**	oh-**lah**
Do you speak English?	**Fala inglês?**	**fah**-lah een-**glaysh**
Do you have a room for...?	**Tem um quarto para...?**	tayn oon **kwar**-too **pah**-rah
...one person	**...uma pessoa**	**oo**-mah peh-**soh**-ah
...two people	**...duas pessoas**	**doo**-ahsh peh-**soh**-ahsh
...tonight	**...esta noite**	**ehsh**-tah **noy**-teh
...two nights	**...duas noites**	**doo**-ahsh **noy**-tehsh

...Friday	...**sexta-feira**	saysh-tah-**fay**-rah
...June 21	...**21 de Junho**	**veen**-teh ee oo<u>n</u> deh **zhoon**-yoo
Yes or no?	**Sim ou não?**	seeng oh no<u>w</u>
I'd like...	**Gostaria...**	goosh-tah-**ree**-ah
...a private bathroom.	...**uma casa de banho privada.**	**oo**-mah kah-zah deh **bahn**-yoo pree-**vah**-dah
...your cheapest room.	...**o quarto mais barato.**	oo **kwar**-too mīsh bah-**rah**-too
...___ bed(s) for ___ people in ___ room(s).	...___ **cama(s) para ___ pessoas no ___ quarto(s).**	___ **kah**-mah(sh) **pah**-rah ___ peh-**soh**-ahsh noo ___ **kwar**-too(sh)
How much is it?	**Quanto custa?**	kwahn-too **koosh**-tah
Anything cheaper?	**Nada mais barato?**	**nah**-dah mīsh bah-**rah**-too
I'll take it.	**Eu fico.**	**eh**-oo **fee**-koo
My name is...	**Chamo-me...**	**shah**-moo-meh
I'll stay / We'll stay...	**Fico / Ficamos...**	**fee**-koo / fee-**kah**-moosh
...for ___ night(s).	...**por ___ noite(s).**	poor ___ **noy**-teh(sh)
I'll come / We'll come...	**Venho / Vimos...**	**vehn**-yoo / **vee**-moosh
...in one hour.	...**dentro de uma hora.**	...**dayn**-troo deh **oo**-mah **aw**-rah
...before 4:00 in the afternoon.	...**antes das quatro da tarde.**	**ahn**-tish dahsh **kwah**-troo dah **tar**-deh
...Friday before 6 p.m.	...**sexta-feira antes das seis horas da tarde.**	saysh-tah-**fay**-rah **ahn**-tish dahsh saysh **aw**-rahsh dah **tar**-deh
Thank you.	**Obrigado[a].**	oh-bree-**gah**-doo

Getting specific:

I'd like a room...	**Gostaria um quarto...**	goosh-tah-**ree**-ah oon kwar-too
...with / without / and	**...com / sem / e**	kohn / sayn / ee
...toilet.	**...casa de banho.**	kah-zah deh **bahn**-yoo
...shower.	**...chuveiro.**	shoo-**vay**-roo
...shower down the hall.	**...chuveiro é no fundo do corredor.**	shoo-**vay**-roo eh noo **foon**-doo doo koo-ray-**dor**
...bathtub.	**...banheira.**	bahn-**yay**-rah
...double bed.	**...cama grande.**	**kah**-mah **grahn**-deh
...twin beds.	**...camas gémeas.**	**kah**-mahsh **zheh**-may-ahsh
...balcony.	**...varanda.**	vah-**rahn**-dah
...view.	**...vista.**	**veesh**-tah
...with only a sink.	**...só com um lavatório.**	saw kohn oon lah-vah-**taw**-ree-oo
...on the ground floor.	**...no rés-do-chão.**	noo **raysh**-doo-show
Is there an elevator?	**Tem elevador?**	tayn eh-leh-vah-**dor**
We arrive Monday, depart Wednesday.	**Vamos chegar segunda-feira, e partir quarta-feira.**	vah-**moosh** shay-**gar** seh-goon-dah-**fay**-rah, ee par-**teer** kwar-tah-**fay**-rah
I have a reservation.	**Tenho reserva.**	**tayn**-yoo ray-**zehr**-vah
Confirm my reservation?	**Confirmar a minha reserva?**	kohn-feer-**mar** ah **meen**-yah ray-**zehr**-vah
I'll sleep anywhere.	**Dormo em qualquer lugar.**	**dor**-moo ayn kwahl-**kehr** loo-**gar**
I have a sleeping bag.	**Tenho um saco de cama.**	**tayn**-yoo oon **sah**-koo deh **kah**-mah

Nailing down the price:

How much is...?	**Quanto custa...?**	**kwahn**-too **koosh**-tah
...a room for ___ people	**...um quarto para ___ pessoas**	oon **kwar**-too **pah**-rah ___ peh-**soh**-ahsh
...your cheapest room	**...o quarto mais barato**	oo **kwar**-too mīsh bah-**rah**-too
Breakfast included?	**Pequeno almoço incluido?**	peh-**kay**-noo ahl-**moh**-soo een-kloo-**ee**-doo
How much without breakfast?	**Quanto custa sem o pequeno almoço?**	**kwahn**-too **koosh**-tah sayn oo peh-**kay**-noo ahl-**moh**-soo
Complete price?	**Preço total?**	**pray**-soo toh-**tahl**
Is it cheaper if I stay ___ nights?	**É mais barato se ficar ___ noites?**	eh mīsh bah-**rah**-too seh fee-**kar** ___ **noy**-tehsh
I'll stay ___ nights.	**Vou ficar ___ noites.**	voh fee-**kar** ___ **noy**-tehsh

Choosing a room:

Can I see the room?	**Posso ver o quarto?**	**paw**-soo vehr oo **kwar**-too
Show me another room?	**Mostre-me outro quarto?**	**mohsh**-treh-meh **oh**-troo **kwar**-too
Do you have something...?	**Tem alguma coisa...?**	tayn ahl-**goo**-mah **koy**-zah
...larger / smaller	**...maior / pequeno**	mī-**yor** / peh-**kay**-noo
...better / cheaper	**...melhor / barato**	mil-**yor** / bah-**rah**-too
...brighter	**...claridade**	klah-ree-**dah**-deh
...in the back	**...nas traseiras**	nahsh trah-**zay**-rahsh
...quieter	**...calmo**	**kahl**-moo

I'll take it.	Eu fico.	eh-oo **fee**-koo
My key, please.	A minha chave, por favor.	ah **meen**-yah **shah**-veh poor fah-**vor**
Sleep well.	Dorme bem.	**dor**-meh bay<u>n</u>
Good night.	Boa-noite.	boh-ah-**noy**-teh

Hotel help:

I'd like...	Gostaria...	goosh-tah-**ree**-ah
...a / another	...um / outro	oo<u>n</u> / **oh**-troo
...towel.	...toalha.	too-**ahl**-yah
...pillow.	...almofada.	ahl-moh-**fah**-dah
...clean sheets.	...lençois limpos.	**layn**-soysh **leem**-poosh
...blanket.	...cobertor.	koo-behr-**tor**
...glass.	...copo.	**koh**-poo
...sink stopper.	...tampa para lava louça.	**tahn**-pah **pah**-rah **lah**-vah **loh**-sah
...soap.	...sabão.	sah-**bow**
...toilet paper.	...papel higiénico.	pah-**pehl** ee-zhee-**ehn**-ee-koo
...crib.	...berço.	**behr**-soo
...small extra bed.	...pequena cama extra.	peh-**kay**-nah **kah**-mah **ish**-trah
...different room.	...quarto diferente.	**kwar**-too dee-feh-**rehn**-teh
...silence.	...silêncio.	see-**layn**-see-oo
Where can I wash / hang my laundry?	Onde é que posso lavar / pendurar a minha roupa?	**ohn**-deh eh keh **paw**-soo lah-**var** / payn-doo-**rar** ah **meen**-yah **roh**-pah

I'd like to stay another night.	**Gostaria de ficar outra noite.**	goosh-tah-**ree**-ah deh fee-**kar** oh-trah **noy**-teh
Where can I park?	**Onde é que estaciono?**	**ohn**-deh eh keh ish-tah-see-**oh**-noo
What time do you lock up?	**A que horas fecha?**	ah keh **aw**-rahsh **fay**-shah
What time is breakfast?	**A que horas é o pequeno almoço?**	ah keh **aw**-rahsh eh oo peh-**kay**-noo ahl-**moh**-soo
Please wake me at 7:00.	**Acorde-me ás sete da manhã, por favor.**	ah-**kor**-deh-meh ahsh **seh**-teh dah ming-**yah** poor fah-**vor**

Hotel hassles:

Come with me.	**Venha comigo.**	**vayn**-yah koo-**mee**-goo
I have a problem in my room.	**Tenho um problema no meu quarto.**	**tayn**-yoo oon proo-**blay**-mah noo **meh**-oo **kwar**-too
It smells bad.	**Cheira mal.**	**shay**-rah mahl
bugs	**insectos**	een-**seh**-toosh
mice	**rato**	**rah**-too
prostitutes	**prostitutas**	proosh-tee-**too**-tahsh
The bed is too soft / hard.	**Esta cama é muito mole / dura.**	**ehsh**-tah **kah**-mah eh **mween**-too **maw**-leh / **doo**-rah
Lamp...	**Candeeiro...**	kahn-dee-**yay**-roo
Lightbulb...	**Lâmpada...**	**lahm**-pah-dah
Key...	**Chave...**	**shah**-veh
Lock...	**Fechadura...**	feh-shah-**doo**-rah

Window...	Janela...	zhah-**neh**-lah
Faucet...	Torneira...	tor-**nay**-rah
Sink...	Lava louça...	**lah**-vah **loh**-sah
Toilet...	Lavatórios...	lah-vah-**taw**-ree-oosh
Shower...	Chuveiro...	shoo-**vay**-roo
...doesn't work.	...não trabalha.	now trah-**bahl**-yah
There is no hot water.	Não hà água quente.	now ah **ah**-gwah **kayn**-teh
When is the water hot?	Quando hà água quente?	**kwahn**-doo ah **ah**-gwah **kayn**-teh

Checking out:

I'll leave...	Parto...	**par**-too
We'll leave...	Partimos...	par-**tee**-moosh
...today / tomorrow.	...hoje / amanhã.	**oh**-zheh / ah-ming-**yah**
...very early.	...muito cedo.	**mween**-too **say**-doo
When is check-out time?	A que horas é preciso pagar a conta e sair?	ah keh **aw**-rahsh eh preh-**see**-zoo pah-**gar** ah **kohn**-tah ee **sah**-eer
Can I pay now?	Posso pagar agora?	**paw**-soo pah-**gar** ah-**gor**-ah
The bill, please.	A conta, por favor.	ah **kohn**-tah poor fah-**vor**
Credit card O.K.?	Cartão de crédito O.K.?	kar-**tow** deh **kreh**-dee-too "O.K."
Everything was great.	Tudo foi óptimo.	**too**-doo foy **awp**-tee-moo
Will you call my next hotel for me?	Pode telefonar para o meu próximo hotel?	**paw**-deh teh-leh-foh-**nar** **pah**-rah oo **meh**-oo **praw**-see-moo oh-**tehl**

Can I...?	**Posso ...?**	**paw**-soo
Can we...?	**Podemos...?**	poo-**day**-moosh
...leave baggage here until ___?	**...deixar a bagagem aqui até ___?**	day-**shar** ah bah-**gah**-zhay<u>n</u> ah-**kee** ah-**teh**

Camping:

tent	**tenda**	**tayn**-dah
camping	**campismo**	kahm-**peesh**-moo
The nearest campground?	**O próximo parque de campismo?**	oo **praw**-see-moo **par**-keh deh kahm-**peesh**-moo
Can I...?	**Posso...?**	**paw**-soo
Can we...?	**Podemos...?**	poo-**day**-moosh
...camp here for one night	**...campar aqui por uma noite**	kahm-**par** ah-**kee** poor **oo**-mah **noy**-teh
Are showers included?	**Os chuveiros estam incluidos?**	oosh shoo-**vay**-roosh ish-**tayn** ee-kloo-**ee**-doosh

Eating

Finding a restaurant:

Where's a good... restaurant?	**Onde hà um bom restaurante...?**	**ohn**-deh ah oon bohn rish-toh-**rahn**-teh
...cheap	**...barato**	bah-**rah**-too
...local-style	**...estilo regional**	ish-**tee**-loo ray-zhee-oh-**nahl**
...untouristy	**...não turistico**	now too-**reesh**-tee-koo
...Chinese	**...chinês**	shee-**naysh**
...fast food	**...comida rápida**	koo-**mee**-dah **rah**-pee-dah
...self-service buffet	**...de auto-serviço**	deh ow-toh-sehr-**vee**-see-oo

Getting a table and menu:

Waiter.	**Criado.**	kree-**ah**-doo
Waitress. (age 35+)	**Senhora.**	sin-**yoh**-rah
Waitress. (under 35)	**Menina.**	meh-**nee**-nah
I'd like...	**Gostaria...**	goosh-tah-**ree**-ah
...a table for one / two.	**...uma mesa para uma / duas.**	oo-mah **may**-zah **pah**-rah oo-mah / **doo**-ahsh
...non-smoking.	**...não fumador.**	now foo-mah-**dor**
...just a drink.	**...só uma bebida.**	saw oo-mah beh-**bee**-dah
...a snack.	**...um petisco.**	oon peh-**teesh**-koo
...a half portion.	**...meia dose.**	**may**-ah **doh**-zeh
...a tourist menu.	**...uma ementa turistica.**	oo-mah ah-**mayn**-tah too-**reesh**-tee-kah
...to see the menu.	**...de ver a amenta.**	deh vehr ah ah-**mayn**-tah
...to order.	**...encomendar.**	ayn-koo-mayn-**dar**

...to eat.	...de comer.	deh koo-**mehr**
...to pay.	...de pagar.	deh pah-**gar**
...to throw up.	...de vomitar.	deh voh-mee-**tar**
What do you recommend?	O que é que recomenda?	oo keh eh keh ray-koo-**mayn**-dah
What's your favorite?	Qual é a sua comida favorita?	kwahl eh ah **soo**-ah koo-**mee**-dah fah-voh-**ree**-tah
Is it...?	Isto é...?	**eesh**-too eh
...good	...bom	bohn
...expensive	...caro	**kah**-roo
...light	...leve	**leh**-veh
...filling	...para encher	pah-rah ayn-**shehr**
What's local?	O que é da região?	oo keh eh dah rayzh-**yow**
What is...?	O que é...?	oo koh eh
...that	...aquilo	ah-**kee**-loo
...fast	...rápido	**rah**-pee-doo
...cheap and filling	...barato e enche	bah-**rah**-too ee **ayn**-sheh
Do you have...?	Tem...?	tayn
...an English menu	...uma ementa em inglês	**oo**-mah ah **mayn** tah ayn een-**glaysh**
...a children's portion	...uma refeição para criança	**oo**-mah reh-fay-**sow** pah-rah kree-**ahn**-sah

Portuguese restaurants are not Spanish—no tapas, but cheaper prices and earlier, more "normal" hours (lunch from noon to 2 p.m., dinner from 7:30 to 10:00 p.m.). Save money by considering the *meia dose* (half portions) and *prato do dia* (menu of the day).

The menu:

menu	**amenta**	ah-**mayn**-tah
tourist menu	**ementa turistica**	ah-**mayn**-tah too-**reesh**-tee-kah
special of the day	**prato do dia**	**prah**-too doo **dee**-ah
specialty of the house	**especialidade da casa**	ish-peh-see-ah-lee-**dah**-deh dah **kah**-zah
breakfast	**pequeno almoço**	peh-**kay**-noo ahl-**moh**-soo
lunch	**almoço**	ahl-**moh**-soo
dinner	**jantar**	zhahn-**tar**
appetizers	**petiscos**	peh-**teesh**-koosh
bread	**pão**	po<u>w</u>
salad	**salada**	sah-**lah**-dah
soup	**sopa**	**soh**-pah
first course	**primeira refeição**	pree-**may**-rah reh-fay-**so<u>w</u>**
main course	**refeição principal**	reh-fay-**so<u>w</u>** preen-see-**pahl**
meat	**carne**	**kar**-neh
poultry	**aves**	**ah**-vish
seafood	**marisco**	mah-**reesh**-koo
side dishes	**pratos á parte**	**prah**-toosh ah **par**-teh
vegetables	**legumes**	lay-**goo**-mish
cheese	**queijo**	**kay**-zhoo
dessert	**sobremesa**	soo-breh-**may**-zah
beverages	**bebidas**	beh-**bee**-dahsh
beer	**cerveija**	sehr-**vay**-zhah
wine	**vinho**	**veen**-yoo

service included	serviço incluido	sehr-**vee**-soo een-kloo-**ee**-doo
service not included	serviço não incluido	sehr-**vee**-soo no<u>w</u> een-kloo-**ee**-doo
with / and / or / without	com / e / ou / sem	koh<u>n</u> / ee / oh / say<u>n</u>

Dietary restrictions:

I'm allergic to...	Sou alérgico[a] a...	soh ah-**lehr**-zhee-koo ah
I cannot eat...	Não posso comer...	no<u>w</u> **paw**-soo koo-**mehr**
...dairy products.	...produtos lácteos.	proh-**doo**-toosh **lahk**-teh-oosh
...meat / pork.	...carne / porco.	**kar**-neh / **por**-koo
...salt / sugar.	...sal / açúcar.	sahl / ah-**soo**-kar
I am diabetic.	Sou diabético[a].	soh dee-ah-**beh**-tee-koo
Low cholesterol?	Colesterol baixo?	koo-**lehsh**-teh-rohl **bī**-shoo
No caffeine.	Descaféenado.	dish-kah-feh-**nah**-doo
No alcohol.	Não alcool.	no<u>w</u> **ahl**-kahl
I'm a...	Sou...	soh
...vegetarian.	...vegetariano[a].	veh-zheh-tar-ree-**ah**-noo
...strict vegetarian.	...rigorosamente vegetariano[a].	ree-goh-roh-zah-**may<u>n</u>**-teh veh-zheh-tar-ree-**ah**-noo
...carnivore.	...carnivoro[a].	kar-nee-**voh**-roo

EATING

Tableware and condiments:

plate	**prato**	**prah**-too
napkin	**guardanapo**	gwar-dah-**nah**-poo
knife	**faca**	**fah**-kah
fork	**garfo**	**gar**-foo
spoon	**colher**	**kool**-yehr
cup	**chávena**	**shah**-veh-nah
glass	**copo**	**kaw**-poo
carafe	**jarro**	**jah**-roo
water	**água**	**ah**-gwah
bread	**pão**	pow
butter	**manteiga**	mahn-**tay**-gah
margarine	**margarina**	mar-gah-**ree**-nah
salt / pepper	**sal / pimenta**	sahl / pee-**mayn**-tah
sugar	**açúcar**	ah-**soo**-kar
artificial sweetener	**açúcar artificial**	ah-**soo**-kar ar-tee-fee-see-**ahl**
honey	**mel**	mehl
mustard	**mostarda**	moosh-**tar**-dah
mayonnaise	**maionese**	mah-yoh-**neh**-zeh

Restaurant requests and regrets:

A little.	**Um pouco.**	oon **poh**-koo
More. / Another.	**Mais. / Outro.**	mīsh / **oh**-troo
The same.	**O mesmo.**	oo **mehsh**-moo
I did not order this.	**Não encomendei isto.**	now ayn-koo-mayn-**day** eesh-too
I've changed my mind.	**Mudei de ideia.**	moo-**day** deh ee-**day**-ah
Is this included with the meal?	**Isto está incluido com a refeição?**	**eesh**-too ish-**tah** een-kloo-**ee**-doo kohn ah reh-fay-**sow**

What time does this open / close?	A que horas é que abre / fecha?	ah keh **aw**-rahsh eh keh **ah**-breh / **fay**-shah
I'm in a hurry.	Estou com pressa.	ish-**toh** koh<u>n</u> **preh**-sah
I must leave at...	Tenho que sair às...	**tayn**-yoo keh sah-**eer** ahsh
When will the food be ready?	Quando é que a comida vai estar pronta?	**kwahn**-doo eh keh ah koo-**mee**-dah vī ish-**tar** **prohn**-tah
Can I get it "to go"?	Posso levar o resto comigo?	**paw**-soo leh-**var** oo **rehsh**-too koo-**mee**-goo
This is...	Isto é...	**eesh**-too eh
...dirty.	...sujo.	**soo**-zhoo
...greasy.	...gorduroso.	gor-doo-**roh**-zoo
...salty.	...salgado.	sahl-**gah**-doo
...undercooked.	...malcozinhado.	mahl-koo-zeen-**yah**-doo
...overcooked.	...queimado.	kay-**mah**-doo
...inedible.	...não comestível.	no<u>w</u> koo-mish-**tee**-vehl
...cold.	...frio.	**free**-oo
Can you heat this up?	Pode aquecer a comida?	**paw**-deh ah-kay-**sehr** ah koo-**mee**-dah
Enjoy your meal!	Bom-apetite!	boh<u>n</u>-ah-poh-**tee** tch
Enough.	Chega.	**shay**-gah
Finished.	Acabado.	ah-kah-**bah**-doo
Do your customers return?	Os seus clientes voltam outra vez?	oosh **seh**-oosh klee-**ayn**-tehsh **vohl**-tay<u>n</u> **oh**-trah vaysh
Yuck!	Porcaria!	poor-kah-**ree**-ah
Delicious!	Delicioso!	deh-lee-see-**oh**-zoo
Very tasty!	Muito gostoso!	**mween**-too goosh-**toh**-zoo

Paying for your meal:

Waiter.	**Criado.**	kree-**ah**-doo
Waitress. (age 35+)	**Senhora.**	sin-**yoh**-rah
Waitress. (under 35)	**Menina.**	meh-**nee**-nah
The bill, please.	**A conta, por favor.**	ah koh<u>n</u>-tah poor fah-**vor**
Together.	**Junta.**	**zhoo<u>n</u>**-tah
Separate.	**Separada.**	seh-pah-**rah**-dah
Credit card O.K.?	**Cartão de crédito O.K.?**	kar-**tow** deh **kreh**-dee-too "O.K."
Is service included?	**O serviço está incluido?**	oo sehr-**vee**-soo ish-**tah** een-kloo-**ee**-doo
This is not correct.	**Isto não está certo.**	**eesh**-too no<u>w</u> ish-**tah** **sehr**-too
Can you explain this?	**Pode-me explicar isto?**	**paw**-deh-meh ish-plee-**kar eesh**-too
What if I wash the dishes?	**E se eu lavar os pratos?**	ee seh **eh**-oo lah-**var** oosh **prah**-toosh
Keep the change.	**Fique com o troco.**	**fee**-keh koh<u>n</u> oo **troh**-koo
This is for you.	**Isto é para si.**	**eesh**-too eh **pah**-rah see

Breakfast:

breakfast	**pequeno almoço**	peh-**kay**-noo ahl-**moh**-soo
bread	**pão**	pow
roll	**rolo**	**roh**-loo
toast	**torrada**	too-**rah**-dah
butter	**manteiga**	mahn-**tay**-gah
jelly	**geláia**	zheh-**lay**-ah

pastry	**pastelaria**	pahsh-teh-lah-**ree**-ah
omelet	**omeleta**	aw-meh-**leh**-tah
eggs...	**ovos...**	**aw**-voosh
...fried	**...estrelados**	ish-treh-**lah**-doosh
...scrambled	**...mexidos**	mish-**ee**-doosh
boiled egg...	**ovo cozido...**	**aw**-voo koo-**zee**-doo
...soft / hard	**...mole / duro**	**maw**-leh / **doo**-roo
ham	**fiambre**	fee-**ahm**-breh
cheese	**queijo**	**kay**-zhoo
yogurt	**yogurte**	yoo-**goor**-teh
cereal	**cereal**	seh-ree-**ahl**
milk	**leite**	**lay**-teh
hot chocolate	**chocolate quente**	shoo-koo-**lah**-teh **kayn**-teh
fruit juice	**sumo de fruta**	**soo**-moo deh **froo**-tah
orange juice	**sumo de laranja**	**soo**-moo deh lah-**rahn**-zhah
coffee / tea (see Drinking)	**café / chá**	kah-**feh** / shah
Is breakfast included?	**O pequeno almoço está incluído?**	oo peh-**kay**-noo ahl-**moh**-soo ish-**tah** een-kloo-**ee**-doo

Soups and salads:

soup (of the day)	**sopa (do dia)**	**soh**-pah (doo **dee**-ah)
broth...	**caldo...**	**kahl**-doo
..chicken	**...de frango**	deh **frang**-goo
..beef	**...de carne**	deh **kar**-neh
...with noodles	**...com massa**	kohn **mah**-sah
..with rice	**...com arroz**	kohn ah-**rohsh**

thick vegetable soup	**sopa de legumes**	**soh**-pah deh lay-**goo**-mish
potato & cabbage soup	**caldo verde**	**kahl**-doo **vehr**-deh
shellfish soup	**açorda de marisco**	ah-**sor**-dah deh mah-**reesh**-koo
green salad	**salada de alface**	sah-**lah**-dah deh ahl-**fah**-seh
mixed salad	**salada mista**	sah-**lah**-dah **meesh**-tah
octopus salad	**salada de polvo**	sah-**lah**-dah deh **pohl**-voo
lettuce	**alface**	ahl-**fah**-seh
tomatoes	**tomates**	too-**mah**-tish
cucumbers	**pepinos**	peh-**pee**-noosh
oil / vinegar	**óleo / vinagre**	**awl**-yoo / vee-**nah**-greh
What is in this salad?	**O que é isto na salada?**	oo keh eh **eesh**-too nah sah-**lah**-dah

Portuguese specialties:

caldo verde	potato and cabbage soup
caracóis	snails (summer only)
chouriços	smoked pork sausage
bacalhau	cod (prepared a thousand different ways)
bolinhos de bacalhau	codfish balls
caldeirada	fish stew
coelho à caçador	rabbit with carrots and potatoes
costeletas de porco à alentejana	pork chops, Alentejo-style, with tomatoes and onions
feijoada	beans with pork and sausage
leitão	small roasted pig
perna de cabrito	roasted leg of baby goat

Seafood:

seafood	**marisco**	mah-**reesh**-koo
assorted seafood	**diversos mariscos**	dee-**vehr**-soosh mah-**reesh**-koosh
fish	**peixe**	**pay**-sheh
cod	**bacalhau**	bah-kahl-**yow**
salmon	**salmão**	sahl-**mow**
trout	**truta**	**troo**-tah
tuna	**atum**	ah-**toom**
herring	**arenque**	ah-**rayn**-keh
sardines	**sardinhas**	sar-**deen**-yahsh
anchovies	**anchovas**	ahn-**shoh**-vahsh
clams	**amêijoas**	ah-**may**-zhoo-ahsh
mussels	**mexilhões**	meh-sheel-**yohnsh**
oysters	**ostras**	**ohsh**-trahsh
shrimp	**camarão**	kah-mah-**row**
prawns	**gambas**	**gahm**-bahsh
crab	**caranguejo**	kah-rahn-**gay**-zhoo
lobster	**lagosta**	lah-**gohsh**-tah
octopus	**polvo**	**pohl**-voo
squid	**lulas**	**loo**-lahsh
Here's looking at you, squid!	**Está a olhar para ti, lulas!**	ish-**tah** ah ohl-**yar** **pah**-rah tee **loo**-lahsh

Poultry and meat:

poultry	**aves**	**ah**-vish
chicken	**frango**	**frang**-goo
stewing chicken	**galinha**	gah-**leen**-yah
turkey	**peru**	peh-**roo**
duck	**pato**	**pah**-too
meat	**carne**	**kar**-neh
beef	**carne de vaca**	**kar**-neh deh **vah**-kah
roast beef	**carne assada**	**kar**-neh ah-**sah**-dah
beef steak	**bife**	**bee**-feh
ribsteak	**costelas**	kohsh-**teh**-lahsh
veal	**vitela**	vee-**teh**-lah
cutlet	**costeleta**	koosh-teh-**lay**-tah
pork	**porco**	**por**-koo
ham	**fiambre**	fee-**ahm**-breh
smoked ham	**presunto**	preh-**zoon**-too
sausage	**salsicha**	sahl-**see**-shah
lamb	**carneiro**	kar-**nay**-roo
baby goat	**cabrito**	kah-**bree**-too
bunny	**coelho**	**kwayl**-yoo
snails	**caracóis**	kah-rah-**koysh**
brains	**miolos**	mee-**oh**-loos
tongue	**lingua**	**leeng**-gwah
liver	**fígado**	**fee**-gah-doo
tripe	**tripas**	**tree**-pahsh
How long has this been dead?	**À quanto tempo é que isto está morto?**	ah **kwahn**-too **tayn**-poo eh keh **eesh**-too ish-**tah mor**-too

How it's prepared:

hot	**quente**	**kayn**-teh
cold	**frio**	**free**-oo
raw	**crú**	kroo
cooked	**cozido**	koo-**zee**-doo
assorted	**diversos**	dee-**vehr**-soosh
baked	**no forno**	noo **for**-noo
boiled	**cozido**	koo-**zee**-doo
fillet	**filé**	fee-**leh**
fresh	**fresco**	**fraysh**-koo
fried	**frito**	**free**-too
grilled	**grilhado**	greel-**yah**-doo
homemade	**caseiro**	kah-**zay**-roo
medium	**melo passado**	**may**-oo pah-**sah**-doo
microwave	**micro ondas**	**mee**-kroo **ohn**-dahsh
mild	**médio**	**meh**-dee-oo
mixed	**mista**	**meesh**-tah
poached	**escalfado**	ish-kahl-**fah**-doo
rare	**mal passado**	mahl pah-**sah**-doo
roasted	**assado**	ah-**sah**-doo
smoked	**fumado**	foo-**mah**-doo
spicy hot	**picante**	pee-**kahn**-teh
steamed	**cozido ao vapor**	koo-**zee**-doo ow vah-**por**
stuffed	**recheio**	reh-**shay**-oo
well-done	**bem passado**	bayn pah-**sah**-doo

EATING

Veggies, pasta, beans, and rice:

vegetables	**legumes**	lay-**goo**-mish
artichoke	**alcachofra**	ahl-kah-**shaw**-frah
asparagus	**espargos**	ish-**par**-goosh
beans	**feijões**	fay-**zhohnsh**
beets	**beterraba**	beh-teh-**rah**-bah
broccoli	**brócolos**	**braw**-koo-loosh
cabbage	**couve**	**koh**-veh
carrots	**cenoura**	seh-**noh**-rah
cauliflower	**couve-flor**	**koh**-veh-flor
corn	**milho**	**meel**-yoo
cucumbers	**pepinos**	peh-**pee**-noosh
eggplant	**berinjela**	beh-reen-**zheh**-lah
French fries	**batatas fritas**	bah-**tah**-tahsh **free**-tahsh
garlic	**alho**	**ahl**-yoo
green beans	**feijões verdes**	fay-**zhohnsh vehr**-dish
lentils	**lentilhas**	layn-**teel**-yahsh
mushrooms	**cogumelos**	koo-goo-**meh**-loosh
olives	**azeitonas**	ah-zay-**toh**-nahsh
onions	**cebolas**	seh-**boh**-lahsh
pasta	**massa**	**mah**-sah
peas	**ervilhas**	ehr-**veel**-yahsh
pepper...	**pimento...**	pee-**mayn**-too
...green / hot	**...verde / picante**	**vehr**-deh / pee-**kahn**-teh
pickle	**pepino de conserva**	peh-**pee**-noo deh kohn-**sehr**-vah
potatoes	**batatas**	bah-**tah**-tahsh
rice	**arroz**	ah-**rohsh**

spaghetti	esparguete	ish-par-**geh**-teh
spinach	espinafre	ish-pee-**nah**-freh
tomatoes	tomates	too-**mah**-tish
zucchini	zukini	zoo-**kee**-nee

Fruits and nuts:

almond	amêndoa	ah-**mayn**-doh-ah
apple	maçã	mah-**sah**
apricot	damasco	dah-**mahsh**-koo
banana	banana	bah-**nah**-nah
canteloupe	melão	meh-**low**
cherry	cereja	seh-**ray**-zhah
chestnut	castanha	kahsh-**tahn**-yah
coconut	coco	**koh**-koo
date	fruto seco	**froo**-too **say**-koo
fig	figo	**fee**-goo
fruit	fruta	**froo**-tah
grapefruit	toranja	toh-**rahn**-zhah
grapes	uvas	**oo**-vahsh
hazelnut	avelã	ah-veh-**lah**
lemon	limão	loo **mow**
orange	laranja	lah-**rahn**-zhah
peach	pêssago	**pay**-sah-goo
peanut	amendoim	ah-**mayn**-**dweem**
pear	pêra	**pay**-rah
pineapple	ananás	ah-nah-**nahsh**
pistachio	pistácio	peesh-**tah**-see-oo
plum	ameixa	ah-**may**-shah
prune	ameixa seca	ah-**may**-shah **say**-kah

EATING

raspberry	**framboesa**	frahm-boo-**ay**-zah
strawberry	**morango**	moo-**rang**-goo
tangerine	**tangerina**	tahn-zheh-**ree**-nah
walnut	**noz**	nawsh
watermelon	**melancia**	meh-**lahn**-see-ah

Just desserts:

dessert	**sobremesa**	soo-breh-**may**-zah
caramel custard	**flan**	flahn
cake	**bolo**	**boh**-loo
ice cream...	**gelado...**	zheh-**lah**-doo
...cone	**...cone**	**koh**-neh
...cup	**...chávena**	**shah**-veh-nah
...vanilla	**...baunilha**	bow-**neel**-yah
...chocolate	**...chocolate**	shoo-koo-**lah**-teh
...strawberry	**...morango**	moo-**rang**-goo
fruit cup	**taça de fruta**	**tah**-sah deh **froo**-tah
tart	**tarte**	**tar**-teh
whipped cream	**chântily**	**shahn**-tee-lee
chocolate mousse	**mousse**	**moo**-seh
pudding	**pudim**	**poo**-deem
pastry	**pastelaria**	pahsh-teh-lah-**ree**-ah
cookies	**bolos**	**boh**-loosh
candy	**rebuçados**	ray-boo-**sah**-doosh
low calorie	**poucas calorias**	**poh**-kahsh kah-loo-**ree**-ahsh
homemade	**caseiro**	kah-**zay**-roo
Exquisite!	**Requintado!**	ray-keen-**tah**-doo
It's heavenly!	**É divinal!**	eh dee-vee-**nahl**

Drinking

Water, milk, and juice:

mineral water...	água mineral...	ah-gwah mee-neh-rahl
...with / without gas	...com / sem gás	kohn / sayn gahsh
tap water	água da torneira	ah-gwah dah tor-nay-ruh
whole milk	leite gordo	lay-teh gor-doo
skim milk	leite magro	lay-teh mah-groo
fresh milk	leite fresco	lay-teh fraysh-koo
hot chocolate	chocolate quente	shoo-koo-lah-teh kayn-teh
fruit juice	sumo de fruta	soo-moo deh froo-tah
orange juice (pure)	sumo de laranja (puro)	soo-moo deh lah-rahn-zhah (poo-roo)
with / without...	com / sem...	kohn / sayn
...sugar	...açúcar	ah-soo-kar
...ice	...gelo	zhay-loo
glass / cup	copo / chávena	kaw-poo / shah-veh-nah
small / large	pequena / grande	peh-kay-nah / grahn-deh
bottle	garrafa	gah-rah-fah
Is this water safe to drink?	Posso beber esta água?	paw-soo beh-behr ehsh-tah ah-gwah

Tap water is free at restaurants—ask for *água da torneira*. If you like mineral water, your big decision is *com* or *sem* *gás* (with or without carbonation). *Com gas* is a taste well worth acquiring. The light, sturdy plastic water bottles are great to pack along and re-use as you travel.

Coffee and tea:

coffee...	café...	kah-**feh**
...with milk	...com leite	koh<u>n</u> **lay**-teh
...with sugar	...com açucar	koh<u>n</u> ah-**soo**-kar
...decaffeinated	...descaféenado	dish-kah-feh-**nah**-doo
...instant	...instantaneo	eensh-tahn-**tahn**-yoo
espresso	bica	**bee**-kah
espresso with milk	garoto	gah-**roh**-too
hot water	água quente	**ah**-gwah **kayn**-teh
tea / lemon	chá / limão	shah / lee-**mow**
herbal tea	chá de ervas	shah deh **ehr**-vahsh
iced tea	chá gelado	shah zheh-**lah**-doo
small / large	pequeno / grande	peh-**kay**-noo / **grahn**-deh
Another cup.	Outra chávena.	**oh**-trah **shah**-veh-nah

Wine:

I would like...	Gostaria...	goosh-tah-**ree**-ah
We would like...	Gostaríamos...	goosh-tah-**ree**-ah-moosh
...a glass	...um copo	oo<u>n</u> **kaw**-poo
...a carafe	...um jarro	oo<u>n</u> jah-roo
...a bottle	...uma garrafa	**oo**-mah gah-**rah**-fah
...of red wine	...de vinho tinto	deh **veen**-yoo **teen**-too
...of white wine	...de vinho branco	deh **veen**-yoo **brang**-koo
...the wine list	...a lista de vinhos	ah **leesh**-tah deh **veen**-yoosh

Wine words:

wine	**vinho**	**veen**-yoo
table wine	**vinho de mesa**	**veen**-yoo deh **may**-zah
cheap house wine	**vinho da casa**	**veen**-yoo dah **kah**-zah
local	**local**	loo-**kahl**
red	**tinto**	**teen**-too
white	**branco**	**brang**-koo
rose	**rosé**	roh-**zeh**
sparkling	**espumante**	ish-poo-**mahn**-teh
sweet	**doce**	**doh**-seh
medium	**médio**	**meh**-dee-oo
dry	**seco**	**say**-koo
very dry	**muito seco**	**mween**-too **say**-koo
cork	**rolha**	**rohl**-yah

For good, cheap wine, try the *vinho de casa* (house wine). A Portuguese specialty is *vinho verde*, a sparkling wine that comes in red or white—while many argue that both are bad, the white is clearly better.

Beer:

beer	**cerveja**	sehr-**vay**-zhah
glass of draft beer	**fino**	**fee**-noo
big glass of draft beer	**caneca**	kah-**neh**-kah
bottle	**garrafa**	gah-**rah**-fah
light / dark	**leve / escura**	**leh**-veh / ish-**koo**-rah
local / imported	**local / importada**	loo-**kahl** / eem-poor-**tah**-dah

small / large	**pequena / grande**	peh-**kay**-nah / **grahn**-deh
cold	**fresca**	**frehsh**-kah
colder	**mais fresca**	mīsh **frehsh**-kah

Bar talk:

What would you like?	**O que é que gostaria?**	oo keh eh keh goosh-tah-**ree**-ah
What is the local specialty?	**Qual é a especialidade local?**	kwahl eh ah ish-peh-see-ah-lee-**dah**-deh loo-**kahl**
Straight.	**Puro.**	**poo**-roo
With / Without...	**Com / Sem...**	kohn / sayn
...alcohol.	**...alcool.**	**ahl**-kahl
...ice.	**...gelo.**	**zhay**-loo
One more.	**Mais uma.**	mīsh **oo**-mah
Cheers!	**Saúde!**	sah-**oo**-deh
Long live Portugal!	**Vida longa Portugal!**	**vee**-dah **lohn**-gah poor-too-**gahl**
I'm...	**Estou...**	ish-**toh**
...a little drunk.	**...um bocado bêbado[a].**	oon boo-**kah**-doo **bay**-bah-doo
...drunk.	**...bêbado[a].**	**bay**-bah-doo

A popular local drink is *água ardente* (firewater), made from grape seeds.

Picnicking

At the market:

Is it self-service?	**É self-service?**	eh "self-service"
Ripe for today?	**Maduro para hoje?**	mah-**doo**-roo **pah**-rah **oh**-zheh
Does it need to be cooked?	**Isto precisa de ser cozinhado?**	**eesh**-too preh-**see**-zah deh sehr koo-zeen-**yah**-doo
A little taste?	**Um pouco do sabor?**	oon **poh**-koo deh sah-**bor**
Fifty grams.	**Cinquenta gramas.**	seeng-**kwayn**-tah **grah**-mahsh
One hundred grams.	**Cem gramas.**	sayn **grah**-mahsh
More. / Less.	**Mais. / Menos.**	mīsh / **may**-noosh
A piece.	**Um pedaço.**	oon peh-**dah**-soo
A slice.	**Uma fatia.**	oo-mah fah-**tee**-ah
Sliced.	**Ás fatias.**	ahsh fah-**tee**-ahsh
Will you make me a sandwich?	**Pode-me fazer uma sande?**	paw-deh-meh fah-**zehr** oo-mah **sahn**-deh
To take out.	**Levar para fora.**	loh **var pah**-rah **for**-rah
Is there a park nearby?	**Há algum parque perto?**	ah ahl-**goon** par-keh **pehr**-too
Is picnicking allowed here?	**É permitido fazer piquenique aqui?**	eh pehr-mee-**tee**-doo fah-**zehr** peek-**neek** ah-**kee**
Enjoy your meal!	**Bom-apetite!**	bohn-ah-peh-**tee**-teh

EATING

Picnic prose:

open air market	**mercado municipal**	mehr-**kah**-doo moo-nee-see-**pahl**
grocery store	**mercearia**	mehr-see-ah-**ree**-ah
supermarket	**supermercado**	soo-pehr-mehr-**kah**-doo
picnic	**piquenique**	peek-**neek**
sandwich	**sande, sanduíche**	**sahn**-deh, sahnd-**wee**-sheh
bread (whole wheat)	**pão (de trigo)**	po<u>w</u> (deh **tree**-goo)
roll	**rolo**	**roh**-loo
ham	**fiambre**	fee-**ahm**-breh
sausage	**salsicha**	sahl-**see**-shah
cheese	**queijo**	**kay**-zhoo
mustard	**mostarda**	moosh-**tar**-dah
mayonnaise	**maionese**	mah-yoh-**neh**-zeh
yogurt	**yogurte**	yoo-**goor**-teh
fruit	**fruta**	**froo**-tah
box of juice	**caixa de sumo**	kī-shah deh **soo**-moo
spoon / fork...	**colher / garfo...**	**kool**-yehr / **gar**-foo
...made of plastic	**...plástica**	**plahsh**-tee-koo
cup / plate...	**chávena / prato...**	**shah**-veh-nah / **prah**-too
...made of paper	**...de papel**	deh pah-**pehl**

You can shop at a *supermercado*, but smaller shops are more fun. Get bread for your *sanduíche* at a *padaria* and order meat and cheese by the gram at a *mercearia*. For a meal on the run on a bun, try a *prego no pão* (meat & egg roll) or a *tosta mista* (toasted cheese & ham sandwich).

Portuguese-English Menu Decoder

This won't contain every word on your menu, but it'll help you get *mexilhões* (mussels) instead of *miolos* (brains).

á parte side dishes
açorda chowder
açúcar sugar
água water
alcachofra artichoke
alcool alcohol
alho garlic
almoço lunch
amêijoas clams
ameixa plum
ameixa seca prune
amêndoa almond
amendoim peanut
amoras berries
ananás pineapple
anchovas anchovies
arenque herring
arroz rice
assado roasted
atum tuna
avelã hazelnut
aves poultry
azeitonas olives
bacalhau cod
batatas potatoes
batatas fritas French fries

baunilha vanilla
bebidas beverages
berinjela eggplant
beterraba beets
bica espresso
bife beef steak
bola scoop
bolo cake
bolos cookies
branco white
brócolos broccoli
cabrito baby goat
cachorro hot dog
café coffee
caldeirada fish stew
caldo broth
camarão shrimp
caneca large draft beer
caracóis snails
caranguejo crab
carne meat
carneiro lamb
casa house
caseiro homemade
castanha chestnut
cebolas onions

cenoura carrots
cereja cherry
cerveija beer
chá tea
chântily whipped cream
chávena cup
chinês Chinese
chocolate quente hot chocolate
chouriços smoked pork sausage
coco coconut
coelho bunny
cogumelos mushrooms
com with
comida food
compota jam
cone cone
copo glass
costelas ribsteak
costeleta cutlet
couve cabbage
couve-flor cauliflower
cozido cooked
crú raw
damasco apricot
de of
descaféenado decaffeinated
diversos assorted
doce sweet
e and
ementa menu
ervas herbs
ervilhas peas
escalfado poached

espargos asparagus
esparguete spaghetti
especialidade speciality
espinafre spinach
espumante sparkling
estilo style
estrelados fried
fatia slice
fatias sliced
feijoada beans with pork &
　　sausage
feijões beans
fiambre ham
fígado liver
figo fig
filé fillet
fino draft beer
flan caramel custard
forno baked
framboesa raspberry
frango chicken
fresco fresh
frio cold
frito fried
fruta fruit
fruto seco date
fumado smoked
galinha stewing chicken
gambas prawns
garrafa bottle
gelado ice cream, iced
geláia jelly
gelo ice

gordura fat
gostoso tasty
grande large
grilhado grilled
importada imported
incluido included
jantar dinner
jarro carafe
lagosta lobster
laranja orange
legumes vegetable
leitão small roasted pig
leite milk
lentilhas lentils
levar para fora "to go"
leve light
limão limon
lingua tongue
lista list
lulas squid
maçã apple
maionese mayonnaise
manteiga butter
margarina margarine
marisco seafood
massa pasta
médio mild
meia dose half portion
mel honey
melancia watermelon
melão canteloupe
mesa table
mexidos scrambled

mexilhões mussels
micro ondas microwave
milho corn
miolos brains
mista mixed
morango strawberry
mostarda mustard
mousse chocolate mousse
não not
no forno baked
noz walnut
óleo oil
omeleta omelet
ostras oysters
ou or
ovos eggs
pão bread
pão de trigo whole wheat bread
pastelaria pastry
pato duck
pedaço piece
peixe fish
pepinos cucumbers
pepinos de conserva pickles
pequeno small
pequeno almoço breakfast
pêra pear
perna de cabrito leg of baby goat
peru turkey
pêssago peach
petiscos appetizers
picante spicy hot
pimento bell pepper

pimento verde green pepper
pistácio pistachio
polvo octupus
porco pork
prato plate
prato do dia special of the day
pratos á parte side dishes
prego no pão meat & egg roll
presunto smoked ham
primeira refeição first course
pudim pudding
puro pure
queijo cheese
quente hot
rebuçados candy
recheio stuffed
refeição meal
refeição principal main course
região local
regional local
rolo roll
sal salt
salada salad
salmão salmon
salsicha sausage
sande sandwich
sardinhas sardines
seco dry

sem without
serviço incluido service included
serviço não incluido service not included
sobremesa dessert
sopa soup
sumo juice
taça de fruta fruit cup
tangerina tangerine
tarte tart
tinto red
tomates tomatoes
toranja grapefruit
torrada toast
tosta mista toasted ham & cheese sandwich
toucinho bacon
tripas tripe
truta trout
uvas grapes
vaca beef
vapor steamed
verde green
vinagre vinegar
vinho wine
vitela veal
yogurte yogurt
zukini zucchini

Sightseeing

Where is...?	Onde é...?	ohn-deh eh
...the best view	...a melhor vista	ah mil-**yor veesh**-tah
...the main square	...a praça principal	ah **prah**-sah preen-see-**pahl**
...the old town center	...a parte da cidade velha	ah **par**-teh dah see-**dah**-deh **vehl**-yah
...the town hall	...a câmara da cidade	ah **kah**-mah-rah dah see-**dah**-dah
...the museum	...o museu	oo moo-**zeh**-oo
...the castle	...o castelo	oo kahsh-**teh**-loo
...the ruins	...as ruínas	ahsh roo-**ee**-nahsh
...a festival	...o festival	oo fehsh-tee-**vahl**
...a fair	...a feira	ah **fay**-rah
...tourist information	...a informação turística	ah een-for-mah-**sow** too-**reesh**-tee-kah
Do you have...?	Tem...?	tayn
...information	...informações	een-for-mah-**sohwsh**
...a guidebook	...um guia	oon **gee**-ah
...a tour	...uma excursão	**oo**-mah ish-koor-**sow**
...in English	...em inglês	ayn een-**glaysh**
When is the next tour in English?	Quando é a próxima excursão em inglês?	**kwahn**-doo eh ah **praw**-see-mah ish-koor-**sow** ayn een-**glaysh**
Is it free?	É grátis?	eh **grah**-teesh
How much is it?	Quanto custa?	**kwahn**-too **koosh**-tah

Is there a discount for...?	**Tem desconto para...?**	tayn dish-**kohn**-too **pah**-rah
...youth	**...jovens**	**zhaw**-vaynsh
...students	**...estudantes**	ish-too-**dahn**-tish
...seniors	**...pessoas de terceira idade**	peh-**soh**-ahsh deh tehr-**say**-rah ee-**dah**-deh
Is the ticket good all day?	**O bilhete é bom para o dia inteiro?**	oo beel-**yeh**-teh eh bohn **pah**-rah oo **dee**-ah een-**tay**-roo
Can I get back in?	**Posso reentrar?**	**paw**-soo reh-ayn-**trar**
What time does this open / close?	**A que horas é que abre / fecha?**	ah keh **aw**-rahsh eh keh **ah**-breh / **fay**-shah
What time is the last entry?	**A que horas é a última entrada?**	ah keh **aw**-rahsh eh ah **ool**-tee-mah ayn-**trah**-dah
PLEASE let me in.	**POR FAVOR deixe-me entrar.**	poor fah-**vor** **day**-sheh-meh ayn-**trar**
I've traveled all the way from...	**Estou a viajar de muito longe...**	ish-**toh** ah vee-ah-**zhar** deh **mween**-too **lohn**-zheh
I must leave tomorrow.	**Tenho que partir amanhã.**	**tayn**-yoo keh par-**teer** ah-ming-**yah**
I promise I'll be fast.	**Prometo que faço rápido[a].**	proo-**may**-too keh **fah**-soo **rah**-pee-doo

In the museum:

Where is...?	**Onde é...?**	**ohn**-deh eh
I'd like to see...	**Gostaria de ver...**	goosh-tah-**ree**-ah deh vehr
Photo / Video O.K?	**Foto / Vídeo O.K.?**	**foh**-too / **vee**-day-oo "O.K."
No flash / tripod.	**Não flash / tripé.**	now flahsh / tree-**peh**

I like it.	Gosto desta.	**gawsh**-too **dehsh**-tah
It's so...	É tão...	eh tow
...beautiful.	...lindo.	**leen**-doo
...ugly.	...feio.	**fay**-oo
...strange.	...estranho.	ish-**trahn**-yoo
...boring.	...enfadonho.	ayn-fah-**dohn**-yoo
...interesting.	...interessante.	een-teh-reh-**sahn**-teh
Wow!	Fiche!	**fee**-sheh
My feet hurt!	Os meus pés estão cansados!	oosh **meh**-oosh pehsh ish-**tow** kahn-**sah**-doosh
I'm exhausted!	Estou estoirado!	ish-**toh** ish-toy-**rah**-doo

Art and architecture:

art	arte	**ar**-teh
artist	artista	ar-**teesh**-tah
painting	pintura	peeng-**too**-rah
self portrait	auto-retrato	ow-too-reh-**trah**-too
sculptor	escultor	ish-kool-**tor**
sculpture	escultura	ish-kool-**too**-rah
architect	arquiteto	ar-kee-**teh**-too
architecture	arquitetura	ar-kee-teh-**too**-rah
original	original	oo-ree-zhee-**nahl**
restored	restaurado	rish-too-**rah**-doo
B.C.	A.C.	ah say
A.D.	D.C.	day say
century	secúlo	seh-**koo**-loo
style	estilo	ish-**tee**-loo
Abstract	abstrato	ahbsh-**trah**-too

Ancient	**antigo**	ahn-**tee**-goo
Art Nouveau	**arte nova**	**ar**-teh **noh**-vah
Baroque	**barroco**	bah-**roh**-koo
Classical	**clássico**	**klah**-see-koo
Gothic	**gótico**	**gaw**-tee-koo
Impressionist	**impressionista**	eem-preh-see-oo-**neesh**-tah
Medieval	**mediaval**	meh-dee-ah-**vahl**
Moorish	**mouro**	**moh**-roo
Renaissance	**renascimento**	reh-nahsh-see-**mayn**-too
Romanesque	**românico**	roo-**mah**-nee-koo
Romantic	**romântico**	roo-**mahn**-tee-koo

Portugal's golden age of trade and exploration gave birth to a lavish, flamboyant Gothic style called "Manueline," named after King Manuel of the early 16th century.

Castles and palaces:

castle	**castelo**	kahsh-**teh**-loo
palace	**palâcio**	pah-**lah**-see-oo
kitchen	**cozinha**	koh-**zeen**-yah
cellar	**celeiro**	seh-**lay**-roo
dungeon	**masmorra**	mahsh-**moh**-rah
moat	**fosso**	**foh**-soo
fortified walls	**fortificação**	for-tee-fee-kah-**sow**
tower	**torre**	**tor**-reh
fountain	**fonte**	**fohn**-teh
garden	**jardim**	zhar-**deem**
king	**rei**	ray
queen	**raínha**	rah-**een**-yah
knights	**cavaleiros**	kah-vah-**lay**-roosh

Religious words:

cathedral	**catedral**	kah-teh-**drahl**
church	**igreija**	ee-**gray**-zhah
monastery	**monestério**	moo-nish-**teh**-ree-oo
mosque	**mesquita**	mehsh-**kee**-tah
synagogue	**sinagoga**	see-nah-**goh**-gah
chapel	**capela**	kah-**peh**-lah
altar	**altar**	ahl-**tar**
cross	**cruz**	kroosh
treasury	**tesoraria**	teh-zoh-**rah**-ree-ah
crypt	**caixão**	kī-**show**
dome	**cúpula**	**koo**-poo-lah
bells	**sinos**	**see**-noosh
organ	**orgão**	or-**gow**
relic	**rélica**	**reh**-lee-kah
saint	**santo[a]**	**sahn**-too
God	**Deus**	**deh**-oosh
Jewish	**Judeu**	**zhoo**-deh-oo
Muslim	**Muçulmano**	moo-**sool**-mah-noo
Christian	**Cristão**	kreesh-**tow**
Protestant	**Protestante**	proh-tish-**tayn**-teh
Catholic	**Católico**	kah-**taw**-lee-koo
agnostic	**agnóstico**	ahg-**naw**-stee-koo
atheist	**ateu**	ah-**teh**-oo
When is the mass / service?	**Quando é que é a missa / serviço?**	**kwahn**-doo eh keh eh ah **mee**-sah / sehr-**vee**-soo
Are there concerts in the church?	**Dão concertos na igreija?**	dow kohn-**sehr**-toosh nah ee-**gray**-zhah

SIGHTSEEING

Shopping

Names of Portuguese shops:

antiques	**antiquário**	ahn-tee-**kwah**-ree-oo
art gallery	**galeria de arte**	gah-leh-**ree**-ah deh **ar**-teh
bakery	**padaria**	pah-dah-**ree**-ah
barber shop	**barbeiro**	bar-**bay**-roo
beauty salon	**cabelareiro**	kah-beh-lah-**ray**-roo
book shop	**livraria**	leev-rah-**ree**-ah
camera shop	**loja fotográfica**	**law**-zhah foh-toh-**grah**-fee-kah
department store	**grande armazen**	**grahn**-deh ar-mah-**zayn**
flea market	**feira**	**fay**-rah
flower market	**mercado de flores**	mehr-**kah**-doo deh **floh**-rish
grocery store	**mercearia**	mehr-see-ah-**ree**-ah
hardware store	**casa de ferragens**	**kah**-zah deh feh-rah-**zhayn**
jewelry shop	**joalheria**	zhoo-ahl-yeh-**ree**-ah
laundromat	**lavandaria**	lah-vahn-dah-**ree**-ah
newsstand	**quiosque**	kee-**awsh**-keh
office supplies	**papelaria**	pah-peh-lah-**ree**-ah
open air market	**mercado municipal**	mehr-**kah**-doo moo-nee-see-**pahl**
optician	**oculista**	aw-koo-**leesh**-tah
pharmacy	**farmácia**	far-**mah**-see-ah

photocopy shop	**casa de fotocopias**	**kah**-zah deh foh-tee-koh-**pee**-ahsh
shopping mall	**centro comercial**	**say<u>n</u>**-troo koo-mehr-see-**ahl**
souvenir shop	**loja de lembranças**	**law**-zhah deh lay<u>n</u>-**brang**-sahsh
supermarket	**supermercado**	soo-pehr-mehr-**kah**-doo
toy store	**loja de brinquedos**	**law**-zhah deh breeng-**kay**-doosh
travel agency	**agência de viagens**	ah-**zhay<u>n</u>**-see-ah deh vee-**ah**-zhay<u>n</u>sh
used bookstore	**loja de livros usados**	**law**-zhah deh **leev**-roosh oo-**zah**-doosh
wine shop	**loja de vinhos**	**law**-zhah deh veen-yoosh

In Portugal, most shops close for lunch from about 13:00 till 15:00, and all day on Sundays.

Shop till you drop:

sale	**saldo**	**sahl**-doo
How much is it?	**Quanto custa?**	**kwahn**-too **koosh**-tah
I'm / We're...	**Estou / Estamos...**	ioh **toh** / ish-**tah**-moosh
...just browsing.	**...só a olhar.**	saw ah ohl-**yar**
I'd like...	**Gostaria...**	goosh-tah-**ree**-ah
Do you have...?	**Tem...?**	tay<u>n</u>
...something cheaper	**...alguma coisa mais barato**	ahl-**goo**-mah **koy**-zah mīsh bah-**rah**-too
...more	**...mais**	mīsh

Can I see...?	Posso ver...?	**paw**-soo vehr
This one.	Este aqui.	**aysh**-teh ah-**kee**
Can I try it on?	Posso exprimentar?	**paw**-soo ish-pree-mayn-**tar**
Do you have a mirror?	Tem um espelho?	tayn oon ish-**payl**-yoo
Too...	Muito...	**mween**-too
...big.	...grande.	**grahn**-deh
...small.	...pequeno.	peh-**kay**-noo
...expensive.	...caro.	**kah**-roo
Did you make this?	Foi você que fez isto?	foy voh-**say** keh fehsh **eesh**-too
What is this made of?	Isto é feito de quê?	**eesh**-too eh **fay**-too deh kay
Is it machine washable?	Posso lavar á máquina?	**paw**-soo lah-**var** ah **mah**-kee-nah
Will it shrink?	Vai encolher?	vī ayn-kohl-**yehr**
Credit card O.K.?	Cartão de crédito O.K.?	kar-**tow** deh **kreh**-dee-too "O.K."
Can you ship this?	Pode enviar isto?	**paw**-deh ayn-vee-**ar** **eesh**-too
Tax-free?	Livre de impostos?	**lee**-vreh deh eem-**pohsh**-toosh
I'll think about it.	Vou pensar.	voh payn-**sar**
What time do you close?	A que horas é que fecha?	ah keh **aw**-rahsh eh keh **fay**-shah
What time do you open tomorrow?	A que horas é que abre amanhã?	ah keh **aw**-rahsh eh keh **ah**-breh ah-ming-**yah**
Is that your best price?	É o seu melhor preço?	eh oo **seh**-oo mil-**yor** **pray**-soo

My last offer.	A minha última oferta.	ah **meen**-yah **ool**-tee-mah oo-**fehr**-tah
I'm nearly broke.	Estou quase sem dinheiro.	ish-**toh kwah**-zeh say<u>n</u> deen-**yay**-roo
My male friend...	O meu amigo...	oo **meh**-oo ah-**mee**-goo
My female friend...	A minha amiga...	ah **meen**-yah ah-**mee**-gah
My husband...	O meu marido...	oo **meh**-oo mah-**ree**-doo
My wife...	A minha mulher...	ah meen-yah **mool**-yehr
...has the money.	...é que tem o dinheiro.	eh keh tay<u>n</u> oo deen-**yay**-roo

Repair:

These handy lines can apply to any repair, whether it's a ripped rucksack, bad haircut, or crabby camera.

This is broken.	Isto está avariado.	**eesh**-too aysh-**tah** ah-vah-ree-**ah**-doo
Can you fix it?	Pode reparar isto?	**paw**-deh reh-pah-**rar eesh**-too
Just do the essentials.	Faça só o que for preciso.	**fah**-sah saw oo keh for preh-**see**-zoo
How much will it cost?	Quanto vai custar?	**kwahn**-too vī koosh-**tar**
When will it be ready?	Quando é que vai estar pronto?	**kwahn**-doo eh keh vī īsh-**tar prohn**-too
I need it by ___.	Preciso até ___.	preh-**see**-zoo ah-**teh**

SHOPPING

Entertainment

What's happening tonight?	O que se passa esta noite?	oo keh seh **pah**-sah **ehsh**-tah **noy**-teh
What do you recommend?	O que é que recomenda?	oo keh eh keh ray-koo-**mayn**-dah
movie...	filme...	**feel**-meh
...original version	...versão original	vehr-**sow** oo-ree-zhee-**nahl**
...in English	...em inglês	ayn een-**glaysh**
...with subtitles	...com legendas	kohn leh-**zhayn**-dahsh
...dubbed	...dobrado	doo-**brah**-doo
music...	música...	**moo**-zee-kah
...live	...ao vivo	ow **vee**-voo
...classical	...clássico	**klah**-see-koo
...folk	...folclore	fool-**klaw**-reh
rock / jazz / blues	rock / jazz / blues	"rock" / zhahz / bloosh
singer	cantor[a]	kahn-**tor**
concert	concerto	kohn-**sehr**-too
show	espetáculo	ish-peh-**tah**-koo-loo
(folk) dancing	dança (folclórica)	**dahn**-sah (fool-**klaw**-ree-kah)
disco	disco	**deesh**-koo
cover charge	entrada	ayn-**trah**-dah

Fado is Portugal's mournful style of folk singing. An evening absorbed in these fishermen's "blues" can leave you with sorrow creases. A good show is powerful stuff. For livelier fun, try Lisbon's *Feira Popular*, a family af-*fair* with lots of food, wine, rides, and friendly chaos.

Phoning

The nearest phone?	O próximo telefone?	oo **praw**-see-moo teh-leh-**foh**-neh
Where is the post office?	Onde é que são os correios?	**ohn**-deh eh keh sow oosh koo-**ray**-oosh
I'd like to telephone...	Gostaria de telefonar para...	goosh-tah-**ree**-ah deh teh-leh-foh-**nar pah**-rah
...the United States.	...os Estados Unidos.	oosh ish-**tah**-doosh oo-nee-doosh
How much per minute?	Quanto custa por minuto?	kwahn-too **koosh**-tah poor mee-**noo**-too
I'd like to make a... call.	Gostaria de fazer uma chamada...	goosh-tah-**ree**-ah deh fah-**zeer oo**-mah shah-**mah**-dah
...local	...local.	loo-**kahl**
...collect	...à cobrança.	ah koo-**brang**-sah
...credit card	...com o meu cartão de crédito.	kohn oo **meh**-oo kar-**tow** deh **kreh**-dee-too
...long distance (within Portugal)	...para fora da cidade.	**pah**-rah **foh**-rah dah see-**dah**-deh
...international	...internacional.	een-tehr-nah-see-oo-**nahl**
It doesn't work.	Não funciona.	now foon-see-**oh**-nah
May I use your phone?	Posso utilizar o seu telefone?	**paw**-soo oo-tee-lee-**zar** oo **seh**-oo teh-leh-**foh**-neh
Can you dial for me?	Pode fazer a ligação por mim?	**paw**-deh fah-**zehr** ah lee-gah-**sow** poor meeng
Can you talk for me?	Pode falar por mim?	**paw**-deh fah-**lar** poor meeng

It's busy.	**Está ocupado.**	ish-**tah** oo-koo-**pah**-doo
Will you try again?	**Pode tentar novamente?**	**paw**-deh tayn-**tar** noo-vah-**mayn**-teh
Hello. (on phone)	**Está.**	ish-**tah**
My name is...	**Chamo-me...**	**shah**-moo-meh
My number is...	**O meu número é...**	oo meh-oo **noo**-may-roo eh
Speak slowly.	**Fale devagar.**	**fah**-leh deh-vah-**gar**
Wait a moment.	**Um momento.**	oon moo-**mayn**-too
Don't hang up.	**Não desligue.**	now dish-**lee**-geh

Key telephone words:

telephone	**telefone**	teh-leh-**foh**-neh
telephone card	**cartão telefónico**	kar-**tow** teh-leh-**foh**-nee-koo
post office	**correios**	koo-**ray**-oosh
operator	**telefonista**	teh-leh-foh-**neesh**-tah
international assistance	**assistência internacional**	ah-seesh-**tayn**-see-ah een-tehr-nah-see-oo-**nahl**
country code	**código do país**	**kaw**-dee-goo doo pah-**eesh**
area code	**código da area**	**kaw**-dee-goo dah ah-**ray**-ah
telephone book	**lista telefónica**	**leesh**-tah teh-leh-**foh**-nee-kah
toll-free	**taxa grátis**	**tah**-shah **grah**-teesh
out of service	**desligado**	dish-lee-**gah**-doo

Use a handy phone card (*cartão telefónico*) instead of coins to make your calls, or try the easy-to-use metered phones at the post office (*correios*). See "Let's Talk Telephones" near the end of this book for more phone tips.

Mailing

English	Portuguese	Pronunciation
Where is the post office?	Onde é que é os correios?	ohn-deh eh keh eh oosh koo-ray-oosh
Which window for...?	Que janela para...?	keh zhah-neh-lah pah-rah
...stamps	...selos	say-loosh
...packages	...embrulhos	ayn-brool-yoosh
To the United States...	Para os Estados Unidos...	pah-rah oosh ish-tah-doosh oo-nee-doosh
...by air mail.	...por avião.	poor ahv-yow
...by surface mail.	...de barco.	deh bar-koo
How much is it?	Quanto custa?	kwahn-too koosh-tah
How many days will it take?	Quantos dias é que demora?	kwahn-toosh dee-ahsh eh keh deh-moh-rah

Handy postal words:

English	Portuguese	Pronunciation
post office	correios	koo-ray-oosh
stamp	selo	say-loo
post card	cartão postal	kar-tow poosh-tahl
letter	carta	kar-tah
aerogram	telegrama aéreo	teh-leh-grah-mah ah-eh-ray-oo
envelope	envelope	ayn-veh-loh-peh
package	embrulho	ayn-brool-yoo
box	caixa	kī-shah
string	cordão	kor-dow

MAILING

tape	**adesivo**	ah-deh-**zee**-voo
mailbox	**caixa postal**	**kī**-shah poosh-**tahl**
air mail	**por avião**	poor ahv-**yow**
express	**expresso**	ish-**preh**-soo
surface mail (slow and cheap)	**de barco**	deh **bar**-koo
book rate	**á tabela do livro**	ah tah-**beh**-lah doo **leev**-roo
weight limit	**limite de peso**	lee-**mee**-teh deh **pay**-zoo
registered	**registrado**	ray-zheesh-**trah**-doo
insured	**seguro**	say-**goo**-roo
fragile	**frágil**	**frah**-zheel
contents	**conteúdo**	kohn-teh-**oo**-doo
customs	**alfândega**	ahl-**fahn**-deh-gah
to / from	**para / de**	**pah**-rah / deh
address	**endereço**	ayn-deh-**ray**-soo
zip code	**código postal**	**kaw**-dee-goo poosh-**tahl**
general delivery	**Posta Restante**	**pawsh**-tah rish-**tahn**-teh

In Portugal, you can often get stamps at a *quiosque* (newsstand) or *tabacaria* (tobacco shop). As long as you know which stamps you need, this is a great convenience.

Red Tape & Profanity

Filling out forms:

Sr. / Sra. / Menina	Mr. / Mrs. / Miss
nome	first name
apelido	last name
endereço	address
rua	street
cidade	city
estado	state
pais	country
nacionalidade	nationality
origem / destino	origin / destination
idade	age
dia de nascimento	date of birth
lugar de nascimento	place of birth
sexo	sex
masculino	male
feminino	female
casado / casada	married man / married woman
solteiro / solteira	single man / single woman
profissão	profession
adulto	adult
criança / rapaz / rapariga	child / boy / girl
crianças	children
familia	family
assinatura	signature
data	date

Portuguese profanity:

In any country, red tape inspires profanity. In case you're wondering what the more colorful locals are saying...

Damn it!	**Maldito seja!**	mahl-**dee**-too **say**-zhah
Go to hell!	**Vá para o inferno!**	vah **pah**-rah oo een-**fehr**-noo
bastard	**bastardo**	bahsh-**tar**-doo
bitch	**puta**	**poo**-tah
breasts (colloq.)	**mamas**	**mah**-mahsh
penis (colloq.)	**caralho**	kah-**rahl**-yoo
shit	**merda**	**mehr**-dah
drunk	**bêbado**	**bay**-bah-doo
idiot	**idiota**	ee-dee-**oh**-tah
imbecile	**tolo[a]**	**toh**-loo
jerk	**palermo[a]**	pah-**lehr**-moo
stupid	**estúpido[a]**	ish-**too**-pee-doo
cretin	**cretino**	kreh-**tee**-noo
Did someone...?	**Alguem deu...?**	**ahl**-gay<u>n</u> **deh**-oo
...fart	**...um peido**	oo<u>n</u> **pay**-doo
...burp	**...um arroto**	oo<u>n</u> ah-**roh**-too

Help!

Help!	Socorro!	soo-**koh**-roo
Help me!	Ajude-me!	ah-**zhoo**-deh-meh
Call a doctor!	Chame um médico!	**shah**-meh oon **meh**-dee-koo
ambulance	ambulância	ayn-boo-**lahn**-see-ah
accident	acidente	ah-see-**dayn**-teh
injured	ferido	feh-**ree**-doo
emergency	emergência	ee-mehr-**zhayn**-see-ah
fire	fogo	**foh**-goo
police	polícia	poo-**lee**-see-ah
thief	ladrão	lah-**drow**
pick-pocket	carteirista	kar-tay-**reesh**-tah
I've been ripped off.	Fui roubado[a].	fwee roh-**bah**-doo
I've lost my...	Perdi o meu...	**pehr**-dee oo **meh**-oo
...passport.	...passaporte.	pah-sah-**por**-teh
...ticket.	...bilhete.	beel-**yeh**-teh
...bag.	...saco.	**sah**-koo
I've lost my...	Perdi a minha...	**pehr**-dee ah **meen**-yah
...purse.	...bolsa.	**bohl**-sah
...wallet.	...carteira.	kar-**tay**-rah
...faith in humankind.	...fé na humanidade.	feh nah oo-mah-nee-**dah**-deh
I'm lost.	Estou perdido[a].	ish-**toh** pehr-**dee**-doo

Help for women:

Leave me alone.	**Deixe-me em paz.**	**day**-sheh-meh ay<u>n</u> pahsh
I *vant* to be alone.	**Quero estar só.**	**keh**-roo ish-**tar** saw
I'm not interested.	**Não estou interessada.**	no<u>w</u> ish-**toh** een-teh-reh-**sah**-dah
I'm married.	**Sou casada.**	soh kah-**zah**-dah
I'm a lesbian.	**Sou lésbia.**	soh **lehzh**-bee-ah
I have a contagious disease.	**Tenho uma doença contagiosa.**	**tayn**-yoo **oo**-mah doo-**ayn**-sah kohn-tah-zhee-**oh**-zah
Don't touch me.	**Não me toque.**	no<u>w</u> meh **taw**-keh
You're disgusting.	**Tu das-me nojo.**	too **dahsh**-meh **noh**-zhoo
Stop following me.	**Pare de me seguir.**	**pah**-reh deh meh seh-**geer**
He is bothering me.	**Ele está a incomodar-me.**	**eh**-leh ish-**tah** ah een-koo-moo-**dar**-meh
Enough!	**Chega!**	**shay**-gah
Get lost!	**Desapareça!**	day-zah-pah-**ray**-sah
Drop dead!	**Quero que morra!**	**keh**-roo keh **moh**-rah
I'll call the police!	**Vou chamar a polícia!**	voh shah-**mar** ah poo-**lee**-see-ah

Health

I am sick.	Estou doente.	ish-**toh** doo-**ayn**-teh
I need a doctor...	Preciso de um médico...	preh-**see**-zoo deh oon meh-dee-koo
...who speaks English.	...que fale inglês.	keh **fah**-leh een-**glaysh**
It hurts here.	Doi aqui.	doy ah-**kee**
I'm allergic to...	Sou alérgico[a] a...	soh ah-**lehr**-zhee-koo ah
...penicillin.	...penecilina.	peh-neh-see-**lee**-nah
I am diabetic.	Sou diabético[a].	soh dee-ah-**beh**-tee-koo
I've missed a period.	Tenho faltar o periodo.	**tayn**-yoo fahl-**tar** oo peh-ree-**oh**-doo
My friend has...	O meu amigo[a]...	oo **meh**-oo ah-**mee**-goo
I have...	Tenho...	**tayn**-yoo
...a burn.	...uma queimadura.	**oo**-mah kay-mah-**doo**-rah
...chest pains.	...uma dor no pcito.	**oo**-mah dor noo **pay**-too
...a cold.	...uma constipação.	**oo**-mah kohnsh-tee-pah-**sow**
...constipation.	...prisão de ventre.	pree-**zow** deh **vayn**-treh
...a cough.	...uma tosse.	**oo**-mah **taw**-seh
...diarrhea.	...diarreia.	dee-ah-**ray**-ah
...dizziness.	...tonturas.	tohn-**too**-rahsh
...a fever.	...febre.	**feh**-breh
...the flu.	...uma gripe.	**oo**-mah **gree**-peh
...the giggles.	...multas guargalhadas.	**mween**-tahsh gwar-gahl-**yah**-dahsh
...hay fever.	...febre dos fenos.	**feh**-breh doosh **feh**-noosh

...a headache.	...uma dor de cabeça.	oo-mah dor deh kah-**beh**-sah
...hemorrhoids.	...hemorróidas.	eh-moh-**raw**-dahsh
...high blood pressure.	...tensão alta.	tay<u>n</u>-**sow** **ahl**-tah
...indigestion.	...uma indigestão.	oo-mah een-dee-zhish-**tow**
...an infection.	...uma infecção.	oo-mah een-fehk-**sow**
...a migraine.	...uma enxaqueca.	oo-mah ay<u>n</u>-shah-**keh**-kah
...nausea.	...tonturas.	toh<u>n</u>-**too**-rahsh
...a rash.	...uma erupção.	oo-mah ee-roop-**sow**
...a sore throat.	...uma dor de garganta.	oo-mah dor deh gar-**gahn**-tah
...a stomach ache.	...uma dor de estômago.	oo-mah dor deh ish-**toh**-mah-goo
...a swelling.	...um inchado.	oo<u>n</u> een-**shah**-doo
...a toothache.	...uma dor de dente.	oo-mah dor deh **day<u>n</u>**-teh
...a venereal disease.	...uma doença venéria.	oo-mah doo-**ay<u>n</u>**-sah veh-**neh**-ree-ah
...worms.	...vermes.	**vehr**-mish
I have body odor.	Tenho cheiro corporal.	**tay<u>n</u>**-yoo **shay**-roo kor-poo-**rahl**
Is it serious?	É grave?	eh **grah**-veh

Handy health words:

pain	dor	dor
dentist	dentista	day<u>n</u>-**teesh**-tah
doctor	doutor[a]	doh-**tor**
nurse	enfermeira	ay<u>n</u>-fehr-**may**-rah

health insurance	**seguro de saúde**	say-**goo**-roo deh sah-**oo**-deh
hospital	**hospital**	ohsh-pee-**tahl**
bandage	**penso**	**payn**-soo
medicine	**medicina**	meh-dee-**zee**-nah
pharmacy	**farmácia**	far-**mah**-see-ah
prescription	**receita**	reh-**say**-tah
pill	**comprimido**	kohn-pree-**mee**-doo
aspirin	**aspirina**	ahsh-pee-**ree**-nah
antibiotic	**antibiótico**	ahn-tee-bee-**aw**-tee-koo
cold medicine	**remedio para constipação**	reh-meh-**dee**-oo **pah**-rah kohnsh-tee-pah-**sow**
cough drops	**rebuçados da tosse**	reh-boo-**sah**-doosh dah **taw**-seh
pain killer	**comprimidos para as dores**	kohn-pree-**mee**-doosh **pah**-rah ahsh **doh**-rish
Preparation H	**Preparação H**	preh-pah-rah-**sow** eh-**gah**
vitamins	**vitaminas**	vee-tah-**mee**-nahsh

Contacts and glasses:

glasses	**oculos**	oo-**koo**-loosh
sunglasses	**oculos de sol**	oo-**koo**-loosh deh sohl
prescription	**receita**	reh-**say**-tah
contact lenses...	**lentes de contacto...**	**lehn**-tish deh kohn-**tahk**-too
...soft	**...flexibeis**	fleh-**shee**-baysh
...hard	**...rigidas**	ree-**zhee**-dahsh
solution...	**solução...**	soo-loo-**sow**
...cleaning	**...de limpeza**	deh leem-**pay**-zah
...soaking	**...para molhar**	**pah**-rah mool-**yar**

Toiletries:

comb	**pente**	**payn**-teh
conditioner	**creme amaciador**	**kreh**-meh ah-mah-see-ah-**dor**
condoms	**preservativos**	pray-zehr-vah-**tee**-voosh
dental floss	**fio dental**	**fee**-oo dayn-**tahl**
deodorant	**desodorizante**	deh-zoo-dor-ee-**zayn**-teh
hairbrush	**escova do cabelo**	ish-**koh**-vah doo kah-**beh**-loo
hand lotion	**creme para as mãos**	**kreh**-meh **pah**-rah ahsh **mowsh**
lip salve	**batão de cierio**	bah-**tow** deh see-**yay**-roo
nail clipper	**corta unhas**	**kor**-tah **oon**-yahsh
razor	**lâmina**	**lah**-mee-nah
sanitary napkins	**pensos higiénicos**	**payn**-soosh ee-zhee-**ehn**-ee-koosh
shampoo	**shampoo**	"shampoo"
shaving cream	**creme de barbear**	**kreh**-meh deh bar-**behr**
soap	**sabão**	sah-**bow**
sunscreen	**protector solar**	proo-tehk-**tor** soo-**lar**
tampons	**tampões higiénicos**	tahn-**powsh** ee-zhee-**ehn**-ee-koosh
tissues	**lenços de papel**	**layn**-soosh deh pah-**pehl**
toilet paper	**papel higiénico**	pah-**pehl** ee-zhee-**ehn**-ee-koo
toothbrush	**escova de dentes**	ish-**koh**-vah deh **dayn**-tish
toothpaste	**pasta dos dentes**	**pahsh**-tah doosh **dayn**-tish
tweezers	**pinça**	**peen**-sah

Chatting

My name is...	Chamo-me...	shah-moo-meh
What's your name?	Como se chama?	koh-moo seh shah-mah
How are you?	Como está?	koh-moo ish-tah
Very well, thanks.	Muito bem, obrigado[a].	mween-too bayn oh-bree-gah-doo
Where are you from?	De onde é que você é?	deh ohn-deh eh keh voh-say eh
What city?	De que cidade?	deh keh see-dah-deh
What country?	De que país?	deh keh pah-eesh
What planet?	De que planeta?	deh keh plah-nay-tah
I am American.	Sou Americano[a].	soh ah-meh-ree-kah-noo
I am Canadian.	Sou Canadiano[a].	soh kah-nah-dee-ah-noo

Nothing more than feelings...

I am / You are...	Estou / Está...	ish-toh / ish-tah
...happy.	...contente.	kohn-tayn-teh
...sad.	...triste.	treesh-teh
...tired.	...cansado[a].	kahn-sah-doo
...thirsty.	...com sede.	kohn say-deh
...hungry.	...com fome.	kohn faw-meh
...lucky.	...afortunado[a].	ah-for-too-nah-doo
...homesick.	...com saudades de casa.	kohn soh-dah-dish deh kah-zah
...cold.	...com frio.	kohn free-oh
...hot.	...com calor.	kohn kah-lor

CHATTING

Who's who:

My... (male / female)	O meu / A minha...	oo **meh**-oo / ah **meen**-yah
...friend.	...amigo / amiga.	ah-**mee**-goo / ah-**mee**-gah
...boyfriend / girlfriend.	...namorado / namorada.	nah-moo-**rah**-doo / nah-moo-**rah**-dah
...husband / wife.	...marido / mulher.	mah-**ree**-doo / mool-**yehr**
...son / daughter.	...filho / filha.	**feel**-yoo / **feel**-yah
...brother / sister.	...irmão / irmã.	eer-**mow** / eer-**mah**
...father / mother.	...pai / mãe.	pī / mow
...uncle / aunt.	...tio / tia.	**tee**-oo / **tee**-ah
...nephew / niece.	...sobrinho / sobrinha.	soo-**breen**-yoo / soo-**breen**-yah
...male / female cousin.	...primo / prima.	**pree**-moo / **pree**-mah
...grandpa / grandma.	...avô / avó.	ah-**voh** / ah-**vaw**
...grandson / granddaughter.	...neto / neta.	**nay**-too / **nay**-tah

Family, school, and work:

Are you married? (asked of a man)	É casado?	eh kah-**zah**-doo
Are you married? (asked of a woman)	É casada?	eh kah-**zah**-dah
Do you have children?	Tem algumas crianças?	tayn ahl-**goo**-mahsh kree-**ahn**-sahsh
How many boys / girls?	Quantos rapazes / raparigas?	**kwahn**-toosh rah-**pah**-zish / rah-pah-**ree**-gahsh

Do you have photos?	Tem fotografias?	tayn foh-toh-grah-**fee**-ahsh
How old is your child?	Que idade tem a sua criança?	keh ee-**dah**-deh tayn ah **soo**-ah kree-**ahn**-sah
Beautiful child!	Linda criança!	**leen**-dah kree-**ahn**-sah
Beautiful children!	Lindas crianças!	**leen**-dahsh kree-**ahn**-sahsh
What are you studying?	O que é que está a estudar?	oo keh eh keh ish-**tah** ah ish-too-**dar**
I'm studying...	Estou a estudar...	ish-**toh** ah ish-too-**dar**
I'm... years old.	Tenho... de idade.	**tayn**-yoo... deh ee-**dah**-deh
How old are you?	Que idade tem?	keh ee-**dah**-deh tayn
Do you have brothers and sisters?	Tem irmãos e irmãs?	tayn eer-**mowsh** ee eer-**mahsh**
Will you teach me a simple Portuguese song?	Pode me ensinar uma canção fácil em português?	**paw**-deh meh ayn-see-**nar** **oo**-mah kahn-**sow** fah-seel ayn poor-too-**gaysh**
I'm a...	Sou...	soh
...student.	...estudante.	ish-too-**dahn**-teh
...teacher.	...professor[a].	proo-feh-**sor**
...worker.	...trabalhador[a].	trah-bahl-yah-**dor**
...professional traveler.	...viajante professional.	vee-ah-**zhahn**-teh proo-feh-see-oo-**nahl**
What is your occupation?	Qual é a sua profissão?	kwahl eh ah **soo**-ah proo-fee-**sow**
Do you like your work?	Gosta do seu trabalho?	**gawsh**-tah doo **seh**-oo trah-**bahl**-yoo

Travel talk:

I am / Are you...?	**Estou / Está...?**	ish-**toh** / ish-**tah**
...on vacation	**...de férias**	deh **feh**-ree-ahsh
...on business	**...em negócios**	ay<u>n</u> neh-**gaw**-see-oosh
How long have you been traveling?	**Á quanto tempo é que tem estado a viajar?**	ah **kwahn**-too **tayn**-poo eh keh tay<u>n</u> ish-**tah**-doo ah vee-ah-**zhar**
day / week	**dia / semana**	**dee**-ah / seh-**mah**-nah
month / year	**mês / ano**	maysh / **ah**-noo
When are you going home?	**Quando é que vai voltar para casa?**	**kwahn**-doo eh keh vī vohl-**tar** pah-rah **kah**-zah
This is my first time in...	**Esta é a minha primeira vez em...**	**ehsh**-tah eh ah **meen**-yah pree-**may**-rah vaysh ay<u>n</u>
Today / Tomorrow I'm going to...	**Hoje / Amanhã vou para...**	**oh**-zheh / ah-ming-**yah** voh **pah**-rah
I'm happy here.	**Estou contente aqui.**	ish-**toh** koh<u>n</u>-**tayn**-teh ah-**kee**
The Portuguese are friendly.	**Os Portugueses são simpáticos.**	oosh poor-too-**gay**-zish so<u>w</u> seeng-**pah**-tee-koosh
Portugal is wonderful.	**Portugal é maravilhoso.**	poor-too-**gahl** eh mah-rah-veel-**yoh**-zoo
To travel is to live.	**A maneira de viver é viajar.**	ah mah-**nay**-rah deh vee-**vehr** eh vee-ah-**zhar**
Have a good trip!	**Boa-viagem!**	boh-ah-vee-**ah**-zhay<u>n</u>

Map talk:

Use these phrases, along with the maps of Iberia, Europe, and the U.S.A. near the end of this book, to delve into family history and explore travel dreams.

I live here.	Eu vivo aqui.	eh-oo vee-voo ah-kee
I was born here.	Eu nasci aqui.	eh-oo nahsh-see ah-kee
My ancestors came from...	Os meus antepassados vieram de...	oosh meh-oosh ahn-teh-pah-sah-doosh vee-eh-rahm deh
I've traveled to...	Ja viajei a...	zhah vee-ah-zhay ah
Next I'll go to...	Em seguida irei...	ayn sehg-ee-dah ee-ray
Where do you live?	A onde vive?	ah ohn-deh vee-veh
Where were you born?	A onde nasceu?	ah ohn-deh nahsh-seh-oo
Where did your ancestors come from?	De onde vieram os vossos antepassados?	deh ohn-deh vee-eh-rahm oosh vaw-soosh ahn-teh-pah-sah-doosh
Where have you traveled?	A onde tem viajado?	ah ohn-deh tayn vee-ah-zhah-doo
Where are you going?	A onde vai?	ah ohn-deh vī
Where would you like to go?	O onde gostaria de ir?	oo ohn-deh goosh-tah-ree-ah deh eer

Favorite things:

What's your favorite...?	**Qual é o seu... favorito?**	kwahl eh oo **seh**-oo... fah-voo-**ree**-too
...hobby	**...passatempo**	pah-sah-**tayn**-poo
...ice cream	**...gelado**	zheh-**lah**-doo
...male singer	**...cantor**	kahn-**tor**
...male movie star	**...actor**	ah-**tor**
...movie	**...filme**	**feel**-meh
...sport	**...desporto**	dish-**por**-too
...vice	**...vício**	**vee**-see-oo
What's your favorite...?	**Qual é a sua... favorita?**	kwahl eh ah **soo**-ah... fah-voo-**ree**-tah
...food	**...comida**	koo-**mee**-dah
...art	**...arte**	**ar**-teh
...music	**...música**	**moo**-zee-kah
...female singer	**...cantora**	kahn-**toh**-rah
...female movie star	**...actriz**	ah-**treesh**

Weather:

What will the weather be like tomorrow?	**Qual é o tempo para amanhã?**	kwahl eh oo **tayn**-poo pah-rah ah-ming-**yah**
sunny / cloudy	**sol / nublado**	sohl / noo-**blah**-doo
hot / cold	**quente / frio**	**kayn**-teh / **free**-oo
muggy / windy	**úmido / ventoso**	**oo**-mee-doo / vayn-**toh**-zoo
rain / snow	**chuva / neve**	**shoo**-vah / **neh**-veh

Responses for all occasions:

Thank you very much.	**Muito obrigado[a].**	**mween**-too oh-bree-**gah**-doo
You are...	**Você é...**	voh-**say** eh
...wonderful.	**...maravilhoso[a].**	mah-rah-veel-**yoh**-zoo
...generous.	**...generouso[a].**	zheh-neh-**roh**-zoo
You've been a great help.	**Você foi uma grande ajuda.**	voh-**say** foy oo-mah **grahn**-deh ah-**zhoo**-dah
I like that.	**Gosto disto.**	**gawsh**-too **deesh**-too
I like you.	**Gosto de si.**	**gawsh**-too deh see
Fantastic!	**Fantástico!**	fahn-**tahsh**-tee-koo
Perfect.	**Perfeito.**	pehr-**fay**-too
Funny.	**Cómico.**	**kaw**-mee-koo
Interesting.	**Interessante.**	een-teh-reh-**sahn**-teh
I don't smoke.	**Não fumo.**	now **foo**-moo
Really?	**A sério?**	ah **seh**-ree-oo
Wow!	**Fiche!**	**fee**-sheh
Congratulations!	**Parabéns!**	pah-rah-**baynsh**
Well done!	**Bem feito!**	bayn **fay**-too
You're welcome.	**Não tem de quê.**	now tayn deh kay
Bless you! (after sneeze)	**Santinho!**	sahn-**teen**-yoo
What a pity.	**É uma pena.**	eh **oo**-mah **pay**-nah
That's life.	**É a vida.**	eh ah **vee**-dah
No problem.	**Não tem problema.**	now tayn proo-**blay**-mah
O.K.	**Está bem.**	ish-**tah** bayn
This is the good life!	**Esta é a boa vida!**	**ehsh**-tah eh ah **boh**-ah **vee**-dah
Good luck!	**Boa-sorte!**	boh-ah-**sor**-teh
Let's go!	**Vamos!**	**vah**-moosh

CHATTING

Create Your Own Conversation

Using these lists, you can have deep (or ridiculous) conversations with the locals.

Who:

I / you	**eu / você**	eh-oo / voh-**say**
he / she	**ele / ela**	eh-leh / **eh**-lah
we / they	**nós / eles**	nawsh / **eh**-lish
my / your...	**meus / seus...**	meh-oosh / **seh**-oosh
...parents / children	**...pais / crianças**	pīsh / kree-**ahn**-sahsh
men / women	**homens / mulheres**	aw-may<u>n</u>sh / mool-**yeh**-rish
rich / poor	**rico / pobre**	ree-koo / **paw**-breh
politicians	**políticos**	poo-**lee**-tee-koosh
big business	**negócio grande**	neh-**gaw**-see-oo **grahn**-deh
mafia	**máfia**	**mah**-fee-ah
military	**militares**	mee-lee-**tah**-rish
Portuguese	**Portugueses**	poor-too-**gay**-zish
Spanish	**Espanhóis**	ish-pahn-**yoysh**
French	**Franceses**	frahn-**say**-zish
Germans	**Alemães**	ah-leh-**may**<u>n</u>sh
Americans	**Americanos**	ah-meh-ree-**kah**-noosh
liberals	**liberais**	lee-**beh**-raysh
conservatives	**conservadores**	koh<u>n</u>-sehr-vah-**doh**-rish
radicals	**radicais**	rah-**dee**-kaysh
travelers	**vijantes**	vee-**zhan**-tish
everyone	**todas as pessoas**	**toh**-dahsh ahsh peh-**soh**-ahsh
God	**Deus**	**deh**-oosh

What:

want / need	querer / precisar	keh-**rehr** / preh-see-**zar**
take / give	tirar / dar	tee-**rar** / dar
love / hate	amar / odiar	ah-**mar** / oo-dee-**ar**
work / play	trabalhar / jogar	trah-bahl-**yar** / zhoo-**gar**
have / lack	ter / faltar	tehr / fahl-**tar**
learn / fear	aprender / temer	ah-prayn-**dar** / teh-**mehr**
help / abuse	ajudar / abusar	ah-zhoo-**dar** / ah-boo-**zar**
prosper / suffer	prósperar / sofrer	prawsh-peh-**rar** / soof-**rehr**
buy / sell	comprar / vender	koh_n_-**prar** / vay_n_-**dar**

Why:

love / sex	amor / sexo	ah-**mor** / **sehk**-soo
money / power	dinheiro / poder	deen-**yay**-roo / poo-**dehr**
work	trabalho	trah-**bahl**-yoo
food	oomida	koo-mee-dah
family	familia	fah-**meel**-yah
health	saúde	sah-**oo**-deh
hope	esperança	ish-peh-**rahn**-sah
education	instrucão	eensh-troo-**sow**
guns	pistolas	peesh-**toh**-lahsh
religion	religião	ray-lee-**zhow**
happiness	felicidade	feh-lee-see-**dah**-deh
marijuana	marijuana	mah-ree-**wah**-nah
democracy	democracia	deh-moo-krah-**see**-ah
taxes	taxas	**tahsh**-ahsh
lies	mentiras	may_n_-**tee**-rahsh
corruption	corrupção	koo-roop-**sow**

CHATTING

pollution	**poluição**	pool-wee-**sow**
television	**televisão**	teh-leh-vee-**zow**
relaxation	**descanso**	dish-**kahn**-soo
violence	**violência**	vee-oo-**layn**-see-ah
racism	**racismo**	rah-**seesh**-moo
respect	**respeito**	rish-**pay**-too
war / peace	**guerra / paz**	**geh**-rah / pahsh
global perspective	**perspectiva mundial**	persh-pehk-**tee**-vah moon-dee-**ahl**

You be the judge:

(no) problem	**(não) á problema**	(now) ah proo-**blay**-mah
(not) good	**(não) bom**	(now) bohn
(not) dangerous	**(não) perigoso**	(now) peh-ree-**goh**-zoo
(not) fair	**(não) justo**	(now) **zhoosh**-too
(not) guilty	**(não) culpado**	(now) kool-**pah**-doo
(not) powerful	**(não) poderoso**	(now) poo-deh-**roh**-zoo
(not) stupid	**(não) estúpido**	(now) ish-**too**-pee-doo
(not) happy	**(não) feliz**	(now) feh-**leesh**
because / for	**porque / para**	**poor**-keh / **pah**-rah
and / or / from	**e / ou / de**	ee / oh / deh
too much	**demasiado**	deh-mah-zee-**ah**-doo
(never) enough	**(nunca é) suficiente**	**(noon**-kah eh) soo-fee-see-**ayn**-teh
same	**mesmo**	**mehsh**-moo
better / worse	**melhor / pior**	mil-**yor** / pee-**or**
here / everywhere	**aqui / em toda parte**	ah-**kee** / ayn **toh**-dah **par**-teh

Assorted beginnings and endings:

I like...	Gosto...	**gawsh**-too
I don't like...	Não gosto...	now **gawsh**-too
Do you like...?	Gosta...?	**gawsh**-tah
I am / Are you...?	Sou / É...?	soh / eh
...an optimist / pessimist	...um optimista / pessimista	oon awp-tee-**meesh**-tah / peh-see-**meesh**-tah
I believe...	Acredito...	ah-kreh-**dee**-too
I don't believe...	Não acredito...	now ah-kreh-**dee**-too
Do you believe...?	Acredita...?	ah-kreh-**dee**-tah
...in God	...em Deus	ayn **deh**-oosh
...in life after death	...vida para além da morte	**vee**-dah pah-rah ah-**lehm** dah **mor**-teh
...in extra-terrestrial life	...que existe vida em outros planetas	keh ee-**zeesh**-teh **vee**-dah ayn **oh**-troosh plah-**nay**-tahsh
...in Santa Claus	...no Pai-Natal	noo pī-nah-**tahl**
Yes. / No.	Sim. / Não.	seeng / now
Maybe. / I don't know.	Talvez. / Não sei.	**tahl**-vaysh / now say
What's most important in life?	O que é a coisa mais importante na vida?	oo keh eh ah **koy**-zah mīsh eem-poor-**tahn**-teh nah **vee**-dah
The problem is...	O problema é...	oo proo-**blay**-mah eh
The answer is...	A resposta é...	ah rish-**pohsh**-tah eh
We have solved the world's problems.	Nós resolvemos os problemas do mundo.	nawsh reh-zool-**vay**-moosh oosh proo-**blay**-mahsh doo **moon**-doo

A Portuguese Romance

Words of love:

I / me / you	**eu / mim / tu**	**eh**-oo / meeng / too
flirt	**namorar**	nah-moo-**rar**
kiss	**beijo**	**bay**-zhoo
hug	**abraço**	ah-**brah**-soo
love	**amor**	ah-**mor**
make love	**fazer amor**	fah-**zehr** ah-**mor**
condom	**preservativo**	preh-zehr-vah-**tee**-voo
contraceptive	**contraceptivo**	koh<u>n</u>-trah-sehp-**tee**-voo
safe sex	**sexo seguro**	**sehk**-soo say-**goo**-roo
sexy	**sexy**	"sexy"
romantic	**romântico**	roh-**mahn**-tee-koo
my tender love	**minha ternura**	**meen**-yah tehr-**noo**-rah
my darling (male, female)	**meu querido / minha querida**	**meh**-oo keh-**ree**-doo / **meen**-yah keh-**ree**-dah
my angel	**meu anjo**	**meh**-oo **ahn**-zhoo
my soft thing (male, female)	**meu fofinho / minha fofinha**	**meh**-oo foh-**feen**-yoo / **meen**-yah foh-**feen**-yah

Ah, amor:

What's the matter?	**O que é que se passa?**	oo keh eh keh seh **pah**-sah
Nothing.	**Nada.**	**nah**-dah

I am / Are you...?	Sou / És...?	soh / ehsh
...straight	...normal	nor-**mahl**
...gay	...maricas	mah-**ree**-kahsh
...undecided	...indeciso[a]	een-day-**see**-zoo
...prudish	...puritano[a]	poo-ree-**tah**-noo
...horny	...excitado[a]	ish-see-**tah**-doo
We are on our honeymoon.	Nós estamos em lua de mel.	nawsh ish-**tah**-moosh ayn **loo**-ah deh mehl
I have a...	Tenho...	**tayn**-yoo
...a boyfriend.	...um namorado.	oon nah-moo-**rah**-doo
...a girlfriend.	...uma namorada.	oo-mah nah-moo-**rah**-dah
I'm married.	Sou casado[a].	soh kah-**zah**-doo
I'm not married.	Não sou casado[a].	now soh kah-**zah**-doo
I'm rich and single.	Sou rico[a] e solteiro[a].	soh **ree**-koo ee sool-**tay**-roo
I'm lonely.	Sinto-me só.	**seeng**-too-meh saw
I have no diseases.	Não tenho nenhuma doença.	now **tayn**-yoo neen-**yoo**-mah doo-**ayn**-sah
I have many diseases.	Tenho muitas doenças.	**tayn**-yoo **mween**-tahsh doo-**ayn**-sahsh
Can I see you again?	Quando é que o posso voltar a ver?	**kwahn**-doo eh keh oo **paw**-soo vool-**tar** ah vehr
Is this an aphrodisiac?	É isto um afrodisíaco?	eh **eesh**-too oon ah-froo-dee-**zee**-ah-koo
This is (not) my first time.	(Não) é a minha primeira vez.	(now) eh ah **meen**-yah pree-**may**-rah vaysh
Do you do this often?	Faz isto regularmente?	fahsh **eesh**-too reh-goo-lar-**mayn**-teh

CHATTING

How's my breath?	**Como é que cheiro da boca?**	koh-moo eh keh **shay**-roo dah **boh**-kah
Let's just be friends.	**Vamos ser só amigos.**	**vah**-moosh sehr saw ah-**mee**-goosh
I'll pay for my share.	**Pagarei somente a minha parte.**	pah-gah-**ray** soo-**mayn**-teh ah **meen**-yah **par**-teh
Would you like a massage for...?	**Gostaria de uma massagem para...?**	goosh-tah-**ree**-ah deh **oo**-mah mah-**sah**-zhayn **pah**-rah
...your back	**...as tuas costas**	ahsh **too**-ahsh **kawsh**-tahsh
...your feet	**...os seus pés**	oosh **seh**-oosh pehsh
Why not?	**Porquê não?**	poor-**kay** now
Try it.	**Experimente.**	ish-pehr-**mayn**-teh
It tickles.	**Isso faz cócegas.**	ee-soo fahsh **kaw**-see-gahsh
Oh my God!	**Ó meu Deus!**	aw **meh**-oo **deh**-oosh
I love you.	**Eu amo-te.**	**eh**-oo **ah**-moo-teh
Darling, will you marry me?	**Querida, queres casar comigo?**	keh-**ree**-dah **keh**-rish kah-**zar** koo-**mee**-goo

Conversing with Portuguese animals:

rooster / cock-a-doodle-doo	**galo / co-coro-cocó**	**gah**-loo / koo-koo-roo-koo-**kaw**
bird / tweet tweet	**pássaro / piu piu**	**pah**-sah-roo / pee-**oo** pee-**oo**
cat / meow	**gato / miau**	**gah**-too / **mee**-ow
dog / woof woof	**cão / ão ão**	kow / ow ow
duck / quack quack	**pato / quac quac**	**pah**-too / kwahk kwahk
cow / moo	**vaca / moo**	**vah**-kah / moo
pig / oink oink	**porco / orn orn (or just snort)**	**por**-koo / orn orn (or just snort)

English-Spanish-Portuguese Dictionary

English	Spanish	Portuguese

A

English	Spanish	Portuguese
above	encima	acima
accident	accidente	acidente
accountant	contador	contador
adaptor	adaptador	adaptador
address	dirección	endereço
adult	adulto	adulto
afraid	miedoso	medo
after	después	depois
afternoon	tarde	tarde
afterwards	después	depois
again	otra vez	outra vez
age	edad	idade
aggressive	agresivo	agressivo
agree	de acuerdo	de acordo
AIDS	SIDA	SIDA
air	aire	ar
air-conditioned	aire acondicionado	ar condicionado
airline	línea aérea	linha aérea
air mail	correo aéreo	correio aéreo
airport	aeropuerto	aeroporto
alarm clock	despertador	despertador
alcohol	alcohol	alcool
allergic	alérgico	alérgico
allergies	alergias	alergias
alone	solo	sozinho
already	ya	já
always	siempre	sempre
ancestors	antepasados	antepassados

English	Spanish	Portuguese
ancient	antiguo	antigo
and	y	e
angry	enfadado	chateado
ankle	tobillo	tornozelo
animal	animal	animal
another	otro	outro
answer	respuesta	resposta
antibiotic	antibiótico	antibiótico
antiques	antigüedades	antiguidades
apartment	apartamento	apartamento
apology	disculpa	desculpa
appetizers	aperitivos	aperitivos
appointment	cita	apontamento
approximately	aproximadamente	aproximadamente
arrivals	llegadas	chegadas
arrive	llegar	chegar
arm	brazo	braço
art	arte	arte
artificial	artificial	artificial
artist	artista	artista
ashtray	cenicero	cinzeiro
ask	preguntar	perguntar
aspirin	aspirina	aspirina
at	a	á
attractive	atractivo	atraente
aunt	tía	tia
autumn	otoño	outono

English	Spanish	Portuguese

B

English	Spanish	Portuguese
baby	niño, niña	bébé
babysitter	niñera	babysitter
backpack	mochila	mochila
bad	malo	mau
bag	bolsa	saco
baggage	equipaje	bagagem
bakery	panadería	padaria
balcony	balcón	varanda
ball	pelota	bola
band-aid	tirita	adesivo
bank	banco	banco
barber	barbero	barbeiro
basement	sótano	porão
basket	canasta	cesto
bath	baño	banho
bathroom	baño	casa de banho
bathtub	bañera	banheira
battery	batería	baterIa
beach	playa	praia
beard	barba	barba
beautiful	bonito[a]	lindo[a]
because	porque	porquê
bed	cama	cama
bedroom	habitación	quarto
bedsheet	sábana	lençol de cama
beef	carne de vaca	bife
beer	cerveza	cerveja
before	antes	antes

English	Spanish	Portuguese
begin	comenzar	começar
behind	detrás	detrás
below	abajo	abaixo
belt	cinturón	cinto
best	mejor	melhor
bib	babero	babeiro
bicycle	bicicleta	bicicleta
big	grande	grande
bill (payment)	cuenta	conta
bird	pájaro	pássaro
birthday	cumpleaños	aniversário
black	negro	preto
blanket	manta	corbetor
blond	rubio	louro
blood	sangre	sangre
blouse	camisa	blusa
blue	azul	azul
boat	barco	barco
body	cuerpo	corpo
boiled	cocido	fervido
bomb	bomba	bomba
book	libro	livro
book shop	librería	livraria
boots	botas	botas
border	orilla	fronteira
borrow	pedir prestado	emprestar
boss	jefe	patrão
bottle	botella	garrafa
bottom	fondo	fundo
bowl	plato hondo	tijela

English	Spanish	Portuguese
box	caja	caixa
boy	chico	rapaz
bra	sujetador	soutien
bracelet	brazalete	pulseira
bread	pan	pão
breakfast	desayuno	pequeno almoço
bridge	puente	ponte
Britain	Gran Bretaña	Grã-Bretanha
broken	roto	partido
brother	hermano	irmão
brown	marrón	castanho
bucket	cubo	balde
building	edificio	prédio
bulb	bombilla	lâmpada
burn (n)	quemadura	queimadura
bus	autobús	autocarro
business	negocio	negócio
but	pero	mas
button	botón	botão
by (via)	en	via

C

English	Spanish	Portuguese
calendar	calendario	calendário
calorie	caloría	caloria
camera	cámara	camara
camping	camping	campismo
can (n)	bote	lata
can (v)	poder	poder
Canada	Canadá	Canadá

English	Spanish	Portuguese
can opener	abridor de latas	abertor de latas
canal	canal	canal
candle	candela	vela
candy	caramelo	doce
canoe	canoa	canoa
cap	gorro	boné
captain	capitán	capitão
car	coche	carro
carafe	garrafa	jarro
card	tarjeta	cartão
cards (deck)	naipe	cartas
careful	cuidadoso	cuidadoso
carpet	alfombra	carpete
carry	llevar	carregar
cashier	cajera	caixa
cassette	cinta	cassete
castle	castillo	castelo
cat	gato	gato
catch (v)	coger	apanhar
cathedral	catedral	catedral
cave	cueva	cave
cellar	bodega	adega
center	centro	centro
century	siglo	século
chair	silla	cadeira
change (n)	cambio	troca
change (v)	cambiar	mudar
charming	lujoso	encantador
cheap	barato	barato
check	cheque	cheque

English	Spanish	Portuguese
Cheers!	¡Salud!	Saúde!
cheese	queso	queijo
chicken	pollo	galinha
children	niños	crianças
Chinese (adj)	chino	chinês
chocolate	chocolate	chocolate
Christmas	Navidad	Natal
church	iglesia	igreija
cigarette	cigarrillo	cigarro
cinema	cine	cinema
city	ciudad	cidade
class	clase	classe
clean (adj)	limpio	limpo
clear	claro	claro
cliff	acantilado	falésia
closed	cerrado	fechado
cloth	tejido	tecido
clothes	ropa	roupa
clothesline	cordón para ropa	linha de roupas
clothes pins	pinzas	broches
cloudy	nuboso	nebuloso
coast	costa	costa
coat hanger	percha	cruzeta
coffee	café	café
coins	monedas	moedas
cold (adj)	frío	frio
colors	colores	cores
comb (n)	peine	pente
come	venir	vir
comfortable	cómodo	confortável

English	Spanish	Portuguese
compact disc	compact disc	compact disco
complain	quejarse	queixar
complicated	complicado	complicado
computer	computadora	computador
concert	concierto	concerto
condom	preservativo	perservativo
conductor	conductor	condutor
confirm	confirmar	confirmar
congratulations	felicidades	parabéns
connection (train)	enlace	conexão
constipation	estreñimiento	prisão de ventre
cook (v)	cocinar	cozinhar
cool	fresco	fresco
cork	corcho	rolha
corkscrew	sacacorchos	sacarolhas
corner	esquina	esquina
corridor	pasillo	corredor
cost	precio	preço
cot	catre	rede
cotton	algodón	algodão
cough (v)	toser	tosser
cough drops	gotas para la tos	rabuçados da tosse
country	país	país
countryside	campo	campo
cousin	primo, prima	primo, prima
cow	vaca	vaca
cozy	cómodo	confortável
crafts	artesanía	artesanato
credit card	tarjeta de crédito	cartão de crédito
crowd (n)	multitud	multidão

English	Spanish	Portuguese
cry (v)	llorar	chorar
cup	taza	chávena

D

English	Spanish	Portuguese
dad	papá	pai
dance (v)	bailar	dançar
danger	peligro	perigo
dangerous	peligroso	perigoso
dark	oscuro	escuro
daughter	hija	filha
day	día	dia
dead	muerto	morto
delay	retraso	atraso
delicious	delicioso	delicioso
dental floss	seda dental	fio dental
dentist	dentista	dentista
deodorant	desodarante	desodorizante
depart	salir	partir
departures	salidas	partidas
deposit	depósito	depósito
dessert	postre	sobremesa
detour	desvío	desvio
diabetic	diabético	diabético
diamond	diamante	diamante
diaper	pañal	fraldas
diarrhea	diarrea	diarreia
dictionary	diccionario	dicionário
die	morir	morrer
difficult	difícil	difícil

English	Spanish	Portuguese
dinner	cena	jantar
direct	directo	directo
direction	dirección	direção
dirty	sucio	sujo
discount	descuento	desconto
disease	enfermedad	doença
disturb	molestar	incomudar
divorced	divorciado[a]	divorciado[a]
doctor	doctor	doutor
dog	perro	cão
doll	muñeca	boneca
donkey	burro	burro
door	puerta	porta
dormitory	dormitorio	dormitorio
double	doble	dobrar
down	abajo	abaixo
dream (n)	sueño	sonho
dream (v)	soñar	sonhar
dress (n)	vestido	vestido
drink (n)	bebida	bebida
drive (v)	conducir	conduzir
driver	conductor	condutor
drunk	borracho	bêbado
dry	seco	seco

E

English	Spanish	Portuguese
each	cada	cada
ear	oreja	orelha
early	temprano	cedo

English	Spanish	Portuguese
earplugs	tapón de oidos	tampões de ouvido
earrings	pendientes	brincos
earth	tierra	terra
east	este	este
Easter	Pascua	Pascoa
easy	fácil	fácil
eat	comer	comer
elbow	codo	cotovelo
elevator	ascensor	elevador
embarrassing	embarazoso	humilhante
embassy	embajada	embaixada
empty	vacío	vazio
engineer	ingeniero	engenheiro
English	inglés	inglês
enjoy	disfrutar	gostar
enough	suficiente	suficiente
entrance	entrada	entrada
envelope	sobre	envelope
eraser	borrador	borracha
Europe	Europa	Europa
evening	la tarde	noitecor
every	todo	todo
everything	todo	tudo
exactly	exactamente	exactamente
example	ejemplo	exemplo
excellent	excelente	excelente
except	excepto	excepto
exchange (n)	cambio	câmbio
excuse me	lo siento	desculpe
exhausted	agotado	esgotado

English	Spanish	Portuguese
exit	salida	saída
expensive	caro	caro
explain	explicar	explicar
eye	ojo	olho

F

face	cara	cara
factory	fábrica	fábrica
fall (v)	caer	cair
false	falso	falso
family	familia	família
famous	famoso	famoso
fantastic	fantástico	fantástico
far	lejos	longe
farm	granja	quinta
farmer	granjero	granjeiro
fashion	moda	moda
fat (adj)	gordo	gordo
father	padre	pai
faucet	grifo	torneira
fax	fax	fax
female	femenino	feminino
ferry	transbordador	barco
festival	festival	festival
fever	fiebre	fevre
few	poco	pouco
field	campo	campo
fight (n)	pelea	luta
fight (v)	discutir	lutar

English	Spanish	Portuguese
fine (good)	bueno	bom
finger	dedo	dedo
finish (v)	terminar	terminar
fireworks	fuegos artificiales	fogo de artificio
first	primero	primeiro
first aid	primeros auxilios	pronto socorro
first class	primera clase	primeira classe
fish	pescado	peixe
fish (v)	pescar	pescar
fix (v)	arreglar	arranjar
fizzy	gaseoso	com gás
flag	bandera	bandeira
flashlight	linterna	lanterna a pilhas
flavor (n)	sabor	sabor
flea	pulga	pulga
flight	vuelo	voo
flower	flor	flor
flu	gripe	gripe
fly	volar	voar
fog	niebla	nevoeiro
food	comida	comida
foot	pie	pé
football	fútbol	futebol
for	para	para
forbidden	prohibido	proibido
foreign	extranjero	estrangeiro
forget	olvidar	esquecer
fork	tenedor	garfo
fountain	fuente	fonte
France	Francia	França

English	Spanish	Portuguese
free (no cost)	gratis	grátis
fresh	fresco	fresco
Friday	viernes	sexta-feira
friend	amigo, amiga	amigo, amiga
friendship	amistad	amizade
frisbee	frisbee	disco voador
from	de	de
fruit	fruta	fruta
fun	diversión	divertido
funeral	funeral	funeral
funny	divertido	divertido
furniture	muebles	mobilias
future	futuro	futuro

G

English	Spanish	Portuguese
gallery	galería	galeria
game	juego	jogo
garage	garaje	garagem
garden	jardín	jardim
gardening	jardineria	jardinagem
gas	gas	gás
gas station	gasolinera	bomba de gasolina
gay	homosexual	homosexual
gentleman	caballeros	cavalheiro
genuine	auténtico	genuíno
Germany	Alemania	Alemanha
gift	regalo	prenda
girl	chica	rapariga
give	dar	dar

English	Spanish	Portuguese
glass	vaso	copo
glasses (eye)	gafas	oculos
gloves	guantes	luvas
go	ir	ir
God	Dios	deus
gold	oro	ouro
golf	golf	golfe
good	bueno	bom
goodbye	adiós	adeus
good day	buenos días	bom-dia
go through	atravesar	atravessar
grammar	gramática	gramática
grandchild	nieto, nieta	neto, neta
grandfather	abuelo	avô
grandmother	abuela	avó
gray	gris	cinzento
greasy	grasiento	gorduroso
great	magnífico	magnifico
Greece	Grecia	Grécia
green	verde	vordo
grocery store	supermercado	mercearia
guarantee	garantía	garantia
guest	invitados	convidados
guide	guía	uma guia
guidebook	guía	um guia
guitar	guitarra	guitarra
gum	chicle	pastilha elástica
gun	pistola	pistola

English	Spanish	Portuguese

H

English	Spanish	Portuguese
hair	pelo	cabelo
hairbrush	cepillo del pelo	escova de cabelo
haircut	corte de pelo	corte de cabelo
hand	mano	mão
handicapped	minusvalidos	aleijados
handicrafts	artesanía	artesanato
handle (n)	tirador	puxador
handsome	guapo	bonito
happy	feliz	feliz
harbor	puerto	porto
hard	difícil	difícil
hat	sombrero	chapéu
hate	odiar	odiar
have	tener	ter
he	él	ele
head	cabeza	cabeça
headache	dolor de cabeza	dor de cabeça
healthy	sano	saudavel
hear	oír	ouvir
heart	corazón	coração
heat (n)	calor	calor
heaven	cielo	céu
heavy	pesado	pesado
hello	hola	olá
help (n)	ayuda	ajuda
help (v)	ayudar	ajudar
hemorrhoids	hemorroides	hemorróidas
here	aquí	aqui

English	Spanish	Portuguese
hi	hola	olá
high	alto	alto
highchair	silla para niños	cadeirinha alta
highway	autopista	autoestrada
hill	colina	subida
history	historia	história
hitchhike	hacer auto-stop	pedir boleia
hobby	pasatiempo	passatempo
hole	agujero	buraco
holiday	festivo	feriado
homemade	hecho en casa	á moda de casa
homesick	morriña	saudade
honest	honesto	honesto
honeymoon	luna de miel	lua de mel
horrible	horrible	horrível
horse	caballo	cavalo
horse riding	montar a caballo	montar a cavalo
hospital	hospital	hospital
hot	calor	calor
hotel	hotel	hotel
hour	hora	hora
house	casa	casa
how many	cuánto	quanto
how much ($)	cuánto cuesta	quanto custa
how	cómo	como
hungry	hambriento	esfomeado
hurry (v)	apresurarse	apressar
husband	marido	marido
hydrofoil	hidroplano	hidroplano

English	Spanish	Portuguese

I

I	yo	eu
ice	hielo	gelo
ice cream	helado	gelado
ill	enfermo	doente
immediately	inmediatamente	imediatamente
important	importante	importante
imported	importado	importado
impossible	imposible	impossível
in	en	em
included	incluido	incluido
incredible	increíble	inacreditável
independent	independiente	independente
indigestion	indigestión	indigestão
industry	industria	industria
information	información	informação
injured	herido	ferido
innocent	inocente	inocente
insect	insecto	insecto
insect repellant	liquido de insectos	repelente de insectos
inside	interior	interior
instant	instante	instante
instead	en vez de	em vez de
insurance	seguro	seguro
intelligent	inteligente	inteligente
interesting	interesante	interresante
invitation	invitación	convite
iodine	yodo	iodo
is	es	ser

English	Spanish	Portuguese
island	isla	ilha
Italy	Italia	Itália
itch (n)	comezón	comichão

J

jacket	chaqueta	casaco
jaw	mandíbula	maxila
jeans	vaqueros	jeans
jewelry	joyas	joalheria
job	trabajo	trabalho
jogging	footing	jogging
joke (n)	chiste	piada
journey	viaje	viagem
juice	zumo	sumo
jump	saltar	saltar

K

keep	guardar	guardar
kettle	olla	chaleira
key	llave	chave
kill	matar	matar
kind	amable	simpático
king	rey	rei
kiss (n)	beso	beijo
kitchen	cocina	cozinha
knee	rodilla	joelho
knife	cuchillo	faca
know	saber	saber

English	Spanish	Portuguese

L

English	Spanish	Portuguese
ladder	escalera de mano	escada
ladies	señoras	senhoras
lake	lago	lago
lamb	cordero	cordeiro
language	lenguaje	língua
large	grande	grande
last	último	último
late	tarde	tarde
later	más tarde	mais tarde
laugh (v)	reír	rir
laundromat	lavandería	lavandaria
lawyer	abogado	advogado
lazy	perezoso	preguiçoso
leather	cuero	cabedal
leave	salir	sair
left	izquierda	esquerda
leg	pierna	perna
lend	prestar	emprestar
letter	carta	carta
library	biblioteca	biblioteca
life	vida	vida
light (n)	luz	luz
light bulb	bombilla	lâmpada
lighter (n)	encendedor	isqueiro
like (v)	gustar	gostar
lip	labio	lábio
list	lista	lista
listen	escuchar	escutar

English	Spanish	Portuguese
liter	litro	litro
little	pequeño	pequeno
live (v)	vivir	viver
local	local	local
lock (v)	cerrar	fechar
lock (n)	cerradura	fechadura
lockers	casilleros	armários
look	mirar	olhar
lost	perdido	perdido
loud	ruidoso	ruidoso
love (v)	amar	amar
lover	amante	amante
low	bajo	baixo
luck	suerte	sorte
luggage	equipaje	bagagem
lukewarm	templado	tépido
lungs	pulmones	pulmões

M

English	Spanish	Portuguese
macho	macho	macho
mad	enfadado	chateado
magazine	revista	revista
mail (n)	correo	correio
main	principal	principal
make (v)	hacer	fazer
male	masculino	masculino
man	hombre	homen
manager	director	gerente
many	mucho	muito

English	Spanish	Portuguese
map	mapa	mapa
market	mercado	mercado
married	casado[a]	casado[a]
matches	cerillas	fosforos
maximum	máximo	máximo
maybe	tal vez	talvez
meat	carne	carne
medicine	medicina	medicina
medium	mediano	médio
men	hombres	homens
menu	menú	ementa
message	recado	recado
metal	metal	metal
midnight	medianoche	meia-noite
mineral water	agua mineral	água mineral
minimum	mínimo	minimo
minutes	minutos	minutos
mirror	espejo	espelho
Miss	Señorita	Menina
mistake	error	erro
misunderstanding	malentendido	malentendido
mix (n)	mixto	mista
modern	moderno	moderno
mom	mamá	mãe
moment	momento	momento
Monday	lunes	segunda-feira
money	dinero	dinheiro
month	mes	mês
monument	monumento	monumento
moon	luna	lua

English	Spanish	Portuguese
more	más	mais
morning	mañana	manhã
mosquito	mosquito	mosquito
mother	madre	mãe
mountain	montaña	montanha
moustache	bigote	bigode
mouth	boca	boca
movie	película	filme
Mr.	Señor	Senhor
Mrs.	Señora	Senhora
much	mucho	muito
muscle	músculo	músculo
museum	museo	museu
music	música	música
my	mi	meu

N

nail clipper	corta uñas	corta unhas
naked	desnudo	nuo
name	nombre	nome
napkin	servilleta	guardanapo
narrow	estrecho	estreito
nationality	nacionalidad	nacionalidade
natural	natural	natural
nature	naturaleza	natureza
nausea	náusea	náusea
near	cerca	perto
necessary	necesario	necessário
necklace	collar	fio

English	Spanish	Portuguese
need	necesitar	necessitar
needle	aguja	agulha
nephew	sobrino	sobrinho
nervous	nervioso	nervoso
never	nunca	nunca
new	nuevo	novo
newspaper	periódico	jornal
next	siguiente	próximo
nice	amable	simpático
niece	sobrina	sobrinha
nickname	apodo	alcunha
night	noche	noite
no	no	não
noisy	ruidoso	barulho
non-smoking	no fumadores	não fumador
noon	mediodía	meio-dia
normal	normal	normal
north	norte	norte
nose	nariz	nariz
not	no	não
notebook	cuaderno	caderno
nothing	nada	nada
no vacancy	completo	cheio
now	ahora	agora

O

occupation	oficio	profissão
occupied	ocupado	ocupado
ocean	océano	oceano

English	Spanish	Portuguese
of	de	de
office	oficina	escritório
O.K.	O.K.	O.K.
old	viejo	velho
on	sobre	sobre
once	una vez	uma vez
one way (street)	dirección única	sentido único
one way (ticket)	de ida	uma ida
only	sólo	só
open (adj)	abierto	aberto
open (v)	abrir	abrir
opera	ópera	ópera
operator	telefonista	operador
optician	óptico	oculista
or	o	ou
orange (color)	naranja	cor de laranja
orange (fruit)	naranja	laranja
original	original	original
other	otro	outro
oven	horno	forno
over (finished)	terminado	acabado
own (v)	poseer	possuir
owner	dueño	dono

P

English	Spanish	Portuguese
pacifier	chupete	chupeta
package	paquete	embalagem
page	página	página
pail	cubo	balde

English	Spanish	Portuguese
pain	dolor	dor
painting	pintura	pintura
palace	palacio	palácio
panties	bragas	cuecas
pants	pantalones	calças
paper	papel	papel
paper clip	clip	clip
parents	padres	pais
park (v)	aparcar	estacionar
park (garden)	parque	parque
party	fiesta	festa
passenger	pasajero	passageiro
passport	pasaporte	passaporte
pay	pagar	pagar
peace	paz	paz
pedestrian	peatón	peão
pen	bolígrafo	caneta
pencil	lápiz	lápis
people	gente	pessoas
percent	porciento	percento
perfect	perfecto	perfeito
perfume	perfume	perfume
period (of time)	período	período
period (woman's)	regla	menstruação
person	persona	pessoa
pet (n)	animal de casa	animal de estimação
pharmacy	farmacia	farmácia
photo	foto	fotografia
pick-pocket	carterista	carteirista
picnic	picnic	piquenique

English	Spanish	Portuguese
piece	pedazo	pedaço
pig	cerdo	porco
pill	píldora	comprimido
pillow	almohada	almofada
pin	alfiler	alfinete
pink	rosa	cor de rosa
pity, it's a	que lástima	que pena
pizza	pizza	pizza
plane	avión	avião
plain	al natural	simples
plant	planta	planta
plastic	plástico	plástico
plastic bag	bolsa de plástico	saco plástico
plate	plato	prato
platform (train)	andén	cais
play (v)	jugar	jogar
please	por favor	por favor
pliers	alicates	alicate
pocket	bolsillo	bolso
point (v)	apuntar	apontar
police	policía	polícia
poor	pobre	pobre
pork	cerdo	porco
Portugal	Portugal	Portugal
possible	posible	possível
postcard	carta postal	cartão postal
poster	cartel	póster
practical	práctico	prático
pregnant	embarazada	grávida
prescription	prescripción	receita médica

English	Spanish	Portuguese
present (gift)	regalo	presente
pretty	bonita	bonita
price	precio	preço
priest	sacerdote	padre
private	privado	privado
problem	problema	problema
profession	profesión	profissão
prohibited	prohibido	proibido
pronunciation	pronunciacion	pronúncia
public	público	público
pull	tirar	tirar
purple	morado	roxo
purse	bolsa	bolsa
push	empujar	empurrar

Q

English	Spanish	Portuguese
quality	calidad	qualidade
quarter (¼)	cuarta parte	quarto
queen	reina	rainha
question (n)	pregunta	pergunta
quiet	tranquilo	calado

R

English	Spanish	Portuguese
R.V.	caravana	roulote
rabbit	conejo	coelho
radio	radio	rádio
raft	balsa	balsa
railway	ferrocarril	caminho de ferro

English	Spanish	Portuguese
rain (n)	lluvia	chuva
rainbow	arco iris	arco íris
raincoat	impermeable	casaco impermeável
rape (n)	violación	violação
raw	crudo	cru
razor	Gilete	Gilete
ready	listo	pronto
receipt	recibo	recibo
receive	recibir	receber
receptionist	recepcionista	recepcionista
recipe	receta	receita
recommend	recomendar	recomendar
red	rojo	vermelho
refund (n)	reembolso	reembolso
relax	relajar	relaxar
religion	religión	religião
remember	recordar	recordar
rent (v)	alquilar	renda
repair	arreglar	reparar
reserve	reservar	reservar
reservation	reserva	reserva
rich	rico	rico
right (direction)	derecha	direita
right (correct)	correcto	certo
ring (n)	sortija	campaínha
ripe	maduro	maduro
river	río	rio
rock (n)	roca	rock
roller skates	patines	patins
romantic	romántico	romântico

English	Spanish	Portuguese
roof	techo	telhado
room	habitación	quarto
rope	cuerda	corda
rotten	podrido	podre
roundtrip	ida y vuelta	ida e volta
rowboat	bote	barco de passeio
rucksack	mochila	mochila
rug	alfombra	carpete
ruins	ruinas	ruínas
run (v)	correr	correr

S

English	Spanish	Portuguese
sad	triste	triste
safe	seguro	seguro
safety pin	imperdible	alfinete de segurança
sailing	barco de vela	barco de vela
sale	rebajas	saldos
same	mismo	mesmo
sandals	sandalias	sandálias
sandwich	bocadillo	sande
sanitary napkins	compresas	pensos higiénicos
Saturday	sábado	sábado
scandalous	escandaloso	escandulo
scarf	bufanda	lenço
school	colegio	escola
science	ciencia	ciência
scientist	científico	cientista
scissors	tijeras	tesouras
scotch tape	cinta adhesiva	fita cola

English	Spanish	Portuguese
screwdriver	destornillador	chave de parafusos
sculptor	escultor	escultor
sculpture	escultura	escultura
sea	mar	mar
seafood	marisco	marisco
seat	asiento	lugar, assento
second	segunda	segunda
second class	segunda clase	segunda classe
secret	secreto	segredo
see	ver	ver
self-service	auto-servicio	auto serviço
sell	vender	vender
send	enviar	enviar
separate	separado	separado
serious	serio	sério
service	servicio	serviço
sex	sexo	sexo
sexy	sexy	sexy
shampoo	champú	xampú
shaving cream	espuma de afeitar	creme de barbear
she	ella	ela
sheet	sábana	lençol
shell	concha	concha
ship (n)	barco	barco
ship (v)	enviar	enviar
shirt	camisa	camisa
shoes	zapatos	sapatos
shopping	compras	compras
short	corto	curto
shorts	pantalones cortos	calções

English	Spanish	Portuguese
shoulder	hombros	ombros
show (v)	enseñar	mostrar
show (n)	espectáculo	espectáculo
shower	ducha	chuveiro
shy	tímido	tímido
sick	enfermo	doente
sign	señal	sinal
signature	firma	assinatura
silence	silencio	silêncio
silk	seda	seda
silver	plata	prata
similar	similar	similar
simple	sencillo	simples
sing	cantar	cantar
singer	cantante	cantor
single	soltero[a]	solteiro[a]
sink	lavabo	lavatório
sir	señor	senhor
sister	hermana	irmã
size	talla	tamanho
skating	patinaje	patinagem
ski (v)	esquiar	esquiar
skin	piel	pele
skinny	delgado	magro
skirt	falda	saia
sky	cielo	céu
sleep (v)	dormir	dormir
sleepy	soñoliento	sonolento
slice	rodaja	fatia
slide (photo)	diapositiva	slide

English	Spanish	Portuguese
slippery	resbaladizo	escorregadio
slow	despacio	devagar
small	pequeño	pequeno
smell (n)	olor	cheiro
smile (n)	sonrisa	sorriso
smoking	fumadores	fumador
snack	pincho	petisco
sneeze (n)	estornudo	espirro
snore	roncar	ressonar
soap	jabón	sabão
soccer	futball	futebol
socks	calcetines	melas
something	alguna cosa	alguma coisa
son	hijo	filho
song	canción	canção
soon	pronto	cedo
sorry	lo siento	desculpe
sour	agrio	azedo
south	sur	sul
3pain	España	Espanha
speak	hablar	falar
speciality	especialidad	especialidade
speed	velocidad	velocidade
spend	gastar	gastar
spider	araña	arranha
spoon	cuchara	colher
sport	deporte	desporto
spring (n)	primavera	primavera
square (town)	plaza	praça
stapler	grapadora	agrafador

DICTIONARY

English	Spanish	Portuguese
stairs	escaleras	escadas
stamp	sello	selo
star (in sky)	estrella	estrela
state	estado	estado
station	estación	estação
stomach	estomago	estômago
stop (n)	parada	parar
stop (v)	parar	parar
storm	tormenta	tempestada
story (floor)	planta	andar
straight	derecho	em frente
strange	extraño	estranho
stream (n)	arroyo	corrente
street	calle	rua
string	cordón	fio
strong	fuerte	forte
stuck	atascado	imobilizado
student	estudiante	estudante
stupid	estúpido	estúpido
sturdy	robusto	sólido
style	estilo	estilo
subway	metro	metro
suddenly	de repente	de repente
suitcase	maleta	mala
summer	verano	verão
sun	sol	sol
sunbathe	tomar el sol	bronzear
sunburn	quemadura	queimadura solar
Sunday	domingo	domingo
sunglasses	gafas de sol	óculos de sol

English	Spanish	Portuguese
sunny	soleado	sol
sunset	puesta de sol	pôr do sol
sunscreen	protección de sol	protector solar
sunshine	luz del sol	brilho de sol
sunstroke	insolación	insolação
suntan (n)	bronceado	bronzeado
suntan lotion	bronceador	creme de bronzear
supermarket	supermercado	supermercado
supplement	suplemento	suplemento
surprise (n)	sorpresa	surpresa
swallow (v)	tragar	engolir
sweat (v)	sudar	suar
sweater	suéter	pullover
sweet	dulce	doce
swim	nadar	nadar
swimming pool	piscina	piscina
swim suit	traje de baño	fato de banho
swim trunks	bañador	calção de banho
Switzerland	Suiza	Suíça
synthetic	sintético	sintético

T

English	Spanish	Portuguese
table	mesa	mesa
tail	rabo	rabo
take	tomar	tomar
take out (food)	para llevar	para levar
talcum powder	polvos de talco	pó de talco
talk	hablar	falar
tall	alto	alto

English	Spanish	Portuguese
tampons	tampones	tampões
tape (cassette)	casete	cassete
taste (n)	sabor	sabor
taste (try)	probar	provar
tax	impuesto	taxa
teacher	profesor	professor
team	equipo	equipa
teenager	joven	jovem
telephone	teléfono	telefone
television	telivisión	televisão
temperature	temperatura	temperatura
tender	tierno	tenro
tennis	tenis	ténis
tennis shoes	tenis	sapatos de ténis
tent	tienda de campaña	tenda
tent pegs	estacas de tienda	estacas de tenda
terrible	terrible	terrível
thanks	gracias	obrigado
theater	teatro	teatro
thermometer	termómetro	termómetro
they	ellos	eles
thick	grueso	grosso
thief	ladrón	ladrão
thigh	muslo	coxa
thin	delgado	magro
thing	cosa	coisa
think	pensar	pensar
thirsty	sediento	sede
thread	hilo	linha
throat	garganta	garganta

English	Spanish	Portuguese
through	a través	através
throw	tirar	atirar
Thursday	jueves	quinta-feira
ticket	billete	bilhete
tight	apretado	apretado
timetable	horario	horário
tired	cansado	cansado
tissues	pañuelos de papel	lenços de papel
to	a	para
today	hoy	hoje
toe	dedo del pie	dedo do pé
together	juntos	juntos
toilet	servicios	casa de banho
toilet paper	papel higiénico	papel higiénico
tomorrow	mañana	amanhã
tonight	esta noche	esta noite
too (much)	demasiado	demasiado
tooth	dientes	dentes
toothbrush	cepillo de dientes	escova de dentes
toothpaste	pasta de dientes	pasta de dentes
toothpick	palillo	palito
total	total	total
tour	viaje	excursão
tourist	turista	turista
towel	toalla	toalha
tower	torre	torre
town	pueblo	cidade
toy	juguete	brinquedo
track (train)	vía	linha
traditional	tradicional	tradicional

English	Spanish	Portuguese
traffic	tráfico	tráfico
train	tren	comboio
translate	traducir	traduzir
travel (v)	viajar	viajar
travel agency	agencia de viajes	agência de viagens
traveler's check	cheque de viajero	cheque de viagem
tree	árbol	árvore
trip	viaje	viagem
trouble	dificultad	problema
T-shirt	camiseta	T-shirt
Tuesday	martes	terça-feira
tunnel	túnel	túnel
tweezers	pinzas	pinsa
twins	gemelos	gêmeos

U

ugly	feo	feio
umbrella	paraguas	guarda-chuva
uncle	tío	tio
under	debajo	debaixo
underpants	calzoncillos	cuecas
understand	entender	entender
unemployed	sin empleo	desempregado
unfortunate	desafortunado	desventurado
United States	Estados Unidos	Estados Unidos
university	universidad	universidade
up	arriba	subida
upstairs	escaleras	escadas
urgent	urgente	urgente

English	Spanish	Portuguese
us	nosotros	nós
use (v)	usar	usar

V

vacancy sign	habitaciónes	quartos
vacant	libre	livre
valley	valle	vale
vegetarian	vegetariano[a]	vegetariano[a]
very	muy	muito
vest	chaleco	colete
video	vídeo	vídeo
video camera	cámara de video	video camera
view	vista	vista
village	aldea	aldeia
vineyard	viñedo	vinhedo
virus	virus	vírus
visit (n)	visita	visita
visit (v)	visitar	visitar
vitamins	vitaminas	vitaminas
voice	voz	voz
vomit	vomitar	vomitar

W

waist	cintura	cintura
wait (v)	esperar	esperar
waiter	camarero	criado
waitress	camarera	senhora, menina
wake up	despertarse	acordar

English	Spanish	Portuguese
walk (v)	andar	andar
wallet	cartera	carteira
want	querer	querer
warm (adj)	caliente	quente
wash	lavar	lavar
watch (n)	reloj	relógio
watch (v)	vigilar	olhar
water	agua	água
water, tap	agua del grifo	água da torneira
waterfall	cascada	queda de água
we	nosotros	nós
weather	tiempo	tempo
wedding	boda	casamento
Wednesday	miércoles	quarta-feira
week	semana	semana
weight	peso	peso
welcome	bienvenido	bem-vindo
west	oeste	oeste
wet	mojado	molhado
what	qué	o quê
wheel	rueda	roda
when	cuándo	quando
where	dónde	donde
white	blanco	branco
who	quién	quem
why	por qué	porquê
widow	viuda	viúva
widower	viudo	viúvo
wife	esposa	esposa
wild	salvaje	salvagem

English	Spanish	Portuguese
wind	viento	vento
window	ventana	janela
wine	vino	vinho
wing	ala	asa
winter	invierno	inverno
wish (v)	desear	desejo
with	con	com
without	sin	sem
woman	mujer	mulher
women	mujeres	mulheres
wood	madera	madeira
wool	lana	lã
word	palabra	palavra
work (n)	trabajo	trabalho
work (v)	trabajar	trabalhar
world	mundo	mundo
worst	peor	pior
wrap (v)	envolver	embrulhar
wrist	muñeca	pulso
write	escribir	escrever

Y / Z

English	Spanish	Portuguese
year	año	ano
yellow	amarillo	amarelo
yes	sí	sim
yesterday	ayer	ontem
you (formal)	usted	você
you (informal)	tú	tu
young	joven	novo

DICTIONARY

English	Spanish	Portuguese
youth hostel	albergue de juventud	albergue de juventude
zero	cero	zero
zip-lock bag	bolsa de cremallera	saco plastico com fecho
zipper	cremallera	fecho
zoo	zoo	zoo

Spanish-English Dictionary

A

a at
a to
a través through
abajo below
abajo down
abierto open (adj)
abogado lawyer
abridor de latas can opener
abrir open (v)
abuela grandmother
abuelo grandfather
acantilado cliff
accidente accident
adaptador adaptor
adiós goodbye
adulto adult
aeropuerto airport
agencia de viajes travel agency
agotado exhausted
agresivo aggressive
agrio sour
agua water
agua del grifo water, tap
agua mineral mineral water
aguja needle
agujero hole
ahora now
aire air

aire acondicionado air-
conditioned
al natural plain
ala wing
albergue de juventud youth hostel
alcohol alcohol
aldea village
Alemania Germany
alergias allergies
alérgico allergic
alfiler pin
alfombra carpet
alfombra rug
algodón cotton
alguna cosa something
alicates pliers
almohada pillow
alquilar rent (v)
alto high
alto tall
amable kind
amable nice
amante lover
amar love (v)
amarillo yellow
amigo, amiga friend
amistad friendship
andar walk (v)
andén platform (train)
animal animal

animal de casa   pet (n)
año   year
antepasados   ancestors
antes   before
antibiótico   antibiotic
antigüedades   antiques
antiguo   ancient
aparcar   park (v)
apartamento   apartment
aperitivos   appetizers
apodo   nickname
apresurarse   hurry (v)
apretado   tight
aproximadamente   approximately
apuntar   point (v)
aquí   here
araña   spider
árbol   tree
arco iris   rainbow
arreglar   fix (v)
arreglar   repair
arriba   up
arroyo   stream (n)
arte   art
artesanía   crafts
artesanía   handicrafts
artificial   artificial
artista   artist
ascensor   elevator
asiento   seat
aspirina   aspirin
atascado   stuck
atractivo   attractive

atravesar   go through
auténtico   genuine
auto-servicio   self-service
autobús   bus
autopista   highway
avión   plane
ayer   yesterday
ayuda   help (n)
ayudar   help (v)
azul   blue

B

babero   bib
bailar   dance (v)
bajo   low
balcón   balcony
balsa   raft
banco   bank
bañador   swim trunks
bandera   flag
bañera   bathtub
baño   bath
baño   bathroom
barato   cheap
barba   beard
barbero   barber
barco   boat
barco   ship (n)
barco de vela   sailing
batería   battery
bebida   drink (n)
beso   kiss (n)

biblioteca library
bicicleta bicycle
bienvenido welcome
bigote moustache
billete ticket
blanco white
boca mouth
bocadillo sandwich
boda wedding
bodega cellar
bolígrafo pen
bolsa bag
bolsa purse
bolsa de cremallera zip-lock bag
bolsa de plástica plastic bag
bolsillo pocket
bomba bomb
bombilla bulb
bombilla light bulb
bonita pretty
bonito[a] beautiful
borracho drunk
borrador eraser
botas boots
bote can (n)
bote rowboat
botella bottle
botón button
bragas panties
brazalete bracelet
brazo arm
bronceado suntan (n)
bronceador suntan lotion

bueno fine (good)
bueno good
buenos días good day
bufanda scarf
burro donkey

C

caballeros gentleman
caballo horse
cabeza head
cada each
caer fall (v)
café coffee
caja box
cajera cashier
calcetines socks
calendario calendar
calidad quality
caliente warm (adj)
calle street
calor heat (n)
calor hot
caloría calorie
calzoncillos underpants
cama bed
cámara camera
cámara de vídeo video camera
camarera waitress
camarero waiter
cambiar change (v)
cambio change (n)
cambio exchange (n)

camisa blouse
camisa shirt
camiseta T-shirt
camping camping
campo countryside
campo field
Canadá Canada
canal canal
canasta basket
canción song
candela candle
canoa canoe
cansado tired
cantante singer
cantar sing
capitán captain
cara face
caramelo candy
caravana R.V.
carne meat
carne de vaca beef
caro expensive
carta letter
carta postal postcard
cartel poster
cartera wallet
carterista pick-pocket
casa house
casado[a] married
cascada waterfall
casete tape (cassette)
casilleros lockers
castillo castle

catedral cathedral
catre cot
cena dinner
cenicero ashtray
centro center
cepillo de dientes toothbrush
cepillo del pelo hairbrush
cerca near
cerdo pig
cerdo pork
cerillas matches
cero zero
cerrado closed
cerradura lock (n)
cerrar lock (v)
cerveza beer
chaleco vest
champú shampoo
chaqueta jacket
cheque check
cheque de viajero traveler's check
chica girl
chicle gum
chico boy
chino Chinese (adj)
chiste joke (n)
chocolate chocolate
chupete pacifier
cielo heaven
cielo sky
ciencia science
científico scientist
cigarrillo cigarette

cine cinema
cinta cassette
cinta adhesiva scotch tape
cintura waist
cinturón belt
cita appointment
ciudad city
claro clear
clase class
clip paper clip
coche car
cocido boiled
cocina kitchen
cocinar cook (v)
codo elbow
coger catch (v)
colegio school
colina hill
collar necklace
colores colors
comenzar begin
comer eat
comezón itch (n)
comida food
cómo how
cómodo comfortable
cómodo cozy
compact disc compact disc
completo no vacancy
complicado complicated
compras shopping
compresas sanitary napkins
computadora computer

con with
concha shell
concierto concert
conducir drive (v)
conductor conductor
conductor driver
conejo rabbit
confirmar confirm
contador accountant
corazón heart
corcho cork
cordero lamb
cordón string
cordón para ropa clothesline
correcto right (correct)
correo mail (n)
correo aéreo air mail
correr run (v)
corta uñas nail clipper
corte de pelo haircut
corto short
cosa thing
costa coast
cremallera zipper
crudo raw
cuaderno notebook
cuándo when
cuánto how many
cuánto cuesta how much ($)
cuarta parte quarter (¼)
cubo bucket
cubo pail
cuchara spoon

cuchillo knife
cuenta bill (payment)
cuerda rope
cuero leather
cuerpo body
cueva cave
cuidadoso careful
cumpleaños birthday

D

dar give
de from
de of
de acuerdo agree
de ida one way (ticket)
de repente suddenly
debajo under
dedo finger
dedo del pie toe
delgado skinny
delgado thin
delicioso delicious
demasiado too (much)
dentista dentist
deporte sport
depósito deposit
derecha right (direction)
derecho straight
desafortunado unfortunate
desayuno breakfast
descuento discount
desear wish (v)

desnudo naked
desodarante deodorant
despacio slow
despertador alarm clock
despertarse wake up
después after
después afterwards
destornillador screwdriver
desvío detour
detrás behind
día day
diabético diabetic
diamante diamond
diapositiva slide (photo)
diarrea diarrhea
diccionario dictionary
dientes tooth
difícil difficult
difícil hard
dificultad trouble
dinero money
Dios God
dirección address
dirección direction
dirección única one way (street)
directo direct
director manager
disculpa apology
discutir fight (v)
disfrutar enjoy
diversión fun
divertido funny
divorciado[a] divorced

doble double
doctor doctor
dolor pain
dolor de cabeza headache
domingo Sunday
dónde where
dormir sleep (v)
dormitorio dormitory
ducha shower
dueño owner
dulce sweet

E

edad age
edificio building
ejemplo example
él he
ella she
ellos they
embajada embassy
embarazada pregnant
embarazoso embarrassing
empujar push
en by (via)
en in
en vez de instead
encendedor lighter (n)
encima above
enfadado angry
enfadado mad
enfermedad disease
enfermo ill

enfermo sick
enlace connection (train)
enseñar show (v)
entender understand
entrada entrance
enviar send
enviar ship (v)
envolver wrap (v)
equipaje baggage
equipaje luggage
equipo team
error mistake
es is
escalera de mano ladder
escaleras stairs
escaleras upstairs
escandaloso scandalous
escribir write
escuchar listen
escultor couplor
escultura sculpture
España Spain
especialidad speciality
espectáculo show (n)
espejo mirror
esperar wait (v)
esposa wife
espuma de afeitar shaving cream
esquiar ski (v)
esquina corner
esta noche tonight
estacas de tienda tent pegs
estación station

estado state
Estados Unidos United States
este east
estilo style
estomago stomach
estornudo sneeze (n)
estrecho narrow
estrella star (in sky)
estreñimiento constipation
estudiante student
estúpido stupid
Europa Europe
exactamente exactly
excelente excellent
excepto except
explicar explain
extranjero foreign
extraño strange

F

fábrica factory
fácil easy
falda skirt
falso false
familia family
famoso famous
fantástico fantastic
farmacia pharmacy
fax fax
felicidades congratulations
feliz happy
femenino female

feo ugly
ferrocarril railway
festival festival
festivo holiday
fiebre fever
fiesta party
firma signature
flor flower
fondo bottom
footing jogging
foto photo
Francia France
fresco cool
fresco fresh
frío cold (adj)
frisbee frisbee
fruta fruit
fuegos artificiales fireworks
fuente fountain
fuerte strong
fumadores smoking
funeral funeral
futball soccer
fútbol football
futuro future

G

gafas glasses (eye)
gafas de sol sunglasses
galería gallery
garaje garage
garantía guarantee

garganta throat
garrafa carafe
gas gas
gaseoso fizzy
gasolinera gas station
gastar spend
gato cat
gemelos twins
gente people
Gilete razor
golf golf
gordo fat (adj)
gorro cap
gotas para la tos cough drops
gracias thanks
gramática grammar
Gran Bretaña Britain
grande big
grande large
granja farm
granjero farmer
grapadora stapler
grasiento greasy
gratis free (no cost)
Grecia Greece
grifo faucet
gripe flu
gris gray
grueso thick
guantes gloves
guapo handsome
guardar keep
guía guide

guía guidebook
guitarra guitar
gustar like (v)

H

habitación bedroom
habitación room
habitaciónes vacancy sign
hablar speak
hablar talk
hacer make (v)
hacer auto-stop hitchhike
hambriento hungry
hecho en casa homemade
helado ice cream
hemorroides hemorrhoids
herido injured
hermana sister
hermano brother
hidroplano hydrofoil
hielo ice
hija daughter
hijo son
hilo thread
historia history
hola hello
hola hi
hombre man
hombres men
hombros shoulder
homosexual gay
honesto honest

hora hour
horario timetable
horno oven
horrible horrible
hospital hospital
hotel hotel
hoy today

I

ida y vuelta roundtrip
iglesia church
imperdible safety pin
impermeable raincoat
importado imported
importante important
imposible impossible
impuesto tax
incluido included
increíble incredible
independiente independent
indigestión indigestion
industria industry
información information
ingeniero engineer
inglés English
inmediatamente immediately
inocente innocent
insecto insect
insolación sunstroke
instante instant
inteligente intelligent
interesante interesting

interior inside
invierno winter
invitación invitation
invitados guest
ir go
isla island
Italia Italy
izquierda left

J

jabón soap
jardín garden
jardineria gardening
jefe boss
joven teenager
joven young
joyas jewelry
juego game
jueves Thursday
jugar play (v)
juguete toy
juntos together
juventude youth

L

la tarde evening
labio lip
ladrón thief
lago lake
lana wool

lápiz pencil
lavabo sink
lavandería laundromat
lavar wash
lejos far
lenguaje language
libre vacant
librería book shop
libro book
limpio clean (adj)
línea aérea airline
linterna flashlight
liquido de insectos insect repellant
lista list
listo ready
litro liter
llave key
llegadas arrivals
llegar arrive
llevar carry
llorar cry (v)
lluvia rain (n)
lo siento excuse me
lo siento sorry
local local
lujoso charming
luna moon
luna de miel honeymoon
lunes Monday
luz light (n)
luz del sol sunshine

M

macho macho
madera wood
madre mother
maduro ripe
magnífico great
malentendido misunderstanding
maleta suitcase
malo bad
mamá mom
mañana morning
mañana tomorrow
mandíbula jaw
mano hand
manta blanket
mapa map
mar sea
marido husband
marisco seafood
marrón brown
martes Tuesday
más more
más tarde later
masculino male
matar kill
máximo maximum
mediano medium
medianoche midnight
medicina medicine
mediodía noon
mejor best
menú menu

mercado market
mes month
mesa table
metal metal
metro subway
mi my
miedoso afraid
miércoles Wednesday
mínimo minimum
minusvalidos handicapped
minutos minutes
mirar look
mismo same
mixto mix (n)
mochila backpack
mochila rucksack
moda fashion
moderno modern
mojado wet
molestar disturb
momento moment
monedas coins
montaña mountain
montar a caballo horse riding
monumento monument
morado purple
morir die
morriña homesick
mosquito mosquito
mucho many
mucho much
muebles furniture
muerto dead

mujer woman
mujeres women
multitud crowd (n)
mundo world
muñeca doll
muñeca wrist
músculo muscle
museo museum
música music
muslo thigh
muy very

N

nacionalidad nationality
nada nothing
nadar swim
naipe cards (deck)
naranja orange (color)
naranja orange (fruit)
nariz nose
natural natural
naturaleza nature
náusea nausea
Navidad Christmas
necesario necessary
necesitar need
negocio business
negro black
nervioso nervous
nieble fog
nieto, nieta grandchild
niñera babysitter

niño, niña baby
niños children
no no
no not
no fumadores non-smoking
noche night
nombre name
normal normal
norte north
nosotros us
nosotros we
nuboso cloudy
nuevo new
nunca never

O

o or
O.K. O.K.
océano ocean
ocupado occupied
odiar hate
oeste west
oficina office
oficio occupation
oír hear
ojo eye
olla kettle
olor smell (n)
olvidar forget
ópera opera
óptico optician
oreja ear

original original
orilla border
oro gold
oscuro dark
otoño autumn
otra vez again
otro another
otro other

P

padre father
padres parents
pagar pay
página page
país country
pájaro bird
palabra word
palacio palace
palillo toothpick
pan bread
panadería bakery
pañal diaper
pantalones pants
pantalones cortos shorts
pañuelos de papel tissues
papá dad
papel paper
papel higiénico toilet paper
paquete package
para for
para llevar take out (food)
parada stop (n)

paraguas umbrella
parar stop (v)
parque park (garden)
pasajero passenger
pasaporte passport
pasatiempo hobby
Pascua Easter
pasillo corridor
pasta de dientes toothpaste
patinaje skating
patines roller skates
paz peace
peatón pedestrian
pedazo piece
pedir prestado borrow
peine comb (n)
pelea fight (n)
película movie
peligro danger
peligroso dangerous
pelo hair
pelota ball
pendientes earrings
pensar think
peor worst
pequeño little
pequeño small
percha coat hanger
perdido lost
perezoso lazy
perfecto perfect
perfume perfume
periódico newspaper

período period (of time)
pero but
perro dog
persona person
pesado heavy
pescado fish
pescar fish (v)
peso weight
picnic picnic
pie foot
piel skin
pierna leg
píldora pill
pincho snack
pintura painting
pinzas clothes pins
pinzas tweezers
piscina swimming pool
pistola gun
pizza pizza
planta plant
planta story (floor)
plástico plastic
plata silver
plato plate
plato hondo bowl
playa beach
plaza square (town)
pobre poor
poco few
poder can (v)
podrido rotten
policía police

pollo chicken
polvos de talco talcum powder
por favor please
por qué why
porciento percent
porque because
Portugal Portugal
poseer own (v)
posible possible
postre dessert
práctico practical
precio cost
precio price
pregunta question (n)
preguntar ask
prescripción prescription
preservativo condom
prestar lend
primavera spring (n)
primera clase first class
primero first
primeros auxilios first aid
primo, prima cousin
principal main
privado private
probar taste (try)
problema problem
profesión profession
profesor teacher
prohibido forbidden
prohibido prohibited
pronto soon
pronunciacion pronunciation

protección de sol sunscreen
público public
pueblo town
puente bridge
puerta door
puerto harbor
puesta de sol sunset
pulga flea
pulmones lungs

Q

qué what
que lástima pity, it's a
quejarse complain
quemadura burn (n)
quemadura sunburn
querer want
queso cheese
quién who

R

rabo tail
radio radio
rebajas sale
recado message
recepcionista receptionist
receta recipe
recibir receive
recibo receipt
recomendar recommend

recordar remember
reembolso refund (n)
regalo gift
regalo present (gift)
regla period (woman's)
reina queen
reír laugh (v)
relajar relax
religión religion
reloj watch (n)
resbaladizo slippery
reserva reservation
reservar reserve
respuesta answer
retraso delay
revista magazine
rey king
rico rich
río river
robusto sturdy
roca rock (n)
rodaja slice
rodilla knee
rojo red
romántico romantic
roncar snore
ropa clothes
rosa pink
roto broken
rubio blond
rueda wheel
ruidoso loud
ruidoso noisy

ruinas ruins

S

sábado Saturday
sábana bedsheet
sábana sheet
saber know
sabor flavor (n)
sabor taste (n)
sacacorchos corkscrew
sacerdote priest
salida exit
salidas departures
salir depart
salir leave
saltar jump
¡Salud! Cheers!
salvaje wild
sandalias sandals
sangre blood
sano healthy
seco dry
secreto secret
seda silk
seda dental dental floss
sediento thirsty
segunda second
segunda clase second class
seguro insurance
seguro safe
sello stamp
semana week

señal sign
sencillo simple
Señor Mr.
señor sir
Señora Mrs.
señoras ladies
Señorita Miss
separado separate
serio serious
servicio service
servicios toilet
servilleta napkin
sexo sex
sexy sexy
si yes
SIDA AIDS
siempre always
siglo century
siguiente next
silencio silence
silla chair
silla para niños highchair
similar similar
sin without
sin empleo unemployed
sintético synthetic
sobre envelope
sobre on
sobrina niece
sobrino nephew
sol sun
soleado sunny
solo alone

sólo only
soltero[a] single
sombrero hat
sonrisa smile (n)
soñar dream (v)
soñoliento sleepy
sorpresa surprise (n)
sortija ring (n)
sótano basement
sucio dirty
sudar sweat (v)
sueño dream (n)
suerte luck
suéter sweater
suficiente enough
Suiza Switzerland
sujetador bra
supermercado grocery store
supermercado supermarket
suplemento supplement
sur south

T

tal vez maybe
talla size
tampones tampons
tapón de oidos earplugs
tarde afternoon
tarde late
tarjeta card
tarjeta de crédito credit card
taza cup

teatro theater
techo roof
tejido cloth
telefonista operator
teléfono telephone
telivisión television
temperatura temperature
templado lukewarm
temprano early
tenedor fork
tener have
tenis tennis
tenis tennis shoes
terminado over (finished)
terminar finish (v)
termómetro thermometer
terrible terrible
tía aunt
tiempo weather
tienda de campaña tent
tierno tender
tierra earth
tijeras scissors
tímido shy
tío uncle
tirador handle (n)
tirar pull
tirar throw
tirita band-aid
toalla towel
tobillo ankle
todo every
todo everything

tomar take
tomar el sol sunbathe
tormenta storm
torre tower
toser cough (v)
total total
trabajar work (v)
trabajo job
trabajo work (n)
tradicional traditional
traducir translate
tráfico traffic
tragar swallow (v)
traje de baño swim suit
tranquilo quiet
transbordador ferry
tren train
triste sad
tú you (informal)
túnel tunnel
turista tourist

U

último last
una vez once
universidad university
urgente urgent
usar use (v)
usted you (formal)

V

vaca cow
vacío empty
valle valley
vaqueros jeans
vaso glass
vegetariano[a] vegetarian
velocidad speed
vender sell
venir come
ventana window
ver see
verano summer
verde green
vestido dress (n)
vía track (train)
viajar travel (v)
viaje journey
viaje tour
viaje trip
vida life
vídeo video
viejo old
viento wind
viernes Friday
vigilar watch (v)
vino wine
viñedo vineyard
violación rape (n)
virus virus
visita visit (n)
visitar visit (v)
vista view

vitaminas vitamins
viuda widow
viudo widower
vivir live (v)
volar fly
vomitar vomit
voz voice
vuelo flight

Y

y and
ya already
yo I
yodo iodine

Z

zapatos shoes
zoo zoo
zumo juice

Portuguese-English Dictionary

A

á at
á moda de casa homemade
abaixo below
abaixo down
aberto open (adj)
abertor de latas can opener
abrir open (v)
acabado over (finished)
acidente accident
acima above
acordar wake up
adaptador adaptor
adega cellar
adesivo band-aid
adeus goodbye
adulto adult
advogado lawyer
aeroporto airport
agência de viagens travel agency
agora now
agrafador stapler
agressivo aggressive
água water
água da torneira water, tap
água mineral mineral water
agulha needle
ajuda help (n)
ajudar help (v)

albergue de juventude youth hostel
alcool alcohol
alcunha nickname
aldeia village
aleijados handicapped
Alemanha Germany
alergias allergies
alérgico allergic
alfinete pin
alfinete de segurança safety pin
algodão cotton
alguma coisa something
alicate pliers
almofada pillow
alto high
alto tall
amanhã tomorrow
amante lover
amar love (v)
amarelo yellow
amigo, amiga friend
amizade friendship
andar story (floor)
andar walk (v)
animal animal
animal de estimação pet (n)
aniversário birthday
ano year
antepassados ancestors

antes before
antibiótico antibiotic
antigo ancient
antiguidades antiques
apanhar catch (v)
apartamento apartment
aperitivos appetizers
apontamento appointment
apontar point (v)
apressar hurry (v)
apretado tight
aproximadamente approximately
aqui horo
ar air
ar condicionado air-conditioned
arco íris rainbow
armários lockers
arranha spider
arranjar fix (v)
arte art
artesanato crafts
artesanato handicrafts
artificial artificial
artista artist
árvore tree
asa wing
aspirina aspirin
assinatura signature
atirar throw
atraente attractive

atraso delay
através through
atravessar go through
auto serviço self-service
autocarro bus
autoestrada highway
avião plane
avô grandfather
avó grandmother
azedo sour
azul blue

B

babeiro bib
babysitter babysitter
bagagem baggage
bagagem luggage
baixo low
balde bucket
balde pail
balsa raft
banco bank
bandeira flag
banheira bathtub
banho bath
barato cheap
barba beard
barbeiro barber
barco boat

barco ferry
barco ship (n)
barco de passeio rowboat
barco de vela sailing
barulho noisy
bateria battery
bêbado drunk
bébé baby
bebida drink (n)
beijo kiss (n)
bem-vindo welcome
biblioteca library
bicicleta bicycle
bife beef
bigode moustache
bilhete ticket
blusa blouse
boca mouth
bola ball
bolsa purse
bolso pocket
bom fine (good)
bom good
bom-dia good day
bomba bomb
bomba de gasolina gas station
boné cap
boneca doll
bonita pretty
bonito handsome
borracha eraser
botão button
botas boots

braço arm
branco white
brilho de sol sunshine
brincos earrings
brinquedo toy
broches clothes pins
bronzeado suntan (n)
bronzear sunbathe
buraco hole
burro donkey

C

cabeça head
cabedal leather
cabelo hair
cada each
cadeira chair
cadeirinha alta highchair
caderno notebook
café coffee
cair fall (v)
cais platform (train)
caixa box
caixa cashier
calado quiet
calção de banho swim trunks
calças pants
calções shorts
calendário calendar
calor heat (n)
calor hot
caloria calorie

cama bed
camara camera
câmbio exchange (n)
caminho de ferro railway
camisa shirt
campaínha ring (n)
campismo camping
campo countryside
campo field
Canadá Canada
canal canal
canção song
oancta pen
canoa canoe
cansado tired
cantar sing
cantor singer
cão dog
capitão captain
cara face
carne meat
caro expensive
carpete carpet
oarpcte rug
carregar carry
oarro car
carta letter
cartão card
cartão de crédito credit card
cartão postal postcard
cartas cards (deck)
carteira wallet
cartelrlsta pick-pocket

casa house
casa de banho bathroom
casa de banho toilet
casaco jacket
casaco impermeável raincoat
casado[a] married
casamento wedding
cassete cassette
cassete tape (cassette)
castanho brown
castelo castle
catedral cathedral
cavalheiro gentleman
cavalo horse
cave cave
cedo early
cedo soon
centro center
certo right (correct)
cerveja beer
ocsto basket
céu heaven
céu sky
chaleira kettle
chapéu hat
chateado angry
chateado mad
chave key
chave de parafusos screwdriver
chávena cup
chegadas arrivals
chegar arrive
cheio no vacancy

cheiro smell (n)
cheque check
cheque de viagem traveler's check
chinês Chinese (adj)
chocolate chocolate
chorar cry (v)
chupeta pacifier
chuva rain (n)
chuveiro shower
cidade city
cidade town
ciência science
cientista scientist
cigarro cigarette
cinema cinema
cinto belt
cintura waist
cinzeiro ashtray
cinzento gray
claro clear
classe class
clip paper clip
coelho rabbit
coisa thing
colete vest
colher spoon
com with
com gás fizzy
comboio train
começar begin
comer eat
comichão itch (n)

comida food
como how
compact disco compact disc
complicado complicated
compras shopping
comprimido pill
computador computer
concerto concert
concha shell
condutor conductor
condutor driver
conduzir drive (v)
conexão connection (train)
confirmar confirm
confortável comfortable
confortável cozy
conta bill (payment)
contador accountant
convidados guest
convite invitation
copo glass
cor de laranja orange (color)
cor de rosa pink
coração heart
corbetor blanket
corda rope
cordeiro lamb
cores colors
corpo body
corredor corridor
correio mail (n)
correio aéreo air mail
corrente stream (n)

correr run (v)
corta unhas nail clipper
corte de cabelo haircut
costa coast
cotovelo elbow
coxa thigh
cozinha kitchen
cozinhar cook (v)
creme de barbear shaving cream
creme de bronzear suntan lotion
criado walter
crianças children
cru raw
cruzeta coat hanger
cuecas panties
cuecas underpants
cuidadoso careful
curto short

D

dançar dance (v)
dar give
de from
de of
de acordo agree
de repente suddenly
debaixo under
dedo finger
dedo do pé toe
delicioso delicious
demasiado too (much)
dentes tooth

dentista dentist
depois after
depois afterwards
depósito deposit
desconto discount
desculpa apology
desculpe excuse me
desculpe sorry
desejo wish (v)
desempregado unemployed
desodorizante deodorant
despertador alarm clock
desporto sport
desventurado unfortunate
desvio detour
detrás behind
deus God
devagar slow
dia day
diabético diabetic
diamante diamond
diarreia diarrhea
dicionário dictionary
difícil difficult
difícil hard
dinheiro money
direção direction
directo direct
direita right (direction)
disco voador frisbee
divertido fun
divertido funny
divorciado[a] divorced

dobrar double
doce candy
doce sweet
doença disease
doente ill
doente sick
domingo Sunday
donde where
dono owner
dor pain
dor de cabeça headache
dormir sleep (v)
dormitorio dormitory
doutor doctor

E

e and
ela she
ele he
eles they
elevador elevator
em in
em frente straight
em vez de instead
embaixada embassy
embalagem package
embrulhar wrap (v)
ementa menu
emprestar borrow
emprestar lend
empurrar push
encantador charming

endereço address
engenheiro engineer
engolir swallow (v)
entender understand
entrada entrance
envelope envelope
enviar send
enviar ship (v)
equipa team
erro mistake
escada ladder
escadas stairs
escadas upstairs
escandulo scandalous
escola school
escorregadio slippery
escova de cabelo hairbrush
escova de dentes toothbrush
escrever write
escritório office
escultor sculptor
escultura sculpture
escuro dark
escutar listen
esfomeado hungry
esgotado exhausted
Espanha Spain
especialidade speciality
espectáculo show (n)
espelho mirror
esperar wait (v)
espirro sneeze (n)
esposa wife

esquecer forget
esquerda left
esquiar ski (v)
esquina corner
esta noite tonight
estação station
estacas de tenda tent pegs
estacionar park (v)
estado state
Estados Unidos United States
este east
estilo style
estômago stomach
estranho strange
estranjeiro foreign
estreito narrow
estrela star (in sky)
estudante student
estúpido stupid
eu I
Europa Europe
exactamente exactly
excelente excellent
excepto except
excursão tour
exemplo example
explicar explain

F

fábrica factory
faca knife
fácil easy

falar speak
falar talk
falésia cliff
falso false
família family
famoso famous
fantástico fantastic
farmácia pharmacy
fatia slice
fato de banho swim suit
fax fax
fazer make (v)
fechado closed
fechadura lock (n)
fechar lock (v)
fecho zipper
feio ugly
feliz happy
feminino female
feriado holiday
ferido injured
fervido boiled
festa party
festival festival
fevre fever
filha daughter
filho son
filme movie
fio necklace
fio string
fio dental dental floss
fita cola scotch tape
flor flower

fogo de artificio fireworks
fonte fountain
forno oven
forte strong
fosforos matches
fotografia photo
fraldas diaper
França France
fresco cool
fresco fresh
frio cold (adj)
fronteira border
fruta fruit
fumador smoking
fundo bottom
funeral funeral
futebol football
futebol soccer
futuro future

G

galeria gallery
galinha chicken
garagem garage
garantia guarantee
garfo fork
garganta throat
garrafa bottle
gás gas
gastar spend
gato cat
gelado ice cream

gelo ice
gêmeos twins
genuíno genuine
gerente manager
Gilete razor
golfe golf
gordo fat (adj)
gorduroso greasy
gostar enjoy
gostar like (v)
Grã-Bretanha Britain
gramática grammar
grande big
grande large
granjeiro farmer
grátis free (no cost)
grávida pregnant
Grécia Greece
gripe flu
grosso thick
guarda-chuva umbrella
guardanapo napkin
guardar keep
guitarra guitar

H

hemorróidas hemorrhoids
hidroplano hydrofoil
história history
hoje today
homen man
homens men

homosexual gay
honesto honest
hora hour
horário timetable
horrível horrible
hospital hospital
hotel hotel
humilhante embarrassing

I

ida e volta roundtrip
idade age
igreija church
ilha island
Imediatamente Immediately
imobilizado stuck
importado imported
importante important
impossível impossible
inacreditável incredible
Incluido included
incomudar disturb
Independente Independent
indigestão indigestion
industria industry
informação information
inglês English
inocente innocent
insecto insect
insolação sunstroke
instante instant
inteligente intelligent

interior inside
interresante interesting
inverno winter
iodo iodine
ir go
irmã sister
irmão brother
isqueiro lighter (n)
Itália Italy

J

já already
janela window
jantar dinner
jardim garden
jardinagem gardening
jarro carafe
jeans jeans
joalheria jewelry
joelho knee
iogar play (v)
jogging jogging
jogo game
jornal newspaper
jovem teenager
juntos together
juventude youth

L

lã wool
lábio lip

ladrão thief
lago lake
lâmpada bulb
lãmpada light bulb
lanterna a pilhas flashlight
lápis pencil
laranja orange (fruit)
lata can (n)
lavandaria laundromat
lavar wash
lavatório sink
lenço scarf
lençol sheet
lençol de cama bedsheet
lenços de papel tissues
limpo clean (adj)
lindo[a] beautiful
língua language
linha thread
linha track (train)
linha aérea airline
linha de roupas clothesline
lista list
litro liter
livraria book shop
livre vacant
livro book
local local
longe far
louro blond
lua moon
lua de mel honeymoon
lugar, assento seat

luta fight (n)
lutar fight (v)
luvas gloves
luz light (n)

M

macho macho
madeira wood
maduro ripe
mãe mom
mãe mother
magnifico great
magro skinny
magro thin
mais more
mais tarde later
mala suitcase
malentendido misunderstanding
manhã morning
mão hand
mapa map
mar sea
marido husband
marisco seafood
mas but
masculino male
matar kill
mau bad
maxila jaw
máximo maximum
medicina medicine
médio medium

medo afraid
meia-noite midnight
meias socks
meio-dia noon
melhor best
Menina Miss
menstruação period (woman's)
mercado market
mercearia grocery store
mês month
mesa table
mesmo same
metal metal
metro subway
meu my
mínimo minimum
minutos minutes
mista mix (n)
mobilias furniture
mochila backpack
mochila rucksack
moda fashion
moderno modern
moedas coins
molhado wet
momento moment
montanha mountain
montar a cavalo horse riding
monumento monument
morrer die
morto dead
mosquito mosquito
mostrar show (v)

mudar change (v)
muito many
muito much
muito very
mulher woman
mulheres women
multidão crowd (n)
mundo world
músculo muscle
museu museum
música music

N

nacionalidade nationality
nada nothing
nadar swim
não no
não not
não fumador non-smoking
nariz nose
Natal Christmas
natural natural
natureza nature
náusea nausea
nebuloso cloudy
necessário necessary
necessitar need
negócio business
nervoso nervous
neto, neta grandchild
nevoeiro fog
noite night

noitecer evening
nome name
normal normal
norte north
nós us
nós we
novo new
novo young
nunca never
nuo naked

O

o quê what
O.K. O.K.
obrigado thanks
oceano ocean
oculista optician
ocúlos glasses (eye)
óculos de sol sunglasses
ocupado occupied
odiar hate
oeste west
olá hello
olá hi
olhar look
olhar watch (v)
olho eye
ombros shoulder
ontem yesterday
ópera opera
operador operator
orelha ear

original original
ou or
ouro gold
outono autumn
outra vez again
outro another
outro other
ouvir hear

P

padaria bakery
padre priest
pagar pay
página page
pai dad
pai father
país country
pais parents
palácio palace
palavra word
palito toothpick
pão bread
papel paper
papel higiénico toilet paper
para for
para to
para levar take out (food)
parabéns congratulations
parar stop (n)
parar stop (v)
parque park (garden)
partidas departures

partido broken
partir depart
Pascoa Easter
passageiro passenger
passaporte passport
pássaro bird
passatempo hobby
pasta de dentes toothpaste
pastilha elástica gum
patinagem skating
patins roller skates
patrão boss
paz peace
pé foot
peão pedestrian
pedaço piece
pedir boleia hitchhike
peixe fish
pele skin
pensar think
pensos higiénicos sanitary
   napkins
ponto oomb (n)
pequeno little
pequeno small
pequeno almoço breakfast
percento percent
perdido lost
perfeito perfect
perfume perfume
pergunta question (n)
perguntar ask
perigo danger

perigoso dangerous
período period (of time)
perna leg
perservativo condom
perto near
pesado heavy
pescar fish (v)
peso weight
pessoa person
pessoas people
petisco snack
piada joke (n)
pinsa tweezers
pintura painting
plor worst
piquenique picnic
piscina swimming pool
pistola gun
pizza pizza
planta plant
plástico plastic
pó de talco talcum powder
pobre poor
poder can (v)
podre rotten
polícia police
ponte bridge
por favor please
pôr do sol sunset
porão basement
porco pig
porco pork
porquê because

porquê why
porta door
porto harbor
Portugal Portugal
possível possible
possuir own (v)
poster poster
pouco few
praça square (town)
praia beach
prata silver
prático practical
prato plate
preço cost
preço price
prédio building
preguiçoso lazy
prenda gift
presente present (gift)
preto black
primavera spring (n)
primeira classe first class
primeiro first
primo, prima cousin
principal main
prisão de ventre constipation
privado private
problema problem
problema trouble
professor teacher
profissão occupation
profissão profession
proibido forbidden

proibido prohibited
pronto ready
pronto socorro first aid
pronúncia pronunciation
protector solar sunscreen
provar taste (try)
próximo next
público public
pulga flea
pullover sweater
pulmões lungs
pulseira bracelet
pulso wrist
puxador handle (n)

Q

qualidade quality
quando when
quanto how many
quanto custa how much ($)
quarta-feira Wednesday
quarto bedroom
quarto quarter (¼)
quarto room
quartos vacancy sign
que pena pity, it's a
queda de água waterfall
queijo cheese
queimadura burn (n)
queimadura solar sunburn
queixar complain
quem who

quente warm (adj)
querer want
quinta farm
quinta-feira Thursday

R

rabo tail
rabuçados da tosse cough drops
rádio radio
rainha queen
rapariga girl
rapaz boy
recado message
receber receive
receita recipe
receita médica prescription
recepcionista receptionist
recibo receipt
recomendar recommend
recordar remember
rede cot
reembolso refund (n)
rei king
relaxar relax
religião religion
relógio watch (n)
renda rent (v)
reparar repair
repelente de insectos insect
   repellant
reserva reservation
reservar reserve

resposta answer
ressonar snore
revista magazine
rico rich
rio river
rir laugh (v)
rock rock (n)
roda wheel
rolha cork
romântico romantic
roulote R.V.
roupa clothes
roxo purple
rua street
ruidoso loud
ruínas ruins

S

sábado Saturday
sabão soap
saber know
sabor flavor (n)
sabor taeto (n)
sacarolhas corkscrew
saco bag
saco plástico plastic bag
saco plastico com fecho zip-lock
   bag
saia skirt
saída exit
sair leave
saldos sale

saltar jump
salvagem wild
sandálias sandals
sande sandwich
sangre blood
sapatos shoes
sapatos de ténis tennis shoes
saudade homesick
saudavel healthy
Saúde! Cheers!
seco dry
século century
seda silk
sede thirsty
segredo secret
segunda second
segunda classe second class
segunda-feira Monday
seguro insurance
seguro safe
selo stamp
sem without
semana week
sempre always
Senhor Mr.
senhor sir
Senhora Mrs.
senhora, menina waitress
senhoras ladies
sentido único one way (street)
separado separate
ser is
sério serious

serviço service
sexo sex
sexta-feira Friday
sexy sexy
SIDA AIDS
silêncio silence
sim yes
similar similar
simpático kind
simpático nice
simples plain
simples simple
sinal sign
sintético synthetic
slide slide (photo)
só only
sobre on
sobremesa dessert
sobrinha niece
sobrinho nephew
sol sun
sol sunny
sólido sturdy
solteiro[a] single
sonhar dream (v)
sonho dream (n)
sonolento sleepy
sorriso smile (n)
sorte luck
soutien bra
sozinho alone
suar sweat (v)
subida hill

subida up
suficiente enough
Suiça Switzerland
sujo dirty
sul south
sumo juice
supermercado supermarket
suplemento supplement
surpresa surprise (n)

T

T-shirt T-shirt
talvez maybe
tamanho size
tampões tampono
tampões de ouvido earplugs
tarde afternoon
tarde late
taxa tax
teatro theater
tecido cloth
telefone telephone
televisão television
telhado roof
temperatura temperature
tempestada storm
tempo weather
tenda tent
ténis tennis
tenro tender
tépido lukewarm
ter have

terça-feira Tuesday
terminar finish (v)
termómetro thermometer
terra earth
terrível terrible
tesouras scissors
tia aunt
tijela bowl
tímido shy
tio uncle
tirar pull
toalha towel
todo every
tomar take
torneira faucet
tornozelo ankle
torre tower
tosser cough (v)
total total
trabalhar work (v)
trabalho job
trabalho work (n)
tradicional traditional
traduzir translate
tráfico traffic
triste sad
troca change (n)
tu you (informal)
tudo everything
túnel tunnel
turista tourist

U

último last
um guia guidebook
uma guia guide
uma ida one way (ticket)
uma vez once
universidade university
urgente urgent
usar use (v)

V

vaca cow
vale valley
varanda balcony
vazio empty
vegetariano[a] vegetarian
vela candle
velho old
velocidade speed
vender sell
vento wind
ver see
verão summer
verde green
vermelho red
vestido dress (n)
via by (via)
viagem journey
viagem trip
viajar travel (v)

vida life
video camera video camera
vídeo video
vinhedo vineyard
vinho wine
violação rape (n)
vir come
vírus virus
visita visit (n)
visitar visit (v)
vista view
vitaminas vitamins
viúva widow
viúvo widower
viver live (v)
voar fly
você you (formal)
vomitar vomit
voo flight
voz voice

X

xampú shampoo

Z

zero zero
zoo zoo

Hurdling the Language Barrier

Don't be afraid to communicate

Even the best phrase book won't satisfy your needs in every situation. To really hurdle the language barrier, you need to leap beyond the printed page, and dive into contact with the locals. Never, never, never allow your lack of foreign language skills to isolate you from the people and cultures you traveled halfway 'round the world to experience. Remember that in every country you visit, you're surrounded by expert, native-speaking tutors. Spend bus and train rides letting them teach you.

Always start a conversation by asking politely in the local language, "Do you speak English?" When you communicate in English with someone from another country, speak slowly, clearly, and with carefully chosen words. Use what the Voice of America calls "simple English." You're talking to people who are wishing it was written down, hoping to see each letter as it tumbles out of your mouth. Pronounce each letter, avoiding all contractions and slang. For bad examples, listen to other tourists.

Keep things caveman-simple. Make single nouns work as entire sentences ("Photo?"). Use internationally understood words ("auto kaput" works in Morocco). Butcher the language if you must. The important thing is to make the effort. To get air mail stamps, you can flap your wings and say "tweet, tweet." If you want milk, moo and pull two imaginary udders. Risk looking like a fool.

If you're short on words, make your picnic a potluck. Pull out a map and point out your journey. Draw what you mean. Bring photos from home and introduce your family. Play cards or toss a Frisbee. Fold an origami bird for kids or dazzle 'em with sleight-of-hand magic.

Go ahead and make educated guesses. Many situations are easy-to-fake multiple choice questions. Practice. Read timetables, concert posters and newspaper headlines. Listen to each language on a multilingual tour. Be melodramatic. Exaggerate the local accent. Self-consciousness is the deadliest communication-killer.

Choose multilingual people to communicate with, such as students, business people, urbanites, young well-dressed people, or anyone in the tourist trade. Use a small note pad to keep track of handy phrases you pick up—and to help you communicate more clearly with the locals by scribbling down numbers, maps, and so on. Some travelers carry important messages written on a small card (vegetarian, boiled water, your finest ice cream).

Easy cultural bugaboos to avoid:

■ When writing numbers, give your sevens a cross (7) and give your ones an upswing (1). European dates are different: Christmas is 25-12-96, not 12-25-96.

■ Commas are decimal points and decimals are commas. So a dollar and a half is 1,50, and there are 5.280 feet in a mile.

■ The Iberian "first floor" is not the ground floor, but the first floor up.

Spanish tongue twisters:

Here are a few *trabalenguas* that are sure to challenge you and amuse your Iberian hosts.

Pablito clavó un clavito. ¿Qué clavito clavó Pablito?

Paul stuck in a stick. What stick did Paul stick in?

Un tigre, dos tigres, tres tigres comían trigo en un trigal. Un tigre, dos tigres, tres tigres.

One tiger, two tigers, three tigers ate wheat in a wheatfield. One tiger, two tigers, three tigers.

El cielo está enladrillado. ¿Quién lo desenladrillará? El desenladrillador que lo desenladrille un buen desenladrillador será.

The sky is bricked up. Who will unbrick it? He who unbricks it, what a fine unbricker he will be.

Portuguese tongue twisters:

O rato roeu a roupa do rei do Roma.

The mouse nibbled the clothes of the king of Rome

Um tigre, dois tigres, três tigres.

One tiger, two tigers, three tigers.

Se cá nevasse fazia-se cá ski, mas como cá não neva não se faz cá ski.

If the snow would fall, we'd ski, but since it doesn't, we don't.

English tongue twisters:

After your Iberian friends have laughed at you, let them try these tongue twisters in English:

If neither he sells seashells, nor she sells seashells,
who shall sell seashells? Shall seashells be sold?

Peter Piper picked a peck of pickled peppers.

Rugged rubber baby buggy bumpers.

The sixth sick sheik's sixth sheep's sick.

Red bug's blood and black bug's blood.

Soldiers' shoulders.

Thieves seize skis.

I'm a pleasant mother pheasant plucker. I pluck mother
pheasants. I'm the most pleasant mother pheasant plucker
that ever plucked a mother pheasant.

International words:

As our world shrinks, more and more words hop across their linguistic boundaries and become international. Savvy travelers develop a knack for choosing words most likely to be universally understood ("auto" instead of "car," "kaput" rather than "broken," "photo," not "picture"). Internationalize your pronunciation. "University," if you play around with its sound (oo-nee-vehr-see-tay) will be understood anywhere. Practice speaking English with a heavy Iberian accent. Wave your arms a lot. Be creative.

Here are a few internationally understood words. Remember, cut out the Yankee accent and give each word a pan-European sound.

Stop	Kaput	Vino	Restaurant
Ciao	Bank	Hotel	Bye-bye
Rock 'n roll	Post	Camping	OK
Auto	Picnic	Amigo	Autobus (boos)
Nuclear	Macho	Tourist	English (Engleesh)
Yankee	Americano	Mama mia	Michelangelo
Beer	Oo la la	Coffee	Casanova (romantic)
Chocolate	Moment	Sexy	Disneyland
Tea	Coca Cola	No problem	Mañana
Telephone	Photo	Photocopy	Passport
Europa	Self-service	Toilet	Police
Super	Taxi	Central	Information
Pardon	University	Fascist	Rambo
American profanity			

Common Iberian Gestures

The Eyelid Pull: Place your extended forefinger below the center of your eye, and pull the skin downward. In Spain this is a friendly warning, meaning: "Be alert, that guy is clever."

The Fingertip Kiss: Bring the thumb and fingers of your right hand together at your lips, kiss gently, and toss them up and away. This usually means praise in Spain, and is used as a form of salutation in Portugal.

The Hand Purse: Straighten the fingers and thumb of one hand, bringing them all together to make an upward point. Your hands can be held still or moved a little up and down at the wrist. In Iberia, this means "lots."

The Cheek Screw: Make a fist, stick out your forefinger and screw it into your cheek. This is used in southern Spain to call someone "effeminate."

The Nose Flick: Thumbing your nose is used as a form of mockery in Spain and Portugal.

Hook 'em Horns: Stick out your index finger and pinky, and hold your two middle fingers down with your thumb. Either you're a Texas Longhorns fan or you're accusing someone of impotence.

The Forearm Jerk: Clench your right fist, and jerk your forearm up as you slap your bicep with your left palm. This is a rude phallic gesture that Iberians use the way Americans give someone "the finger." This extra-large version says, "I'm superior."

Counting on fingers: Counting begins with the thumb, so if you hold up two fingers, someone will sell you three of something.

To beckon someone: In Iberia, wave your hand palm downward.

Tell me what you think.

Your feedback will do a lot to improve future editions of this phrase book. To help tomorrow's travelers travel smarter, please send me any ideas, phrases, and suggestions as they hit you during your travels. *¡Gracias! Obrigado!*

Rick Steves
Europe Through the Back Door
120 Fourth Ave. N, PO Box 2009
Edmonds, WA 98020

APPENDIX

Let's Talk Telephones

Using Iberian telephones

Smart travelers use the telephone every day. Hotel room phones are reasonable for local calls, but a terrible rip-off for long distance calls (unless you're calling the USA with your calling card's local access number). In Spain, a *Telefónica* is an easy-to-use "talk now, pay later" telephone office. You'll also find fair, metered phones in post offices in both Spain and Portugal.

When you're at a public phonebooth, remember that it's much easier to use a telephone card than coins for local and long distance calls. Buy a card on your first day to force yourself to find smart reasons to use the local phones. The cards, costing from $8 to $15, are available at post offices and tobacco shops. The older coin-operated phones (commonly found in bars and restaurants) will work if you have the necessary change.

Calling the USA from a pay phone is easy if you have a phone card, or an ATT, MCI or SPRINT calling card. Or you can make a short call using coins ($1 for 15 seconds) and ask the other person to call you back at your hotel at a specified time. Iberia-to-USA calls are twice as expensive as direct calls from the States. Midnight in California is breakfast in Iberia.

If you plan to call home often, get an ATT, MCI or SPRINT card. Each card company has a toll-free number in each European country which puts you in touch with an American operator who takes your card number and the

number you want to call, puts you through, and bills your
home phone number for the call (at the cheaper USA rate
of about a dollar a minute plus a $2.50 service charge). If
you talk for at least 3 minutes, you'll save enough to make
up for the service charge.

Important numbers:	**Spain**	**Portugal**
International access code (calling from):	07	00
Country code (calling to):	34	351
Directory assistance:	003	13
ATT operator:	900-99-0011	05-017-1288
MCI operator:	900-99-0014	05-017-1234
SPRINT operator:	900-99-0013	05-017-1877

Dial away:

If you're dialing direct, here's the sequence of numbers
you'd dial:

USA to Spain: 011 - 34 - area code (without the prefix 9) - local number
USA to Portugal: 011 - 351 - area code (without the prefix 0) - local number
Spain to Portugal: 07 - 351 - area code - local number
Portugal to Spain: 00 - 34 - area code - local number
Long distance within Spain: 9 - area code - local number
Long distance within Portugal: 0 - area code - local number

Country telephone codes:

Austria:	43	Germany:	49	Norway:	47
Belgium:	32	Greece:	30	Portugal:	351
Britain:	44	Hungary:	36	Spain:	34
Canada:	1	Ireland:	353	Sweden:	46
Czech Rep.:	42	Italy:	39	Switzerland:	41
Denmark:	45	Morocco:	212	Turkey:	90
France:	33	Netherlands:	31	USA / Canada:	1

Major Iberian area codes:

Madrid:	1	Sevilla:	54	Granada:	58
Barcelona:	3	Toledo:	25	Lisbon:	1

Metric conversions (approximate)

1 inch = 25 millimeters   1 foot = .3 meter
1 yard = .9 meter   1 mile = 1.6 kilometers
1 sq. yard = .8 sq. meter 1 acre = 0.4 hectare
1 quart = .95 liter   1 ounce = 28 grams
1 pound = .45 kilo   1 kilo = 2.2 pounds
1 centimeter = 0.4 inch   1 meter = 39.4 inches
1 kilometer = .62 mile

Miles = kilometers divided by 2 plus 10%
(120 km ÷ 2 = 60, 60 +12 = 72 miles)
Fahrenheit degrees = double Celsius + 30
32° F = 0° C, 82° F = about 28° C

Faxing your hotel reservation

Most hotel managers know basic "hotel English." Use this handy form for your fax.

. . . .

One page fax   My fax #:_____
To: Today's date: ____ / ____ / ____
From: day month year

Dear Hotel _____,
    Please make this reservation for me:

Name: _____
Total # of people: ____   # of rooms: ____   # of nights: ____

Arriving: ____ / ____ / ____   Time of arrival (24-hour clock): _____
          day month year   (I will telephone if later)
Departing: ____ / ____ / ____
           day month year

Room(s): Single Double Twin   Triple   Quad   Quint
With: Toilet   Shower   Bath   Sink only
Special needs: View   Quiet   Cheapest room   Ground floor
Credit card: Visa   Mastercard   Amex
Card #: _____   Exp. date: _____
Name on card: _____

If a deposit is necessary, you may charge me for the first night. Please fax or mail me confirmation of my reservation, the type of room reserved, the price, and whether the price includes breakfast. Thank you.
Signed: _____   Phone: _____
Address: _____

Weather

First line is average daily low (°F.); second line is average daily high (°F.); third line, days of no rain.

	J	F	M	A	M	J	J	A	S	O	N	D
Madrid	33	35	40	44	50	57	62	62	56	48	40	35
	47	51	47	64	71	80	87	86	77	66	54	48
	22	19	20	21	22	24	28	29	24	23	20	22
Barcelona	42	44	47	51	57	63	69	69	65	58	50	44
	56	57	61	64	71	77	81	82	67	61	62	57
	26	21	24	22	23	25	27	26	23	23	23	25
Costa del Sol	47	48	51	55	60	66	70	72	68	61	53	48
	61	62	64	69	74	80	84	85	81	74	67	62
	25	22	23	25	28	29	31	30	28	27	22	25
Lisbon	46	47	49	52	56	60	63	64	62	57	52	47
	56	58	61	64	69	75	79	80	76	69	62	57
	22	20	21	23	25	28	30	30	26	24	20	21
Algarve	47	57	50	52	56	60	64	65	62	58	52	48
	61	61	63	67	73	77	83	84	80	73	66	62
	22	19	20	24	27	29	31	31	28	26	22	22

Tear-out Spanish cheat sheet

Hello.	Hola.	**oh**-lah
Do you speak English?	**¿Habla usted inglés?**	**ah**-blah oo-**stehd** een-**glays**
Yes. / No.	**Sí. / No.**	see / noh
I don't speak Spanish.	**No hablo español.**	noh **ah**-bloh ay-spahn-**yohl**
I'm sorry.	**Lo siento.**	loh see-**ehn**-toh
Please.	**Por favor.**	por fah-**bor**
Thank you.	**Gracias.**	**grah**-thee-ahs
It's (not) a problem.	**(No) hay problema.**	(noh) ī proh-**blay**-mah
Very good.	**Muy bien.**	moo-ee bee-**yehn**
You are very kind.	**Usted es muy amable.**	oo-**stehd** ays **moo-ee** ah-**mah**-blay
Goodbye.	**Adiós.**	ah-dee-**ohs**
Where is a...?	**¿Donde hay un...?**	**dohn**-day ī oon
...hotel	**...hotel**	oh-**tel**
...youth hostel	**...albergue de juventud**	ahl-**behr**-gay day hoo-behn-**tood**
...restaurant	**...restaurante**	ray-stoh-**rahn**-tay
...supermarket	**...supermercado**	soo-pehr-mehr-**kah**-doh
...bank	**...banco**	**bahn**-koh
Where is the...?	**¿Dónde está la...?**	**dohn**-day ay-**stah** lah
...pharmacy	**...farmacia**	far-mah-**thee**-ah
...train station	**...estación de trenes**	ay-stah-thee-**ohn** day **tray**-nays
...tourist information office	**...Oficina de Turismo**	oh-fee-**thee**-nah day too-**rees**-moh
Where are the toilets?	**¿Dónde están los servicios?**	**dohn**-day ay-**stahn** lohs sehr-bee-**thee**-ohs
men / women	**hombres / mujeres**	**ohm**-brays / moo-**heh**-rays

CHEAT SHEET

How much is it?	¿Cuánto cuesta?	**kwahn**-toh **kway**-stah
Write it?	¿Me lo escribe?	may loh ay-**skree**-bay
Cheap(er).	(Más) barato.	(mahs) bah-**rah**-toh
Cheapest.	El más barato.	ehl mahs bah-**rah**-toh
Is it free?	¿Es gratis?	ays grah-**tees**
Is it included?	¿Está incluido?	ay-**stah** een-kloo-**ee**-doh
Do you have...?	¿Tiene...?	tee-**ehn**-ay
I would like...	Quería...	keh-**ree**-ah
We would like...	Queríamos...	keh-**ree**-ah-mohs
...this.	...esto.	**ay**-stoh
...just a little.	...un poquito.	oon poh-**kee**-toh
...more.	...más.	mahs
...a ticket.	...un billete.	oon bee-**yeh**-tay
...a room.	...una habitación.	**oo**-nah ah-bee-tah-thee-**ohn**
...the bill.	...la cuenta.	lah **kwayn**-tah

one	uno	**oo**-noh
two	dos	dohs
three	tres	trays
four	cuatro	**kwah**-troh
five	cinco	**theen**-koh
six	seis	says
seven	siete	see-**eh**-tay
eight	ocho	**oh**-choh
nine	nueve	**nway**-bay
ten	diez	dee-**ayth**

At what time?	¿A qué hora?	ah kay **oh**-rah
Just a moment.	Un momento.	oon moh-**mehn**-toh
Now.	Ahora.	ah-**oh**-rah
Soon. / Later.	Pronto. / Más tarde.	**prohn**-toh / mahs **tar**-day
Today. / Tomorrow.	Hoy. / Mañana.	oy / mahn-**yah**-nah

Tear-out Portuguese cheat sheet

Hello.	Olá.	oh-lah
Do you speak English?	Fala inglês?	fah-lah een-glaysh
Yes. / No.	Sim. / Não.	seeng / now
I don't speak Portuguese.	Não falo português.	now fah-loo poor-too-gaysh
I'm sorry.	Desculpe.	dish-kool-peh
Please.	Por favor.	poor fah-vor
Thank you.	Obrigado[a].	oh-bree-gah-doo
It's (not) a problem.	(Não) á problema.	(now) ah proo-blay-mah
Very good.	Muito bem.	mween-too bayn
You are very kind.	É muito simpático[a].	eh mween-too seeng-pah-tee-koo
Goodbye.	Adeus.	ah-deh-oosh
Where is...?	Onde é que é...?	ohn-deh eh keh eh
...a hotel	...um hotel	oon oh-tehl
...a youth hostel	...uma pousada de juventude	oo-mah poh-zah-dah deh zhoo-vayn-too-deh
...a restaurant	...um restaurante	oon rish-toh-rahn-teh
...a supermarket	...um supermercado	oon soo-pehr-mehr-kah-doo
...a pharmacy	...uma farmácia	oo-mah far-mah-soo-ah
...a bank	...um banco	oon bang-koo
...the train station	...a estação de comboio	ah ish-tah-sow deh kohn-boy-yoo
...tourist information	...a informação turistica	ah een-for-mah-sow too-reesh-tee-kah
...the toilet	...a casa de banho	ah kah-zah deh bahn-yoo
men / women	homens / mulheres	aw-maynsh / mool-yeh-rish
How much is it?	Quanto custa?	kwahn-too koosh-tah
Write it?	Escreva?	ish-kray-vah

Cheap(er).	**(Mais) barato.**	(mīsh) bah-**rah**-too
Cheapest.	**O mais barato.**	oo mīsh bah-**rah**-too
Is it free?	**É grátis?**	eh **grah**-teesh
Is it included?	**Está incluído?**	ish-**tah** een-kloo-**ee**-doo
Do you have...?	**Tem...?**	tayn
I would like...	**Gostaria...**	goosh-tah-**ree**-ah
We would like...	**Gostaríamos...**	goosh-tah-**ree**-ah-moosh
...this.	**...isto.**	**eesh**-too
...just a little.	**...só um bocadinho.**	saw oon boo-kah-**deen**-yoo
...more.	**...mais.**	mīsh
...a ticket.	**...um bilhete.**	oon beel-**yeh**-teh
...a room.	**...um quarto.**	oon **kwar**-too
...the bill.	**...a conta.**	ah **kohn**-tah

one	**um**	oon
two	**dois**	doysh
three	**três**	traysh
four	**quatro**	**kwah**-troo
five	**cinco**	**seeng**-koo
six	**seis**	saysh
seven	**sete**	**seh**-teh
eight	**oito**	**oy**-too
nine	**nove**	**naw**-veh
ten	**dez**	dehsh

At what time?	**A que horas?**	ah keh **aw**-rahsh
Just a moment.	**Um momento.**	oon moo-**mayn**-too
Now.	**Agora.**	ah-**goh**-rah
Soon.	**Em breve.**	ayn **bray**-veh
Later.	**Mais tarde.**	mīsh **tar**-deh
Today.	**Hoje.**	**oh**-zheh
Tomorrow.	**Amanhã.**	ah-ming-**yah**

Major Iberian transportation connections

Spain and Portugal

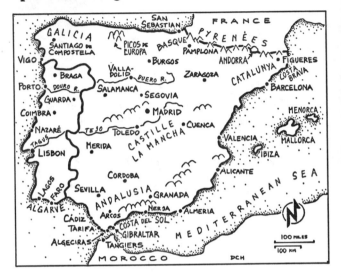

Rick Steves' Europe Through the Back Door Catalog

All of these items have been specially designed for independent budget travelers. They have been thoroughly field tested by Rick Steves and his globe-trotting ETBD staff, and are completely guaranteed. Prices include shipping and a free subscription to Rick's quarterly newsletter/catalog.

Back Door Bag convertible suitcase/backpack $75

At 9"x21"x13" this specially-designed, sturdy, functional bag is maximum carry-on-the-plane size (fits under the seat), and your key to foot-loose and fancy-free travel. Made in the USA from rugged, water-resistant 1000 denier Cordura nylon, it converts from a smart-looking suitcase to a handy backpack. It has hide-away padded shoulder straps, top and side handles, and a detachable shoulder strap (for toting as a suitcase). Beefy, lockable perimeter zippers allow easy access to the roomy (2500 cubic inches) main compartment. Two large outside pockets are perfect for frequently used items. A nylon stuff bag is also included. Over 50,000 Back Door travelers have used these bags around the world. Rick Steves helped design this bag, and lives out of it for 3 months at a time. Comparable bags cost much more. Available in black, grey, navy blue and très chic teal green.

European railpasses

...cost the same everywhere, but only ETBD gives you a free hour-long "How to get the most out of your railpass" video, free advice on your 1-page itinerary, and your choice of one of Rick Steves' regional guidebooks or phrasebooks. For starters, call 206/771-8303, and we'll send you a free copy of Rick Steves' Annual Guide to European Railpasses.

Moneybelt $8

Absolutely required no matter where you're traveling! An ultra-light, sturdy, under-the-pants, one-size-fits-all nylon-cotton pouch, our svelte moneybelt is just the right size to carry your passport, airline tickets and traveler's checks comfortably. Made to ETBD's exacting specifications, this moneybelt is your best defense against theft—when you wear it, feeling a street urchin's hand in your pocket becomes just another interesting cultural experience.

Prices include shipping within the USA/Canada, and are good through 1997—maybe longer. Orders will be processed within 2 weeks. For rush orders (which we process within 48 hours), please add $10. Washington residents please add 8.2% sales tax. Send your check to:

Rick Steves' Europe Through the Back Door

120 Fourth Ave. N, PO Box 2009
Edmonds, WA 98020

More books by Rick Steves...

Now more than ever, travelers are determined to get the most out of every mile, minute and dollar. That's what Rick's books are all about. He'll help you have a better trip because you're on a budget, not in spite of it. Each of these books is published by John Muir Publications, and is available through your local bookstore, or through Rick's free Europe Through the Back Door newsletter/catalog.

Rick Steves' Europe Through The Back Door

Updated every year, *ETBD* has given thousands of people the skills and confidence they needed to travel through the less-touristed "back doors" of Europe. You'll find chapters on packing, itinerary-planning, transportation, finding rooms, travel photography, keeping safe and healthy, plus chapters on Rick's favorite back door discoveries.

Mona Winks: Self-Guided Tours of Europe's Top Museums

Let's face it, museums can ruin a good vacation. But *Mona* takes you by the hand, giving you fun and easy-to-follow self-guided tours through Europe's 20 most frightening and exhausting museums and cultural obligations. Packed with more than 200 maps and illustrations.

Europe 101: History and Art for the Traveler

A lively, entertaining crash course in European history and art, *101* is the perfect way to prepare yourself for the rich cultural smorgasbord that awaits you.

Rick Steves' Spain & Portugal
Rick Steves' Europe
Rick Steves' Great Britain & Ireland
Rick Steves' France, Belgium & the Netherlands
Rick Steves' Italy
Rick Steves' Germany, Austria & Switzerland
Rick Steves' Scandinavia
Rick Steves' Baltics & Russia

For a successful trip, raw information isn't enough. In his regional guidebooks, Rick Steves weeds through each region's endless possibilities to give you candid, straightforward advice on what to see, where to sleep, how to manage your time, and how to get the most out of every dollar. Rick personally updates these guides every year.

Rick Steves' European Phrase Books: French, Italian, German, Spanish/Portuguese, and French/Italian/German

Finally, a series of phrase books written specially for the budget traveler! Each book gives you the words and phrases you need to communicate with the locals about room-finding, transportation, food, health—you'll even learn how to start conversations about politics, philosophy and romance—all spiced with Rick Steves' travel tips, and his unique blend of down-to-earth practicality and humor.

Find Rick on the Web!

Rick Steves' Europe Through the Back Door Home Page is packed full of travel tips, late-breaking book updates, and more. We're at http://www.ricksteves.com.

What we do at Europe Through the Back Door

At ETBD we value travel as a powerful way to better understand and contribute to the world in which we live. Our mission at ETBD is to equip travelers with the confidence and skills necessary to travel through Europe independently, economically, and in a way that is culturally broadening. To accomplish this, we:

■ Teach budget European travel skills seminars (often for free);

■ Research and write guidebooks to Europe;

■ Write and host a Public Television series;

■ Sell European railpasses, our favorite guidebooks, maps, travel bags, and travel accessories;

■ Provide European travel consulting services;

■ Organize and lead free-spirited Back Door tours of Europe, France, Italy, Turkey, and beyond;

■ Run a Travel Resource Center in espresso-correct Edmonds, WA;

...and we travel a lot.

Back Door 'Best of Europe' tours

If you like our independent travel philosophy but would like to benefit from the camaraderie and efficiency of group travel, our Back Door tours may be right up your alley. Every year we lead friendly, intimate 'Best of Europe in 21 Days' tours, free-spirited 'Bus, Bed & Breakfast' tours, and special regional tours of Italy, France, Turkey, Britain, nd other fun places. For details, call 206/771-8303 and ask for our free newsletter/catalog.

Other Books from John Muir Publications

Ordering Information

Please check your
local bookstore for
our books, or call
1-800-888-7504
to order direct and to
receive a complete
catalog. A shipping
charge will be added
to your order total.

Send all inquiries to:
John Muir
Publications
P.O. Box 613
Santa Fe, NM
87504